Ọ̀ṣun Ṣẹ̀ẹ̀gẹ̀sí

Worshippers with statue of *Ọ̀ṣun* at Ọ̀ṣun River

Òsun Sèègèsí:

The Elegant Deity
of
Wealth, Power, and Femininity

Diedre L. Bádéjọ

Africa World Press, Inc.

P. O. Box 1892

P. O. Box 48

Trenton, New Jersey 08607   Asmara, ERITREA

Africa World Press, Inc.

P. O. Box 1892
Trenton, New Jersey 08607

P. O. Box 48
Asmara, ERITREA

Typesetting: *Your World International, Inc., Louisville, KY 40223*

Cover Design: *Linda Nickens*

Photo credits: p. xxii — *Osogbo Local Government, Osogbo, Oyo State, Nigeria;* **p. 15** — *Andrea Benton Rushing;* **p. 46 (lower)** — *Babalawo Yemi Eleburuibon;* **pp. ii, xii, 46 (upper), 124, 125, 126, 127, 128, 129, and 130** — *Author.*

Maps: p. xi — *Museum for African Art, New York, N.Y.* (reprinted with permission); **pp. 112, 113** — *Author.*

Library of Congress Cataloging-in-Publication Data

Badejo, Diedre,
    Osun Seegesi: the elegant deity of wealth, power, and femininity
/ Diedre Badejo.
      p.   cm.
    Includes bibliographical references and index.
    ISBN 0-86543-354-2 (cloth : alk. paper). -- ISBN 0-86543-355-0
(paper : alk. paper)
      1. Osun (Yoruba deity)   I. Title.
BL2480. Y6B34 1996
299'. 68333--dc20

95-51678
CIP

DEDICATION

FOR MY CHILDREN — KIM, ADEWALE, AND ADEBAYO

who have journeyed with me through universities, and archives, West Africa and America, through the wonderful world in which we live, and dwell, and have our Being. And for my grandchildren, Andre and Chase Nelson who are our future spirit travellers. And for those unborn generations for whom we now live. Thank you.

Contents

Frontispiece..ii
List of Illustrations......................................x
Preface..xiii
Acknowledgments..xix
Introduction..xxiii

Chapter One
SPEAKING IN Ọ̀ṢUN'S VOICE.....................1

Translation of *Oríkì Ọ̀ṣun* 5
Phase One of the Chant — Yorùbá 16
Phase One of the Chant — English 17
Phase Two of the Chant — Yorùbá 18
Phase Two of the Chant — English 19
Phase Three of the Chant — Yorùbá 20
Phase Three of the Chant — English 23
Linguistic Notes 26

Chapter Two
THE ÒRÌṢÀ SYSTEM: AN OVERVIEW OF
   YORÙBÁ COSMOLOGY 47

Festival Drama as an Expression of Cultural Literacy 53
Viewing the Ọ̀rìṣà System 55
Yorùbá Social Discourse in Ritual and Festival Drama 63
Notes 64

Chapter Three
Ọ̀ṢUN IN YORÙBÁ COSMOLOGY 67

A Woman of Power 73
Ọ̀ṣun — Leader of the Àjẹ́ 77
Fertility, Power, and Cosmic Harmony 80
Ọ̀ṣun — Leader of Women 85
Ọ̀ṣun and the Art of Divination 89
Ọ̀ṣun and the Settling of Òṣogbo 97
Ọ̀ṣun, Yorùbá Cosmology, and Festival Drama 98
Notes 99

Chapter Four
THE Ọ̀ṢUN FESTIVAL: STRUCTURE AND MEANING 103

The Preparation and Paraphernalia for the Ọ̀ṣun Festival 104
Olójùmẹ̀rìndínlógún: The Lighting of the Sixteen Lamps ... 109
A Cast of Thousands: The Ọ̀ṣun Grove as the Setting for
  Festival Drama 114
Ọ̀ṣun's Representatives 115
Music: Communication Between Deity and Humanity 117
The Ọ̀ṣun Festival Proper 118
Notes 122

Chapter Five
THE DRAMATIZATION OF THE Ọ̀ṢUN FESTIVAL 131

Ritual Drama 135

Secular Drama 138
Symbiosis as the Essence of Dramatic Art 147
Notes 151

Chapter Six
THE SOCIAL VISION OF THE *ỌṢUN*
FESTIVAL DRAMA 155

Historical Themes 156
Political Themes 159
Sociocultural Themes 166
Cosmological Themes 170
Notes 173

Chapter Seven
GENDER, POWER, AND AFRICAN
FEMINIST THEORY 175

Notes 185

Pronouncination Key 187
Glossary 191
Bibliography 197
Index 205

ILLUSTRATIONS

Frontispiece ii
Map of Yorubaland xi
Ọ̀ṣun River xii
Ìyá Ọ̀ṣun with Ọ̀ṣun Shrine xxii
Ìyá Ọ̀ṣun with Òsì Áwo and Ọ̀tùn Áwo 15
Ìyá Alajéré casting Mẹ́rìndínlógún 15
Sanctuary in Ọ̀ṣun Grove 46
Babaláwo Yẹmi Ẹlẹ́bùrûíbọn 46
Staging the Ọ̀ṣun Festival in Central Òṣogbo Township. 112
Staging the Olódùmẹ́rìndínlógún 113
Olójùmẹ́rìndínlógún 124
Atáója celebrating Olójùmẹ́rìndínlógún 124
Ilú Àyàn 125
Crowd in Palace Courtyard 125
Ìyá Ọ̀ṣun dancing and greeting Atáója in Ọ̀ṣun Grove 126
Atáója, his wives, Beaded Crown, and Ọ̀pá Ọba 126
Atáója's Stage 127
Praise Singer 127
Ọmọde Ọ̀ṣun 128
Women in Aṣo Ẹgbẹ 128
Female Egúngún Dancers 129
Stilt Dancers 129
Cheering Ọ̀ṣun's acceptance of the communal offering 130
Collecting the sacred waters of the Ọ̀ṣun River 130

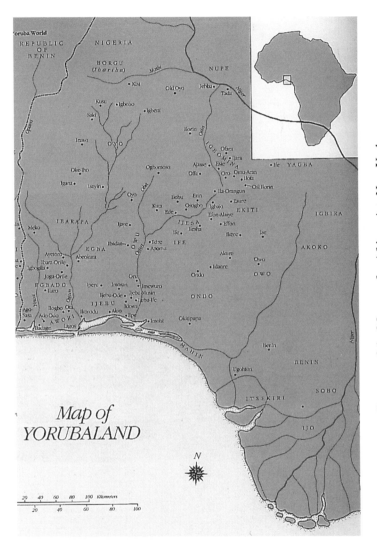

Courtesy of the Museum for African Art, New York

Yorùbá speaking territory in western Nigeria

Ọ̀ṣun River   Photo by author

PREFACE

I stood on the banks of the Ọ̀ṣun river breathing the fresh smells of moist earth and rich soil. I crossed the weakened bridge to the other side, and waded in the water. The waters of the Ọ̀ṣun river felt cool, tasted sweet, and I bathed myself, splashing my face repeatedly with her waters. Ọ̀ṣun, tell me, what is it that you are saying to me. What do you want me to say in return? What message of yours do you want me to carry? Why have you allowed me here? On the several occasions when I aimed towards the Ọ̀ṣun Grove in Òṣogbo, I felt drawn, compelled, yes, permitted to enter. Then there were times when I would walk down that same road toward the Grove, reach its gates, only to be turned away. The pervasive presence of Ọ̀ṣun and the other spiritual forces dwelled there, and I followed their guidance. In respecting the sanctity of the Ọ̀ṣun Grove, I came in greater contact with its spirituality and mine. It has taken me several years to begin to sort out what Ọ̀ṣun wants me to say — this work is only a small beginning.

The journey to the Ọ̀ṣun river and her shrine was neither smooth nor straight. It began with my great grandmother, Nana Mrs. Daisy Estella Carpenter Young, who made me know, feel, and understand that my primary knowledge base was just that — primary in the sense of being first and foremost, and knowledge in the sense that what she and the other old folks knew, and taught represented permanent, sustaining truths, and a base in the sense that this primary knowledge would carry me throughout my life. In short, I inherited the worldview of the African diaspora which is rooted, of course, in the Motherland.

The first challenge to this primary knowledge base came in Catholic school which condemned my non-Catholic Nana to

purgatory if not hell because she wasn't Catholic. I didn't understand, even in the second grade, how a good woman could be
condemned by any god. My time spent in the coat closet for
questioning the catechism did little to change my mind. The
second challenge came through the television. The whole black
world according to the evolving American mass media was
bracketed between Beulah and Tarzan. The African American
maid character, Beulah, was insular, neutered, and unlike any of
the women that I knew, maids or otherwise. The African male
characters who provided the backdrop for the white Tarzan were
unintelligible, purposeless, and also unlike the men that I knew
either as a communal group or as individual members of my
family. Like many of my age mates, I was rescued from this
miasma of contradictions and negation by the Black Power and
Black Studies Movement which gained momentum during the
late sixties.

Nevertheless, mainstream religious and social ideologies
placed women and men of African descent in precarious positions
with respect to their sense of manhood and womanhood, as well
as their sense of Africanness. This attempt to negate African
worldviews had been continuously challenged by some scholars
of African descent both from the continent and from the diaspora.
Here, Warren Cuney's poem, "No Images," resonates in my mind,
but with a difference. For us, the dilemma is "wrong images"
rather than "no images." Not just because those images are
European, but because we lacked the specific details of the "right
images."

Because of political and economic domination, the imposed
European images were featured consistently and became perhaps
even reliable, albeit only because they were most available. In
addition, the code for understanding, debating, modifying,
developing, and evolving such European codes was made available
through a panoply of sources, and at such a level that even when

dismantled or fought against, new "images" evolved from that same Eurocentric base.

Thankfully, the key to African worldviews remains within reach. The primary knowledge base which is the iconography of African images persists like African American spirituals and sayings in its own orature. Unlike the African American spirituals and sayings, however, Africa's ethnolinguistic cultures were, and are, upheld by the presence of institutionalized structures such as her myriad cultural festivals, her extensive oral literary corpora, and her quintessential socio-political practices, all of which are thoroughly interwoven throughout the philosophy and fabric of African living. In the diaspora, Africa's external ethnolinguistic cultures evolved in opposition to the type of institutionalized support which they enjoyed in the womb of the Motherland. Indeed, these cultures and the people who transmitted them became ancillary, so-called subcultures under the maelstrom of enslavement and colonialism in the Americas and the Caribbean. Undoubtedly then, African worldviews persist in Africa and the diaspora.

To feel the spiritual ambience of the Òṣun Grove is a matter of shifting locale, removing the opaque filter which threatens visual clarity, listening once again to birds and the wind, to enjoy the invigorating scent of the earth after the rains, and to add to this, the first taste of Òṣun's sweet waters. It was to reconnect with my great grandmother, and a source of her second generation born in American African knowledge. It was, and is, to refresh the soul.

The orature and festival drama of Òṣun presented here is exemplary of such primary knowledge base. The festival drama is the context for the historical and cultural knowledge imparted during the sixteen-day celebration. The oriki or praise-poem which is annotated in the first chapter codifies this knowledge through a series of complex, compressed images; historical place

and personal names; succinct symbols of power, femininity, and
fecundity, allusions to warfare, healing, and cosmological beliefs.
In this regard, the subsequent chapters may be viewed as continuous
analysis, confirmation, and elaboration of the oríkì itself. On the
other hand, it is the celebration of the annual festival which renews
its meaning.

Festival, then, is context for the verbal as well as the visual
and performing arts. It is the context for judging the quality of
performance, for accepting new religious and artistic practitioners
into their respective professional ranks. Festival is source and
sustenance for artistry, values and civic celebration. With respect
to the Ọ̀ṣun Festival, it is a place to begin to unravel the reasons
why women of African descent in Ghana, Nigeria, and the United
States stand with their hands on their hips in a pose that speaks,
as Sister Mari Evans says, across time, place, and circumstance.

By the time that I had completed undergraduate degree,
my teachers had made it very clear that Africa was as diverse and
culturally rich as the folks on Lenox Avenue. I studied both
Yorùbá and Akan cultures closely, reading about their histories,
literatures, languages, folklores, political, social, and economic
structures, and finally, chose to concentrate more specifically on
Yorùbá culture, literature, and language. Like the Akan, the
Yorùbá left an indelible mark on the so-called New World. But the
specifics were hazy, and the images became generic African ones
with the passage of time.

My attempt here is to present "a corner, in the dark, of the
tip of the iceberg." Ọ̀ṣun is a powerful, indeed empowering,
Yorùbá goddess. She is feminine, beautiful, a warrior, a leader of
powerful beings, a giver of children, a model of the attributes of
the Yorùbá pantheon, an intelligent, wealthy worker. And none of
these aspects of Ọ̀ṣun are in conflict or contradictory. Nor is her
femininity and power hostile to the masculinity and power of male
òrìṣà (deities). Rather they are complementary and challenging.

In much of the oral literature that I collected, in visiting the House of the ʾIyá Ọ̀ṣun, and in observing the festival, I witnessed the visible signs of this balance between the sexes, and the consequences of gender imbalance. The oral literature confirms that Olódùmarè, The Supreme Being, gave Ọ̀ṣun her powers. The male Ọ̀ṣun priests and musicians accompanied the priestesses and women during the presentation of the oral literature at the House of the ʾIyá Ọ̀ṣun. And the juxtaposition of the *Atáójá* (ruler of Ọ̀ṣogbo) with the ʾIyá Ọ̀ṣun (chief priestess of Ọ̀ṣun) and the *Arugbá* (sacrifice carrier) during the festival illustrates this balance, and is counterpoised against the stoic presence of the Atáója's wives.

Nonetheless, the power of Ọ̀ṣun and her female followers remains independent of male dominance and, as documented, evolves autonomously. What this says is that women and men possess their own separate sources of power which are interwoven like *aṣọ ọke* and *kente* into the complex fabric of existence. What it also says is that the balance between these gender based sources of power that keeps the world advancing, is the objective of gender reciprocity which, in the words of the late Professor Sterling Brown, "keeps a people coming." What it says is that a feminist can be for women without being against men. What it says is that imbalance and disharmony affect the entire social composition. What Ọ̀ṣun wanted me to say is that women are powerful in and of themselves, and that power exists to ensure our continuity, and that controlling our lives and our destiny is a joint effort not to be diminished by male dominance or female antagonism. In short, Ọ̀ṣun wants to negotiate a truce, and bring the Town of Women back to the community of men and women so we can ensure our survival and growth.

ACKNOWLEDGEMENTS

The world is truly a remarkable place full of remarkable people. I've been fortunate to meet many of them in many of the world's places. To Ms. Beah Richards who first encouraged me to continue to explore the connections and to open new ways for Black Women to speak and tell our story. To Dr. Akosua Aidoo whose historical insight, integrity, and direction gave me some of the tools for excavating Africa's historical complexity. To Professor Mazizi Kunene for teaching so many of us about the sheer power and beauty of the oral tradition and performance. To the late Professor John Povey for believing in my oral literary and historical quest strongly enough to support the earlier dissertation research from which this manuscript eventually grew. To Professor Beverly Robinson, for the keys to the African American theater kingdom which provided grounding in my approach to festival and written drama. To Professor Lloyd Brown for his wonderful classes and lectures in Comparative Black Literature, and to Professor Abdul-Rahman for his encouragement in my undergraduate study of African and African American religions. To the late Dr. W.E.B. DuBois whose intellectual depth and social responsibility remains a beacon for my evolving scholarly pursuits.

To the òrìṣà Ọ̀ṣun for permitting me to understand her myriad Beings. To Babaláwo Yẹmí Ẹlẹ́búrùìbọ́n for teaching me how to understand Ọ̀ṣun and Ifá through the odù Ifá, and for preparing the way for me to enter the Ọ̀ṣun shrine to meet with the Ìyá Ọ̀ṣun, the priests, and priestesses there. To Ìyá Ọ̀ṣun for granting permission for me to enter the shrine, and record the oríkì Ọ̀ṣun and the orin odún. To Mrs. Ṣàngótúndùn Àṣàbi for her beautiful a capella voice and for allowing me to record her chanting the oríkì annotated here. To the caretakers and custodians who watched over me during my solo sojourns to the Òṣun River to meditate and pray for guidance. To all the babaláwo and ìyálọ̀ṣa who safeguard this amazing storehouse of traditional African wisdom and knowledge, mo pe Ẹ ṣè púpọ̀.

To Dr. Jacob Olúpọ̀nà for encouraging the completion of this work, and reviewing it in its final stages despite his own exhaustive writing and publishing schedule. Your own devotion to the discipline and expertise has enhanced this work. To Dr. Rowland Abíódún for spending hours with me on the telephone as I unraveled the linguistic and artistic marvels of the Yorùbá language. Thank you for your time and articles that you sent to me. And to Professor Wándé Abímbọ́lá whose insisted that I begin the book in Òṣun's voice. Professor Abímbọ́lá, that was the greatest and most rewarding challenge in this entire endeavor. Every line of the oríkì Òṣun is another wealth of knowledge. Thank you. To Professor Olábiyi Babalọ́lá Yai

To my family in Nigeria, the Bádéjọ, especially Mr. and Mrs. Stephen Bádéjọ for their love, warmth, and support during my research years in Òṣogbo. For my sisters, brothers, and children of the Bádéjọ family thank you for your kindness and love. To Mr. Peter Bádéjọ for sharing his amazing talent and gifts in the performing arts, may your blessings continue.

To my Ghanaian family, for their on-going support and encouragement of my work in general and the revisions of this book during my Fulbright year at the University of Ghana, Institute of African Studies and the W.E.B. DuBois Memorial Center for Pan-African Culture. To Mrs. Efua Sutherland for her insight, wisdom, and knowledge about African oral traditions and criticism. To Professor J.O. Apronte for his guest lectures during my graduate year at IAS. To my friend, sister, and colleague, Mrs. Esi Sutherland-Addy. Our mutual passion for African oral literature has been a constant companion and refreshing watering-hole for thought and discussion. To the faculty at the Institute of African Studies, thank you for your insight and teaching excellence. To the staff at the University of Ghana at Legon, and the W.E.B. DuBois Memorial Center for providing supportive assistance.

To my best friends and colleagues, Dr. David L. Horne and Dr. Andrea B. Rushing -- there wherever there is. What more can I say! Your reading, listening, discussing, and critiquing of this work are of immeasurable value to me. To my colleague and friend, Dr. Phanuel Egejuru who listened to me almost everyday while we were in Rhode Island. To my friend, Babaláwo Bolú Fátumíṣẹ who agreed to the arduous task of check the tonal marks in the final manuscript. And to my mentor, Dr. Vivian O. Windley for her love of life which she so generously shares, and for reading the manuscript in its final stages.

Finally, to my parents for the gift of life, and to the computer world for making the completion of this book easier than its inception. The development of the language fonts for the Yorùbá tonal marks will make the writing lives of those of us who love African languages, literatures, and philosophies much easier. To Dr. Patrick W. Flanagan, Dean of the Graduate School, University of Louisville for the grant which allowed me to complete the technical production of this book.

Ìyá Òṣun with Òṣun Shrine

INTRODUCTION

In diverse ways the powerful pull of the motherland on those who, having been separated from her for centuries, are dispersed on distant continents oceans away, demands to be heeded. They return to re-embrace their roots, to draw sustenance from the source, and to experience the affirmation of the reality, the truth, and the worth of a way of being that the complex of processes called colonization (and neocolonialism after it) had sought to deny or at least denigrate. In many instances, the dispersed sons and daughters of the soil had near to hand, even in their separation and dispersal, reminders of what they left behind, in the form, for example, of culinary recipes and herbal remedies they took with them, of relational habits predicated on mutuality, of languages whose preservation also preserved their identity, or of gods and goddesses they held on to, together with their lore and rituals.

Among the last is the cult of Oxun (sometimes Ochun) that is to be found as a consort of Xango (sometimes Chango or Shango) in the Americas. They are respectively the Yorùbá Ọ̀ṣun and her husband Ṣàngó, the god of thunder. The cults of the god and goddess are not nearly as strong in the United States of America as they are in Latin America, but despite their attenuation in her country, Dr. Diedre Badejo was nevertheless drawn powerfully to Ọ̀ṣun, the river goddess whose main shrine and worship are located in the Yorùbá town of Ọ̀ṣogbo in western Nigeria. Her response to the call, which she says was boosted by her great grandmother, has been both personal and intellectual. She began by seeking knowledge which she found, but in the process, she also entered into a communion with the goddess, drinking the sweet water of the Ọ̀ṣun river, and bearing away a message the goddess enjoined her to communicate to the world.

This message is affirmative, as the reader of the pages that follow will discover. The account of the sixteen-day annual festival of Òṣun is enough reward for the time the reader devotes to the study, but even more important is the understanding of certain aspects of Yorùbá (and by extension African) worldview it purveys. The notion is still pervasive, among African intellectuals no less than among uninformed non-Africans, that Africans need schooling under European (or Western) tutelage in practically all areas of life and living, that African institutions and habits are contrary or perverse, and must be abandoned in favor of Western alternatives, or at least ameliorated by a decisive infusion of Western elements. The most pertinent area in this instance, since the study is of a goddess, is the regard of femininity of the Yoruba scheme.

Western feminism has followed other earlier tendencies in casting the African world as the worst imaginable hell for women. From a basis of ignorance and culturally ingrained racism, it has invented pathological misogyny as essentially African, and has sucessfully sold the fiction even to Africans whose knowledge about their own cultures derives from Western misrepresentations. Dr. Badejo's study of Òṣun provides a welcome corrective. This female diety, whose annual festival is the grandest in the year of sacred festivals, is a warrior and a shield, the mother figure who became a watery barrier between her wards and their pursuing enemies. Independently powerful, she is subservient to no male authority, but neither does she harbor any antagonism towards the masculine gender. Above all, she champions balanced and equitable co-existence, and as Dr. Badejo tells us, she negotiates a truce between the two genders.

This study achieves what the author set out to do — to counterpoise the right images of Africa to the wrong ones the colonizes and their surrogates have erected. She has done more than that. I lived the first fourteen years of my life in Oṣogbo, and I recall the incomparable excitement that attended the annual festival of Òṣun, especially that of the climatic day of the *arugba's* regal procession to the Grove, that day when it seemed as though all the roads in the world converged on the town. Dr. Badejo's account brings the memories back most powerfully, and affords those who have not been privileged to personally experience the excitement a worthy substitute. She also goes a long way in offering her readers an insight into the accommodating and reciprocative ways of the Yoruba.

 This is a work that deserves a place in the library of every serious scholar of the Yoruba and the African world.

Dr. Oyekan Owomoyela
Professor of English
University of Nebraska, Lincoln

Òṣun Ṣèègèsí

Chapter One

SPEAKING IN Ọ̀ṢUN'S VOICE

The oral literature and festival drama of the Yorùbá deity Ọ̀ṣun is beautiful, powerful, and exceedingly rich. In Yorùbá cosmology, Ọ̀ṣun is known as a powerful woman, the owner of the beaded comb, Ṣẹ̀ẹ̀gẹ̀sí, which she uses to part the pathways to human and divine existence. Her full appellation is Ọ̀ṣun Ṣẹ̀ẹ̀gẹ̀sí Olóòyà-iyùn, which means Ọ̀ṣun, the owner of the flawless, perfectly carved beaded comb. She is the giver of children, the leader of the àjẹ́ (powerful beings), a wealthy and beautiful woman, an herbalist and dyer. Ọ̀ṣun is also a diviner who learned the mẹ́rìndínlógún (sixteen-cowries divination) from Ọ̀rúnmìlà, the Ifá divination deity of wisdom and knowledge. The symbolism and, therefore, the meaning of Ọ̀ṣun is complicated by her uncompromising femininity, for Ọ̀ṣun loves bathing in cool waters, pampering herself with fragrant soaps and oils, and wearing and changing her elegant clothing several times a day. When we listen to Ọ̀ṣun's voice in her orature (oral literary corpus) and witness her cosmology reenacted during the annual festival in Òṣogbo, we learn that her uncompromising femininity is an aspect of her innate, uncompromising powers, that she is a warrior-woman and protectress of the covenants by which the àjẹ́ ensnarl and release their victims, that she is a consummate being.

The oral poem included in this chapter introduces Ọ̀ṣun Òṣogbo to us. It is only one of several oríkì (praise-poems), and orin odún (festival songs) that I recorded and collected in Òṣogbo from the priestesses and priests of the Ọ̀ṣun shrine, professional praise-singers, and poets of Òṣogbo. Ṣàngótuńduǹ Àṣàbí, a wife and mother, professional praise-singer, market-woman, and Ọ̀ṣun devotee from Òṣogbo intoned and chanted this particular poem. Unfortunately, the printed page cannot satisfactorily transmit the richness and elegance of Mrs. Àṣàbí's *a cappella* voice to the reader, nor can mere description approximate it. Instead, by transliterating and annotating the Yorùbá text, I am attempting to elicit the symbolism, imagery, and meaning embedded in the complex praise-names and lines of the poem.

Although chapters two and three detail Yorùbá cosmology and Ọ̀ṣun's place in it, to fully appreciate this particular praise poem some highlights from those chapters are necessary. Let me note here that the Yorùbá word *oríkì* means to greet one's head or destiny, and refers to both praise-*poems* and praise-*names*. According to the Yorùbá, the *Ifá* corpus is the most comprehensive and authoritative body of knowledge about their people, genealogy, history, belief systems, and philosophy. As chapter three shows, the *ẹṣẹ Ifá* (*Ifá* divination poems) tells us that Ọ̀ṣun is the only female among the first seventeen òrìṣà (divinities) to descend from ọ̀run (heaven) to ayé (earth) to prepare the world for human habitation. Art historian and critic, Professor Rowland Abiodun notes in his article, "Woman in Yorùbá Religious Images," that Ọ̀ṣun is the seventeenth òrìṣà and owner of the beaded comb, hence her nickname, Ṣẹ̀ẹ̀gẹ̀sí Olóòyà-iyuǹ. The *odù Ifá* (*Ifá* chapter), *OsẹTura*, tells us that Olódùmarè, the Supreme Creator, assigned these seventeen òrìṣà referred to as *Irún Imọlẹ̀* (often written as *IrùnMọlẹ̀*) the task of establishing an orderly world for human habitation. The other sixteen òrìṣa ignore Ọ̀ṣun during their deliberations, it states, because she is a woman. However, they are unaware at that time she is àjẹ́, and leader of the àjẹ́, thus she embodies her own special powers given to her and sanctioned by Olódùmarè. Because they shun her, she arrests their progress, and their plans fail. When they consult with the Supreme Creator, Olódùmarè asks about Ọ̀ṣun. They report that

they did not include her in the planning of the world order because she is a woman. *Olódùmarè* advises them to counsel with
Òṣun. Having done so, they offer `ibà` (sacrifice or restitution) to
Òṣun. The Great Mother *Òṣun* demands initiation, and advises
them to initiate all "women like her" as compensation for their
actions. In the introductory oríkì cited here, allusions to her awesome power are enhanced by her image as a nurturing mother,
ruler, and warrior, and complemented by such *orîkì* (praise
names) as *Ṣọlágbadé Èwùjí* (meaning "the wealthy one receives
the crown, a pleasing feeling, an awakening"). This orîkì symbolizes that *Òṣun* is also a wealthy, powerful, sensual, and saga-
cious woman.

The inclusion of this particular *orîkì* allows *Òṣun* to speak for
herself. The annotation and analysis of this poem documents
Òṣun's literary, historical, social, and political prowess. Inscribed
in its beautiful language and symbolism are reflections of a cosmology that strives to keep the spiritual and mundane worlds in
balance, to keep all of its myriad forces harmonized despite the
vagaries of existence, and to keep humanity attuned to its own
potentialities and pitfalls. Inscribed also are historical events,
social concerns, political issues, and the perfected artistry that is
associated with all African orature.

Repetition embellishes the literary style employed here. The
poem is intoned in three phases, the first of which introduces
Òṣun to the listeners by a series of references to the townships
where she is worshipped, townships through which the Òṣun
River flows, and townships which have other historical connections to *Òṣun Òṣogbo*. This *orîkì* enshrines the primacy of *Òṣun*
of Òṣogbo as the chief archetype of *Òṣun* found elsewhere. The
first phase also provides an overview of her images as a river, as
an *àjẹ́*, as an *òrìṣà*, as an entrepreneur, and as a woman. Here also
are included images which reflect the natural attributes of the
Òṣun Grove, its flora and fauna. Phase two illustrates *Òṣun's*
roles as a wife, mother, ruler, and divinity. Phase three pays homage to the lineage of *Ìyá Òṣun Òṣogbo*, to *Òṣun's* role as ances-

tor, and leader of women. This *oríkì* is comprehensive in its presentation while allowing the audience to become familiar with the attributes of the divinity *Ọ̀ṣun*. Changes between the various phases of the chant are signaled through the repetition of certain groups of lines indicated in the annotation below.

Literarily more significant, this *oríkì* **is** *Ọ̀ṣun*'s voice because the sweet-sounding, high pitched, wavering *a cappella* voice in which the praise-singer renders her song reflects the majestic flow and ambrosial taste of the Ọ̀ṣun River. That is, its style and language are indicative of the divine being *Ọ̀ṣun* herself. Such is the nature of orature. Its distinctiveness is found not only in its orality but, more importantly, in the style, iconography, and pitch that signals a shift in genre and theme. In this oríkì we also find the keys to *Ọ̀ṣun*'s character, talents, and nature. It tells us where to find her as she, in her riverain manifestation, flows through western Nigeria. It tells us what she subscribes to and what she abhors in her human and divine personas. In her own sweet *a cappella* voice rendered through the praise-singer, *Ọ̀ṣun* illustrates the critical roles that women have always played in the social order, especially those roles played prior to enslavement, colonialism, and westernization.

The *oríkì* prepares the reader for the subsequent references to the orature of the deity *Ọ̀ṣun* herself, to the analysis of the *Ọ̀ṣun Òṣogbo* Annual Festival, and other oral literary works which comprise the seven chapters of this book. The annotation of this poem is from the original text, and its transcription includes the tonal marks that distinguish high-, mid-, and low-toned syllables. For the tonal markings, I relied on the expertise of Dr. Yíwọlá Awolayé and Dr. Kéhìndé Olúpọ̀nà. For contextual accuracy and verification, I relied on Dr. Rowland Abíọdún. Our combined efforts are reflected in the translations. Drs. Awolayé, Olúpọ̀nà, Abíọdún and I combined our linguistic, historical-religious, aesthetic, and literary and historical expertise, respectively, to present a translation and transliteration of the highest possible quality and integrity. The interpretation, its blessings and faux pas are mine alone. This *oríkì* along with the *orin ọdún* and the *ẹsẹ Ifá*, comprise the basis for the discourse found in this analysis of *Ọ̀ṣun* and my other publications of African feminism. The following is a transcription, transliteration, and translation, of the *oríkì* chanted by Mrs. Àṣabí mentioned above. She rendered the oríkì at the home of Bàbá Ìbejì Yẹmí Ẹlẹburúibon, a *babaláwo* (*Ifá* priest-diviner) in Òṣogbo. For clarification, low-tones are indicated by (ˋ) marks, and are equivalent to *do* on the musical scale, mid-tones are without a mark in modern Yoruba orthography, and are equivalent to *re* on the musical scale, and high-tones are indicated by (ˊ) marks, and are equivalent to *mi* on the musical scale. The musicality of the language, then, lends itself easily to the musicality of the chant. Please note that we followed the tonality and inflection as chanted and as spoken in the Òṣogbo dialect of the Yorùbá language. Tonality and pronunciation varies from region to region. A Yorùbá word followed by a colon mark indicates a general explanation. These various punctuation and grammatical indicators are meant to facilitate the meaning of the annotation. For the sake of clarity, references are included within the body of the annotation where appropriate.

Translation of *Oríkì Ọ̀ṣun*

As mentioned earlier, the following translation of the *oríkì* is the culmination of efforts of Drs. Awolayé, Olúpọ̀nà, Abíọ́dún, and myself. Dr. Awolayé is a professor of *Yorùbá* language and linguistics at Ilorin University in Nigeria, and was visiting professor in residence at Boston University for the 1986-1987 academic year. His own work focuses on Yorùbá orthography, ideophones, and stylistics. Dr. Kẹ́hindé Olúpọ̀nà is a professor of History of Religions, African and African American Studies at the University of California at Davis and was visiting senior scholar of African religion at Harvard University's Center for the Study of World Religions during the Fall 1993 semester. His work focuses on traditional Yorùbá religious historiography and oral tradition. Dr. Rowland Abíọ́dún is professor of art history and chair of Black Studies at Amherst College, and his work focuses on Yorùbá art and aesthetics. My work, of course, focuses on Yorùbá and Akan orature, festival drama, and history with special emphasis on the goddess Ọ̀ṣun. Various consultative sessions included linguistic and cultural discussions and information. Each of us brought our expertise to bear upon the transcription, transliteration, and translation of the original text. Because of the exclusivity of each òrìṣà practice, the iconography and literary analysis was specifically determined by the cultural nuances and ideology related to the Ọ̀ṣun shrine and the Ifá corpus. Please note the direct English translation and transliteration of the Yorùbá text is annotated and included herein. The line numbers and the notational numbers correspond in both the Yorùbá and English texts. References and notes remain in the Yorùbá annotation solely. My literary analysis reflects the cultural and linguistic nuances, ideology, symbolism, and iconography of Ọ̀ṣun Òṣogbo.

Let me note here that although I am knowledgeable about the Ọ̀ṣun and other Yorùbá practices in Brazil, Cuba, and Haiti, the images, symbols, and nuances here are strictly from the Ọ̀ṣun shrine in Òṣogbo, Nigeria. I have deliberately maintained exclusivity here to ensure the integrity of this particular work, and to give readers a firm basis for a richer analysis with these other cultural regions and comparative studies.

The praise-singer opens her chant by calling the deity Ọ̀ṣun by her oríkì, Ṣọlágbadé Ẹ̀wùjí, which means "the wealthy one captures a crown." These first five lines quickly alert the listener to the attributes of Ọ̀ṣun. They stress that she is at the root and the apex of all human and divine affairs because she is the Great Mother who perpetually (Pèrègún) gives life with ease and frequency. This line also suggests that she does difficult tasks graciously. This concept is a recurrent theme in her oríkì. The àyàn and coconut trees also engender rich literary images associated with *Òṣun*. The *ìlù àyàn (àyàn* drums) belonging to the *babaláwo (Ifá* priests) are the made from this tree. *Òṣun's* first husband, *Òrúnmìlà*, is the patriarch of the *babaláwo* who are the owners and caretakers of these drums. Also, coconut milk resembles breast milk in color and texture, thus alluding again to motherhood.

Lines 6 through 16 are key to *Òṣun's* preeminence in Yorùbá cosmology. Her appellation, *Òṣun Ṣèègèsí Olóòyà-iyùn* acknowledges that she is the owner of the beaded comb which she uses to part the pathways of destiny. This section suggests that she gives birth with ease and frequency, alluding to her strength and fecundity. Women are encouraged to accept labor pains with similar ease, and to have many children to insure one's place in human and spiritual society. As *Ṣèègèsí*, she sculpts or decorates the hard metal, brass, with the same ease that she sculpts or decorates a calabash, a more pliant material. Yorùbá artists often sculpt or decorate calabashes for various purposes. The roundness of the calabash and the many seeds it contains also alludes to pregnancy, the world itself, and the many human beings who occupy it. As noted above, the *Pèrègún* plant is a perennial suggesting *Òṣun's* perennial nature. Lines 17 through 30 refer to townships and materials that are specific to *Òṣun* and *Òṣun* worship. Èfòn, Anké, Ilèṣà, and Ìjùmú are all affiliated with *Òṣun* Òṣogbo through resources and trade. Òṣogbo was originally settled as an outpost to Ibadan, and became a great trading center. Kola nuts from Ìjèṣà region, beads from Èfòn and Èjigbà, and brass from Ìjùmú are plentiful in Òṣogbo. Coral beads and brass are associated mainly with *Òṣun* worshippers. *Òṣun* and *Òṣun* worshippers are known for their prowess with herbs and medicinal infusions. The reference to dogs implies that the untutored do not know the value of coral beads. The use of coral and Èjigbà beads symbolizes unity among the *Òṣun* worshippers. Unity is a dominant theme in *Òṣun* worship because the women form an *ẹgbẹ́* or society of women. Their loyal and faithful practice of *Òṣun* generates innumerable rewards symbolized by rolling on brass, loading shelves with beads, and filling the ear lobes with coral beads. *Ọṣun's* generosity is also a major theme in both her *oríkì* and in certain *odù Ifá* relevant to her. The highly compressed imagery here links several Ọṣun towns and chieftaincy titles together. It suggests *Ọṣun's* military and sociopolitical roles as *Ìyálóde*, mother of the outside, *Ìyálójà*, mother of the marketplace, and *ọba*, ruler. According to Abrahams and Johnson, *Ìyálóde* is a title for women rulers who call the women's meetings in each township, and who supply the warriors with the weapons and other supplies as needed. The ruling *Ìyálóde* has her own right and left flank military personnel. The *Ìyá Ọṣun*, chief priestess of *Ọṣun*, has a parallel command and is the *Ìyálóde* for Òṣogbo township. She is also the commander-in-chief for the women's military in the township. Ìdòwú notes that the plant, *pèrègún*, is one of the emblems of *Ògún*, the deity of war and iron. Since *pèrègún* is another appellation for *Ọṣun Òṣogbo*, it confirms her military role and relationship to *Ògún* whose shrine guards the entrance to Óṣogbo's marketplace. References to the various towns in Ìjèṣà suggest the breadth of *Ọṣun's* influence in that region of Yorubáland. This section corroborates and enhances her claims to political, social, and economic leadership. Moreover, according to her mythology, *Ọṣun* is from Ìjèṣà region of which Ilèṣà is a major town. Like *Ọṣun*, Ìjèṣà is a very wealthy region, and it seems much of their wealth results from rich palm-oil and kola nut farms. *Ọṣun* as an *oba* or ruler is linked to the title of the Ìjèṣà rule, *'Bokun*, or *Obokun*, the name of the Ìjèṣà's sacred river. Together lines 31 thru 42 symbolize *Ọṣun's* role as a superior, wealthy market woman who demonstrates great business acumen. Line 35 signals the audience that we are entering a new phase of the *oríkì*.

Phase Two of the *oríkì* summarizes *Ọṣun's* womanly roles as wife, mother, healer, and ruler by focusing on her divine and human power. Lines 43 through 56 signal *Ọṣun's* prowess as a mother and guardian. Her ability to accomplish tasks great and small draws great admiration from all who embrace her in worship and in practice. Water is the dominant image here, and *Òṣun* flows along sensually and aggressively. Although the child evolves in the secrecy of the womb (*Awọ́mọ́dàá*) and remains within the uterus invisible to the human eye, water ushers in its life and sustains it. Medicinal preparations are made from the sacred waters of the blessed Òṣun River which is believed to have healing powers, especially after the completion of the Festival itself. The elegant, powerful deity also has the power (*àṣẹ*) to rescue those needing assistance. Deliverance, then, embraces images of childbirth as well as health and salvation.

The merger of male and female images here consummate *Òṣun's* role as a giver of children and a mother of females and males alike. It subtly acknowledges what the *Akan* of Ghana acknowledge about the critical role of the *Ohenemahene* (Queen Mother) in the selection of the three top candidates for kingship. In 1991, an *okyeame* (King's counselor and advisor) in the Kyebi region told me that through the womb of woman all humanity passes, so it is woman as mother who is responsible for knowing the character of men and, of course, other women. Therefore, the Queen Mother is responsible for knowing who has the best character and stamina for the responsibility that kingly leadership entails. Female power, then, is celebrated by powerful men, and together comprise the intrinsic power of humanity.

In the *Òṣun* imagery, the mysterious consummation of life is a power that ever humbles rulers and followers alike. *Òṣun*, as giver of life, also calls upon the ruler of Ará, another Yorùbá township, from the top of the palm nut tree, possibly to remind him of the critical importance of having offspring. Palm nut soup prepared throughout western Africa is a nourishing, rich dish. It provides a meal fit for a ruler and his or her offspring. The beautiful red palm nuts cluster together at the top of the tree nestling among the palm fronds. References to vegetables also symbolize women's power in sustaining her family, that is, by preparing their meals. The humble praise-singer also awaits *Òṣun's* bountiful blessings which are too plentiful to carry in her arms and hands alone. Images such as spreading clothes, harvesting vegetables, and hiding or planting money reinforce Ọ̀ṣun's abundance and the bestowing of her bounty upon those who worship and emulate her. The invitation to people to join in celebrating Ọ̀ṣun parallels an earlier invitation to the òrìṣà to celebrate with her. Since human continuity is central to both òrìṣà (deities) and èniyàn (human beings), Ọ̀ṣun is central to the continuous existence. In fact, a Yorùbá proverb confirms Èniyàn kò sí, kò sí 'Mọlẹ̀, meaning, "If human beings do not exist, deities do not exist." Consequently, we all should greet Ọ̀ṣun Òṣogbo as a bridge between humanity and deity.

The ancestor spirits (egúngún) of previous Àtáọ́ja, Adénlé and Látọnà Àjàdí, and the living human beings (èniyàn) as well as enemies of Ọ̀ṣun's people north of the Niger River (Oyèká) all gather together to salute and praise her power, wealth, fecundity, and courage. As one of the seventeen primary deities, Ọ̀ṣun herself is an ancestor as well. These lines suggest that since we know Ọ̀ṣun's greatness, we can assuredly ask for her blessings and her assistance in reaching our goals.

The very cogent passage (lines 81 and 82), "Who doesn't know that it is Ọ̀ṣun Òṣogbo who helps Àtáọ́ja rule Òṣogbo?" signifies the reciprocal balance of power between female and spiritual worlds (Ọ̀ṣun), and between male and physical worlds (Àtáọ́ja). It should be pointed out that the intrinsic or covert power of the womb is more awesome than the external or overt power of political position. This passage then signals the transfer of overt political power from female to male rulership in the Yorùbá region of western Africa. Women, of course, maintain the more cogent internal power. In another version of the origins of the male cofounders, Olútìmíhìn from Ẹ̀dẹ settled drought victims and Laróòyè from Èkìtì settled slave-raiding refugees near the banks of the Ọ̀ṣun River. According to legend, Olútìmíhìn and Laróòyè made a treaty with Ọ̀ṣun, who was then the ruler, to settle their people outside of her grove. In exchange for her permission to settle there, the newcomers were to conserve the plants and animals in the Ọ̀ṣun Grove, and celebrate her annually. Lines 87 through 91 enhance Ọ̀ṣun's image as a wife and mother. In her domestic responsibilities, she protects and nurtures her household. Indeed, her intrinsic power becomes more potent because she is a very attentive, caring mother and wife. Phase Three of the *oríkì* emphasizes the power of *ìbà* (homage) to one's ancestors, elders, and authority figures. Ọ̀ṣun occupies these roles simultaneously as a divinity and as a human being. In Yorùbá cosmological thought, *òrìṣa* (divinities) and *enìyàn* (human beings) are mirror images of each other. Aside from the major òrìṣa (*IrúnMọlẹ̀*) who participated in the organization of the world, other divinities who become ineffective are replaceable. These correlating concepts place the *òrìṣà* in juxtaposition to *enìyàn*, and seem to underscore the belief that the *àṣẹ* of the *òrìṣà* exist solely to benefit *enìyàn*.

This section also elaborates Ọ̀ṣun's femininity, beauty, and strength as aspects of her maternal power. Oils, white powder (also used on the *Ifá* divination tray), and camwood for bodily adornment, fine clothing, and *femme fatale* expression create an ambiance of mystery and awe. Maternal power and female power are mysterious, intrinsic secrets. Thus, *Ọ̀ṣun is* mother, *The Good Mother,* and she demands homage, respect, and supplication if her powers are to be placated and accessed. Ọ̀ṣun as ancestor is mysterious, offering an awe-inspiring presence. Phase three alludes to Yorùbá political, economic, and cultural themes. These and other literary aspects of Ọ̀ṣun's *oríkì* are discussed throughout the later chapters of the book.

The praise singer begins by acknowledging her predecessors who trained her, and who provide the tradition through which she, and others like her, express their own talents, and acquire part of their wealth. Wealth, health, and children demonstrate prosperity in Yorùbá culture and are a dominant theme in Yorùbá orature. The praise-singer acknowledges Ádétayùn, one of the earliest priestesses of Ọ̀ṣun, thus sealing her link with her ancestral heritage. Since Ádétayùn also means "a source from which royalty purchases beads," this name also indicates that wealth is a key element of the Yorùbá traditional heritage. The references to inheritance also suggest the perennial nature of motherhood, which is also symbolized by the perègún tree in the Ọ̀ṣun Grove. Since mother's role is to nurture and protect her offspring, supplying warriors with military necessities fulfills that role and adds to the women's material wealth. Additionally, the various images of the flora and fauna found in the Grove allude to the natural, everlasting nature of motherhood itself. The reference to olóbò-tujẹ̀ (bot., jatropha curcas), an aloe vera type of healing plant and cognomen for the female genitals in Yorùbá, draws attention to Ọ̀ṣun's role as a healer and a sensual, fertile woman. Thus, Ọ̀ṣun is the mother among mothers who is beautiful, sensual, nurturing, prosperous, and eternal.

The central theme in lines 102 through 112 focuses on Ọ̀ṣun's greatness and the relationship between children and wealth, which are inextricably tied. The numerous cultural responsibilities surrounding marriage, childbirth, naming ceremonies, and childrearing require a continuous source of wealth. When people pray for children, they also pray for the wealth to enable them to fulfill their social obligations as well as the daily upkeep of the children themselves. Women like Ọ̀ṣun with good business acumen are viewed as exceedingly good mothers because they can avail their children and extended families of the benefits of these numerous social obligations. These, of course, are reciprocated by the adult children, the extended families, and the society itself. Thus, line 112 states that people are greater than money. To give life without the resources to sustain it is unheard of.

Self-adornment, especially by nursing mothers during their "outdooring," is most pleasing and expected. These lines express the pinnacle of femininity. Beautiful adornment, shyness, and greatness combine to suggest a component of ideal Yorùbá femininity. Shyness because of white powder, which is associated with Ọ̀rìṣà-Ńlá, suggests anticipation because of a wedding engagement perhaps, or the first knowledge of pregnancy. Lines 120 through 129 demonstrate the proper acknowledgement of a performer's predecessors. To ignore this cultural obligation is harmful to the performer herself and embarrassing to her children. Paying homage or *júbà* precedes all major events. It acknowledges one's literary and performance inheritance and demonstrates respect and humility. Failure to do so brings disfavor to one's children, who fail to learn respect for their heritage and their elders. Conversely, when one pays homage, one's children emulate such behavior and, therefore, receive the blessings of the *òrìṣà.*

References to *Ọ̀ṣun's* role as a divinator and healer are found in lines 129 through 144. White powder, *ïyẹ̀rẹ̀-òsùn*, is used for divination and healing purposes. *Ọ̀ṣun* is the owner of the *mẹ́rìndínlógún* (sixteen cowries divination) given to her by *Òrúnmìlà*, the deity of wisdom and knowledge, and *Ọ̀ṣun's* first husband. *Àïwẹ́* or medicinal herbs can also include *ïyẹ̀rẹ̀-osùn.* White powder and medicinal herbs suggest *Ọ̀ṣun's* combined powers in her *oríkì,* Àṣekunlà, "meaning creative power (*àṣẹ*) enhances wealth (*ọlá*), again uniting material and maternal wealth." Okra (line 138) are full of seeds, hence the image of prosperity.

The potent imagery in lines 139 through 150 pictures *Ọ̀ṣun* and *Ọ̀ṣun's* worshippers as *àjẹ́,* powerful beings. They derive this power from *àṣẹ,* or the creative power of the universe. With it, *Ọ̀ṣun* and other *Ọ̀ṣun* practitioners produce children and wealth, cure illnesses especially childhood and female complaints, and in this manner, they inherit the privilege and rights of wealth, eldership, and ancestry. References to *Ọ̀ṣun's* role as a diviner and healer are found here as well. She is potent as salt, and her worshippers seek to emulate her effectiveness. Here, white powder also symbolizes *Ọ̀ṣun's* relationship to *Ọbatálá,* for he shapes the human forms that *Ọ̀ṣun* holds in her womb during gestation. Since white powder is also used on the *Ifá* divination tray of *Òrúnmìlà, Ọ̀ṣun's* husband, the passage reminds us that *Òrúnmìlà* recognized *Ọ̀ṣun's* talent for divination, and taught her the *mẹ̀rìndínlógún* or sixteen cowrie divination. The culmination of these talents create *àjẹ́*, powerful beings whom *Òṣun* leads. Having had many children and properly demonstrated their own appreciation to *Òṣun*, the worshippers can then spread their arms and cloths to receive her blessings that are as plentiful as okra seeds. Having led a fruitful and prosperous life filled with many children and countless offspring, the worshippers and others who wish to emulate *Òṣun,* are worthy of becoming beneficent ancestors.

In line 134, *Òṣun* is celebrated as the "confidante of twins". In line 144, the invitation is again open to join in celebrating the Great Mother *Òṣun* and the sacredness of motherhood. Among the ten lines of this passage are found the special place in the religious and social structure accorded twins. *Ìbejì* (twins) are celebrated annually, and are highly prized by the Yorùbá. Delivering twins therefore signifies perfection in childbearing. Self-control is mastered during childbirth by bearing labor pains in silence. The *Òṣun* practitioner who demonstrates self-mastery as well as practices divination and healing has the power *(àṣẹ)* to do the impossible. This reference symbolizes the mystery of gestation, while the delivery of twins suggests perfection in childbearing. Bearing labor silently, divining, healing and accumulating wealth gives practitioners mastery even over the dead of night when the *egún* and *àjẹ́* are most active. Like *Òṣun,* her followers become nurturers and protectors of human beings. Lines 134 through lines 160 then summarize the purpose and power of *Òṣun* worship.

Courtesy of Andrea Benton Rushing

Ìyá Ọ̀ṣun with *Òṣì Awo* and *Ọ̀tún Awo*

Courtesy of Andrea Benton Rushing

Ìyá Alajéré casting *Mẹ́rìndínlóngún*

Phase One of the Chant – Yorùbá

1.   Ṣọlágbadé[1] Ẹ̀wùjí,[2] mo kóre Yèyé[3] f' Ọ̀ṣun!
   Ṣọlágbadé, Abídẹbabo bẹ́ẹ̀ran![4]
   Ìyáà mi,[5] Pèrèguń[6] Ilé Ìjámọ̀![7]
   Òòṣa[8] t'ó l'Òke Àyan[9] t'ó nidí agbọn[10]
5.   Mo kóre[11] Yèyé f' Ọ̀ṣun.
   Èèyàn tó bá tète kóre Yèyé ní í j'ẹgbẹ[12]
   Èèyàn tó bá tète kóre Yèyé ní ó j'ọ̀ọ̀ọ̀[13]
   Èèyàn tó bá tète kóre Yèyé ní ó yà gbowó[14] yà gbọmọ.[15]
   Ṣọlágbadé Ẹ̀wùjí, mo kóre Yèyé f' Ọ̀ṣun.
10.   Abídẹ́baabo bí ẹran[16]
    Ìyáà mí, Pèrèguń Ilé Ìjámọ̀.
    Asáde bí ẹ ń ṣagbá[17]
    Mo kóre Yèyé f' Ọ̀ṣun.
    Ìyáà mí Ẹ̀wùjí, Ọlọ́rọ̀,[18] Ọba Ìjẹ̀ṣà[19]
15.   Ẹ̀wùji n Ìyá òní[20]
    Mo kóre Yèyé f'Ọ̀ṣun.
    Ìyáà mí, t'Ẹ̀fọn,[21] t'Ànkẹ́,[22] t'onílẹ̀-obì,[23]
    Bẹ́ẹ̀ ni mo torí ilẹ̀kẹ̀[24] Ẹ̀fọntẹ́,[25]
    Tí mo bá wọn[26] l'ọ́rùn gungùn.[27]
20.   Ṣọlágbadé o, Ìyáà mi,
    Mo torí idẹ, mo bọn'ọn[28] lọ́wọ́ gbọgbọọgbọ.[29]
    Èjigbà ilẹ̀kẹ̀[30] ni ń ṣá mi lọ́rùn n'Íjùmú.[31]
    Idẹ ń ṣá mi lọ́wọ́ ere abọ[32]
    Mo ṣúdẹ, mo i lerí idẹ.
25.   Èjigbà ilẹ̀kẹ̀ mo ï tàkìtì l'oke Ẹ̀fọn[33]
    Para OníJùmú mọ ṣọ̀dẹ.[34]
    Ọ̀dẹdẹ Ìya Oníjùmú sòlẹ̀kẹ̀.[35]
    Àarin gungùn Ìjùmú l'ó ṣako iyùn hátí.[36]
    Aja ṣe tań, ajà ṣe béégun ni[37].
30.   Ileerèe mi abọn[38]!
    Ta ní ó mọ̀ si bá n
    Jólóye[39] dùn òyé nì 'Bokun[40] epo[41]

Phase One of the Chant – English

1. *Ṣọlágbadé¹ Èwùjí,² I* salute the Great Mother,³ *Ọ̀ṣun!*
   Ṣọlágbadé, the one who gives birth like a female animal
      with ease and frequency!
   My mother,⁵ the *Pèrègún⁶* who hails from `Ijámọ̀!`⁷
   The Deity⁸ who tops the Àyàn tree⁹ who is at the bottom
      of the coconut tree,¹⁰
5. I salute¹¹ the Great Mother, *Ọ̀ṣun!*
   Only human beings who eagerly and quickly salute the
      Great Mother will eat preserved yam;¹²
   Only human beings who eagerly and quickly salute the
      Great Mother will eat yam cake;¹³
   Only human beings who eagerly and quickly salute the
      Great Mother will receive money,¹⁴ will receive children.¹⁵
   Ṣọlágbadé Èwùjí, I salute the Great Mother, *Ọ̀ṣun,*
10. Who gives birth like a female animal with ease and grace,¹⁶
   My mother, *Pèrègún,* who hails from `Ijámọ̀!`
   The One who sculpts or decorates brass like a calabash or a
      whole world.¹⁷
   I salute the Great Mother, *Ọ̀ṣun!*
   My Mother, *Èwùjí, Qlọ́rọ̀.*¹⁸ *Ọbá Ìjẹ̀ṣà,*¹⁹
15 *Èwùjí* is the Great Mother, today,²⁰
   I salute the Great Mother, *Ọ̀ṣun!*
   My Mother from Èfọn,²¹ from Ànké,²² from the land of
      kolanuts²³
   Certainly I, for the sake of coral beads²⁴ from Èfòntẹ́,²⁵
   Grow a long neck²⁷ like others who worship *Ọ̀ṣun.*²⁶
20. *Ṣọlágbadé o!* My Mother!
   I, for the sake of brass, join others²⁸ in growing very long hands,²⁹
   Bundles of Èjìgbà beads³⁰ flow down my neck in Ìjùmú,³¹
   Brass bangles rattle on my hands like the herbs for medical
      infusion.³²
   I revel in brass, I roll in brass.

25.   Bundles of beads I use to somersault among the hills of Ẹ̀fọn.[33]
      Wọ̀n`in mọ̀mọ̀ jólóye dún' yàá mi nȋ 'Bokun epo.[42]
      `Ijẹ̀sà t'ó ní sòre, ọmọ ilẹ̀ obì.[43]
35.   Ẹ̀ è jẹ́ á re 'lé Ọ̀sun Òṣogbo.[44]
      Awọ́mọ́ọ̀dá[45] Ọ̀sun Òṣogbo
      Aṣadẹ-bi-ẹ-ń-ṣagbá.[46]
      Oree Yèyé f' Ọ̀sun, Ṣọlágbadé Ẹ̀wùji
      Mo kóre Yèyé f' Ọ̀sun.
40.   Ẹ̀wùji, mo kóre Yèyé f' Ọsun
      `Iyaá mi, t'Ẹ̀fọn, t'Àǹke, t'onílẹ̀-obì
      Ṣọlágbadé Ẹ̀wùji, mo kóre Yèyé f' Ọ̀sun.[47]

Phase Two of the Chant – Yorùbá

      Ọ̀sun Òṣogbo òòò!
      Awọ́mọ́daa, Ọ̀sun Òṣogbo!
45.   Òwọruru-f'ara-l'ako![48]
      Òwọruru-f'ara-l'àpáta![49]
      Oníkíi Awoyegunlẹ̀![50]
      Ṣọlágbadé Ẹ̀wùji,
      Mo tuń kóre Yèyé f'Ọ̀sun,[51] Ọ̀sun Òṣogbo!
50.   `Iyaá mí, Ọ̀sun Òṣogbo.
      Abidẹ́ẹ̀-báábo-ẹran.
      `Iyáà mí, mọ̀ọ̀ [52] gbà mí ò!
      Ṣọlágbadé Ẹ̀wùji,
      Mo ké mọ̀gbà[53] lọ́dọ̀ omi.[54]
55.   Ọ̀sun Òṣogbo mọ̀mọ̀ gbà mí
      Mo ké mọ̀gbà lọ́dọ̀ rẹ [55] o!
      Ọ̀sun Òṣogbo ò!
      `Iyáà mi làkùkọ [56] gaǹgaǹraǹ[57]
      T'ó ròrí ọpẹ rèé kọ̀lé sí[58]
60.   Bẹ́ẹ naà ni, ibẹ wọ́n[59] ń gbé p'Alárá[60] tantan.
      Mo dúró ọwọ́ ò tó ò![61]
      Ọ̀sun Òṣogbo!

Ọ̀ṣun Òṣogbo Òròki,⁶² mo téṣọ,⁶³
Oníjùmú 's shelves bear brass (like fruit hanging down
    from a tree);³⁴
The living room of *Oníjùmu*'s mother bears beads (like fruit);³⁵
The very center of *Ìjùmú* fills its ear lobes with coral beads.³⁶
But later, dogs thought the coral beads were bones.³⁷
30.   *"Ìléèréè mi àbọ́n!"*³⁸
And who will be with me
To dance *Jólóye*³⁹ happily to celebrate the chieftancy
    title, *'Bòkun*⁴⁰ (owner of) palm-oil?⁴¹
They know in *'Bòkun*, the land of palm-oil, that *Jólóye*
    dance is sweet to my Mother.⁴²
Ìjẹ̀sà who demonstrates kindness, the offspring of kolanut land.⁴³
35.   Let us now go with goodness to the home of *Ọ̀ṣun Òṣogbo.*⁴⁴
The secret child is created⁴⁵ — *Ọ̀ṣun Òṣogbo!*
Who sculpts brass like a calabash with ease and grace.⁴⁶
Homage to the Great Mother *Ọ̀ṣun, Ṣọlágbadé Èwùjí!*
I greet the Great Mother, *Ọ̀ṣun.*
40.   Èwùjí, I salute the Great Mother, *Ọ̀ṣun*
My Mother from *Èfọ̀n*, from *Àŋké*, from the land of kolanuts,
Ṣọlágbadé Èwùjí! I salute the Great Mother, *Ọ̀ṣun!*⁴⁷

Phase Two of the Chant — English

Ọ̀ṣun Òṣogbo òòò!
The secret child is created, *Ọ̀ṣun Òṣogbo!*
45.   The one who in flowing majestically along hits her body
    against grass.⁴⁸
The one who in flowing majestically along hits her body
    against rocks.⁴⁹
*Oníkìí Awoyèguńlẹ̀!*⁵⁰
Ṣọlágbadé Èwùji
I again salute the Great Mother *Ọ̀ṣun,*⁵¹ *Ọ̀ṣun Òṣogbo!*
50.   My Mother, *Ọ̀ṣun Òṣogbo,*
Who gives birth like a female animal with ease and grace.
My Mother, please⁵² deliver and rescue me!

Èmí ó gbà si ò![64]

65. Ṣọlágbadé, ọwayanrin-wayanrin-kówó-sí![65]
E wáá w' Ọ̀ṣun Òṣogbo![66]
Ìyáá mi, abiyamọ[67] tí í retí igbee[68]
Ìyáá mi, Ṣawẹlolú[69], Olọ́rọ̀, Ọba Ijẹ̀ṣà[70]
Ibunnu má sùn ![71]

70. Mo kóre Yèyé f' Ọ̀ṣun!
Iwin Adénlé[72], mo kóre Yèyé f' Ọ̀ṣun!
Iwin Látọ̀nà Àjàdí[73], mo kóre Yèyé f' Ọ̀ṣun!
Èèyàn tó bá tètè kóree Yèyé f'Ọ̀ṣun[74]!
Èmí mọ̀ tètè kóree Yèyé f' Ọ̀ṣun[75]

75. Mo yà gbowó [76], mo yà gbọmọ[77]!
Ṣọlágbadé Ẹ̀wùjí, mo kóre Yèyé f' Ọ̀ṣun
Iwin Oyewálé[78], mo kóre Yèyé f' Ọ̀ṣun.
Gbogbaara Òkèyá [79], ẹ kóree Yèyé f' Ọ̀ṣun!
Ìyáá mi t' Ẹ̀fọn, t' Àǹké, t' onílẹ̀-obì

80. Ṣọlágbadé Ẹ̀wùjí, mo kóree Yèyé f' Ọ̀ṣun!
Taa ní ò mọ̀mọ̀ [80] p' Ọ́ṣun Òṣogbo
Níí b' ọbáá ṣèlú Òṣogbo o?[81]
Ọ̀ṣun Òṣogbo ni óo bá mi
Ṣèyí ní tèmi.

85. Ọ̀ṣun Òṣogbo ní ó mọ̀mọ̀[82] bá mi
Ṣèyí tí mi o lè ṣe!
Nítorí ọmọ níí fi í retí igbe[83]
'Torí àmàlà,[84] in níí fi í wá Ṣàngó ó ká.[85]
Baáléè mi,[86] ọkọ̀ mi![87]

90. Nitori ọmọ níí fi í gba yánrin[88]
Ṣọlágbadé Ẹ̀wùjí, mo kóre Yèyé f' Ọ̀ṣun.

Phase Three of the Chant – Yorùbá

Ṣọlágbadé Ẹ̀wùjí!
Ẹ tú, kóree Yèyé f' Ọ̀ṣun!

Ṣọlágbadé Ẹ̀wùjí!
I cried "deliverance"[53] through the water[54]

55.   Ọ̀ṣun Òṣogbo, please deliver me!
I cried "deliverance" to you![55]
Ọ̀ṣun Òṣogbo òo!
My Mother is the giant[57] cock[56]
Who climbed to the top of the palm nut tree top to
build her house.[58]

60.   Yes, it is from there she[59] calls on *Aláráá* [60] with a loud voice.
I stand to wait (for *Ọ̀ṣun*'s blessings), my hands are not
enough.[61]
Ọ̀ṣun Òṣogbo!
Ọ̀ṣun Òṣogbo greetings,[62] I spread my clothes,[63]
I will certainly receive more.[64]

65.   Ṣọlágbadé, the one who digs sand, and digs sand to hide
money![65]
Come and look at Ọ̀ṣun Òṣogbo![66]
My Mother, the nursing mother[67] who eagerly listens to
noise![68]
My Mother, Ṣàwẹlolú,[69] Ọlọ́rọ Ọba Ìjẹ̀ṣà, [70]
In the dead of night, please do not sleep[71]

70.   I salute the Great Mother, Ọ̀ṣun!
The spirit of Adénlé,[72] I salute the Great Mother, Ọ̀ṣun!
The spirit of Látònà Àjàdí,[73] I salute the Great Mother,
People who quickly eagerly salute the Great Mother, Ọ̀ṣun![74]
Iwin Adénlé,[89] ẹ tún kóree Yèyé f' Ọ̀ṣun!
I very eagerly salute the Great Mother, Ọ̀ṣun![75]

75.   I receive money,[76] I receive children.[77]
Ṣọlágbadé Ẹ̀wùjí, I salute the Great Mother, Ọ̀ṣun.
The spirit of *Oyèwálé*,[78] I salute the Great Mother, Ọ̀ṣun.
All the people of *Òkèyá*,[79] salute the Great Mother, Ọ̀ṣun!
My Mother, from *Èfọn*, from *Ànké*, from the land of
kolanuts.

80.   Ṣọlágbadé Ẹ̀wùjí, I salute the Great Mother, Ọ̀ṣun.
Who does not know[80] that it is the Ọ̀ṣun Òṣogbo

95.   Iwin Adúnní,[90] ẹ tún kóree Yèyé f' Ọ̀ṣun![91]
      Ìbà [92] ni n ó f'ojọ́ òni jú óó!
      Ṣọlágbadé Ẹ̀wùji, mo ríbà orin mí![93]
      Adétayùn,[94] Ìyáá mí !
      Abíyamọ̀[95] nínùu l'àhàloho[96]
100.   Ìyá mí l'obìnrin gbàgọ̀[97] nínú olóbò-tújẹ   [98]
      Egbin[99] nínùu rérè![100]
      N ó mọ̀ mọ̀ sì b'ọlọ́mọ ṣ'ọ̀ṣọ́ r'ode[101]
      Ìyáá mí, mọmọ̀ gba mí,
      Mo b'ọlọ́mọ, ṣ'ọ̀ṣọ́ r'ode o!
105.   Adéta o![102] Ìyáá mi gìlọ̀gìlọ̀[103]
      Tíi paraÀwó l' ádìẹ jẹẹ![104]
      Ẹgbẹ́róngbé[105] tijú ẹfun,[106]
      Ọ̀bàrà-gẹṣin-làlú,[107] ènìyán-ju-owó![108]
      Ìyáá mi mọmọ sa l'énìyán-ju-owó!
110.   Adéta l'énìyán-jú-abíkú![109]
      Ọmọ ń bẹ nínú arúgbo,[110]
      Ènìyán-jù-mí,[111] Ọ̀ṣun Òṣogbo ò !
      Awọ-mọ-dàá
      Òwọ́rùrù-f'ara-l'àkó
115.   Òwórùrù-f'ara-l'àpáta
      Ìbùnnú má sùn
      Mo tún kóree Yèyé f' Ọ̀ṣun.
      Ìbà tún ni n ó f'ojọ́ òni jú o!
      Ṣọlágbadé Ẹ̀wùji![112]
120.   Mo tún júbà[113] orin mí.
      Ìbà l'óde òni aláré![114]
      Àdàṣe nàa níí hun'mọ [115]
      Ìbà ò níí gbọdọ̀ hun'mọ.[116]
      Bàbàa mí, tí mo ríbà orin mi
125.   Ọmọ l'ójúu ṣẹbọra![117]
      Ìgbà tí mo tún ríbà orin mi!
      Ìbà nì n ó f'ojọ́ òni jú!
      Mo ríbà lọ́dọ̀ rẹ!
      Ẹgbẹ́róngbé, mo ríbà lọ́dọ̀ rẹ.

Who helps the *Obá* manage or rule Ọ̀ṣogbo?[81]
Ọ̀ṣun Ọ̀ṣogbo is the one who will help me
Accomplish this one of mine.
85.   *Ọ̀ṣun Ọ̀ṣogbo* is the one who will definitely[82] help me
Accomplish what I cannot accomplish on my own!
It is because of children that she eagerly listens to noise![83]
It is because of *àmàlà* [84] that she looks for *Ṣàngó*.[85]
My father of the house,[86] my husband![87]
90.   It is because of children that she receives *iyánrin*.[88]
Ṣọlágbadé Ẹ̀wùji, I salute the Great Mother, *Ọ̀ṣun!*

Phase Three of the Chant – English

Ṣọlágbadé Ẹ̀wùji!
I again salute the Great Mother, *Ọ̀ṣun!*
The spirit of *Adénlé*,[89] I again salute the Great Mother, *Ọ̀ṣun!*
95.   The spirit of *Àdùnní*,[90] I again salute the Great Mother, *Ọ̀ṣun!*[91]
It is homage[92] that I will use today to pay respect to my
predecessors.
Ṣọlágbadé Ẹ̀wùji, I pay homage for my songs![93]
Adétayùn,[94] my Mother,
The Nursing Mother[95] who suffers for the sake of her child.[96]
100.   My Mother is the woman who wiggles[97] inside *olóbò-tújẹ̀*,[98]
A gazelle[99] inside goodness.[100]
I will certainly adorn myself to go on an outdooring with
the one who has children.[101]
My Mother, please deliver me!
In beautiful adornment, I go on an outdooring with the
one who has children!
105.   *Adéta* o![102] My very radiant Mother[103]
Who slaughters Iwo people's chickens for food.[104]
Ẹgbẹ́róngé[105] who is shy of white powder.[106]
Ọ̀bàrà-gẹṣin-lálù,[107] the one with business acumen who
knows that people are greater than wealth![108]
My Mother definitely knows that people are greater than money!

130.   Ẹgbẹ́róngbé tijú ẹfun
       Ọ̀ bá mọ̀mọ̀ gbà mí,
       Tí mo ríbà orin mí.[118]
       Ìbà ni n ó f ọjọ́ òní jú![119]
       Ará Òoreé Àgbọn
135.   Ìyáa mi t'osùn[120] tààwẹ́[121]
       Ọmọ Aṣekunlà[122]
       Lóreé àgbọnmọ[123]
       Onírúlá n gbogbo
       Ọ̀sun mi Àìwẹ ọmaajẹbiyọ̀[124]
140.   Gbà tá i bá jẹbí yọ[125] l àïwẹ́[126]
       Ìgba tí n ó jẹbî yọ[127]
       Mo gb'ọwọ̀ ijó gẹngẹ́[128]
       Ọ̀sun-l'Àïwẹ́[129]
       N ó máa pè 'Yáa mi
145.   L'óoreè àìgbọn 'mọ.[130]
       Irúlá[131] n wọ́n ń gb'óko kii
       Mo sùn, mo yẹ òjẹ̀[132]
       Tani ó mọ̀mọ̀ ba mí délé Ìyáa mi o?[133]
       Ará t Olólò ẹdun[134]
150.   Ibú alẹ o![135]
       Loro ẹdun, mo siwo tan![136]
       Mo yáa m'ojú le koko![137]
       Bẹ́ẹ, mo ṣawo[138] mo ṣẹ ṣègùn[139]
       Mo s àìbọ́dọ̀-ràn[140]
155.   Ta ní ó mọ̀mọ̀ bá mí dẹlẹ Ìyáa mí?
       Ọ̀tuǹ-uǹ mí, imú-ń-kelé[141]
       Bẹ́ẹ ni, òsì mí n fa bàbà[142]
       Agbedeméjì mí ń mú ṣẹrẹ l'ọwọ̀.[143]
       Ẹ̀ bá mọ̀ sì yáa bá mi
160.   Kóree Yèyé f' Ọ̀sun![144]
       Ṣọlágbadé Ẹ̀wùjí!
       Mo kóree Yèyé f' Ọ̀sun![145]

The original Yorùbá *oríkì Ọ̀sun* ends here.

110.　*Adéta*, the living child is greater than the *àbíkú* child![109]
　　There are children inside the aged,[110]
　　One who is greater than me,[111] *Ọ̀ṣun Ọ̀ṣogbo o*!
　　The secret child is created!
　　The one who, in flowing along majestically, hits her
　　　　body against grass,
115.　The one who, in flowing along majestically, hits her
　　　　body against rocks,
　　In the dead of night, please do not sleep!
　　I again salute the Great Mother, *Ọ̀ṣun*!
　　It is homage again that I will use today to pay my respects!
　　Ṣọlágbadé Èwùjí![112]
120.　I again pay homage[113] for my songs.
　　I pay homage today, entertainers of the *òrìṣà*.[114]
　　Solo performance can be harmful[115] to one's offspring,
　　Homage must not be harmful.[116]
　　My Father, when I pay homage for my songs
125.　Offspring who becomes the favorite of the Gods![117]
　　I pay homage to you (entertainers of the *òrìṣà*)!
　　When I pay homage again for my songs –
　　It is homage that I will use today to pay
　　Egbẹ́rongbé, I pay homage to you!
130.　*Egbẹ́rongbé* who is shy of white powder,
　　Please, you must deliver me
　　When I find homage for my songs.[118]
　　It is homage that I will use to pay today.[119]
　　Goodness of the people,
135.　My Mother of white powder[120] and of healing water.[121]
　　The child/daughter of *Aṣèkunlà*,[122] –
　　Goodness/blessings of obedient children[123]
　　All of them are owners of okra seeds!
　　My *Ọ̀ṣun* of healing waters, one who is as effective as salt.[124]
140.　When we are as effective as salt[125] in using the healing waters,[126]
　　When I am *àjẹ́*, I am as effective as salt,[127]
　　I proudly grow long arms and hands for dancing.[128]

Ọ̀ṣun-l' Áǐwẹ̀![129]
I will be calling on my Mother!
145. For the goodness and blessing of disobedient children,[130]
It is okra seeds[131] they carry all over the farm.
I slept, I am fit to become an ancestor.[132]
Who will come with me to my Mother's house?[133]
The one who is the confidante of twins.[134]
150. Dead of Night![135]
In Órò Ẹdùn, I finished finally.[136]
I quickly toughen my face![137]
Yes, I practice the secrets[138] I practice as a healer;[139]
I even did the unexpected.[140]
155. Who will definitely come with me to enter my Mother's house?
On my right, I hold on to *kele* beads;[141]
Yes, on my left, I pull copper (brass);[142]
In my very center, I carry the rattle in my hands;[143]
You should hurriedly help me
160. Salute the Great Mother, Ọ̀ṣun![144]
Ṣọlágbadé Ẹ̀wùjí!
I salute the Great Mother, Ọ̀ṣun.[145]

Linguistic Notes

The sequence of this annotation corresponds to the matching numerical superscripts [1-145] internal to both the Yorùbá and the English texts.

1. **Ṣọlágbadé** is one of several cognomens and praise-names (*oríkì*) for Ọ̀ṣun Ṣe-olá-gba-adé means "the wealthy one captures or receives a crown." These refer to Ọ̀ṣun's royal status, and her wealth in children and in business which allows her to capture the crown, a position of power and authority. Because of her affluence she receives the crown.

2. *Èwùjí* is another cognomen and praise-name for *Ọ̀ṣun*. It is also the name of a town, possibly one where *Ọ̀ṣun* is worshipped. It also means a pleasing feeling; *jí* means awakening.

3. *Yèyé* is another cognomen and praise-name frequently used for *Ọ̀ṣun*. *Yèyé* means "The Good Mother."

4. *Abídébabo-bééran* is a praise name for *Ọ̀ṣun*. *A-bí-idé-bí-abo-bi-ẹran* means "one who gives birth as a female animal with ease and frequency". This refers to *Ọ̀ṣun*'s role as giver of children. Because of her combined power, strength, and femininity, all of *Ọ̀ṣun*'s endeavors are accomplished with grace, frequency, and ease.

5. *Ìyáà mí* means "my Mother." The term applies respectfully to the *àjẹ́* (powerful beings) as well as to *Ọ̀ṣun*, and is used in a plural sense as "our Mothers." *Ọ̀ṣun* is the leader of the *àjẹ́*. Some writers have interpreted the *àjẹ́* as witches, which connotes a negative use of power only. However, the *àjẹ́*, as we find in the cosmology of *Ọ̀ṣun* and in the *Ifá* corpus, are given this power by *Olódumarè* and it is used variously. My colleagues and informants made it clear that any person of ability, insight, leadership or other forms of observable power can be considered *àjẹ́*. Consequently, the translation, "witch", is singularly misleading and conceptually incorrect.

6. *Pèrègún* is another praise-name for *Ọ̀ṣun*. According to Abrahams Yorùbá Dictionary, *dracaena fragrans* is a sweet-smelling plant or tree that never dies. It is always found in the sacred *Ọ̀ṣun* grove in *Ọ̀ṣogbo*, and is often used as a boundary or fence plant. As a perennial, it is ever-growing, and like *Ọ̀ṣun*, it is ever-flowering and has many offspring. Ìdòwú states that it is also one of the emblems of *Ògún*, the *òrìṣà* of war and iron. The allusion here is to *Ọ̀ṣun*'s military role and prowess.

7. *Ilé Ìjámọ̀*: *ilé* means earth or land. According to one tradition, Ìjámọ̀ and Èwùjí were towns settled by the earliest Yorùbá twins. Both towns are now part of Oǹdó,

8. **Òòṣà**: òrìṣà means divinity (also used in the plural).
9. **Òkè Àyàn** means "at the top of the àyàn tree." The ìlú àyàn (àyàn drums) of the babaláwo (Ifá priest-diviners and scholars) is made from this tree. These drums are used on the first night of the Ọ̀ṣun festival when the mẹ́rìndínlógún (sixteen candles) are lit to call the òrìṣà to join Ọ̀ṣun in her celebration. Also, the staff of authority depicts a bird or birds atop a tree. Birds are symbols of the àjẹ́, and Ọ̀ṣun.
10. **nìdì agbọ̀n**: nì-idí agbọ̀n means "at the bottom of the coconut tree." It seems the allusion here is to the root which evolves from the soil, Mother Earth. The coconut tree bears many fruits or offspring, and it contains a liquid that resembles breast milk.
11. **k'óre**: kí ore meaning "to greet kindly" or "to salute".
12. **j'ẹ̀gbẹ**: jẹ̀ ẹ̀gbẹ means "to eat preserved yam," an honor reserved for special guests.
13. **j'ọsọsọ**: jẹ̀ ọsọsọ means "to eat yam cake," one of Ọṣun's favorite foods.
14. **gb'owó**: gba owó means "to receive money (wealth)."
15. **gb'ọmọ**: gba ọmọ means "to receive children (also considered wealth)."
16. **Abídẹ́baabo-bí-ẹ́ran** see line 4 above for translation. Note here the stylistic difference. In line 4, bẹ́ẹ́ran is used instead of bí-ẹran which is the literal form meaning "as an animal."
17. **Aṣádẹ-bí-ẹ-ń-ṣǎgbá** a-ṣá-idẹ-bí-ẹni-tí-ó-ń-ṣá-igbá which means "one who sculpts brass like someone who is sculpting a calabash or a whole world." An oríkì for Ọ̀ṣun, brass is one of her symbols. This praise-name implies Ọ̀ṣun's fertility, and links her material wealth to her maternal wealth. Furthermore, since the flesh of the calabash is pliable, it is relatively easy to sculpt, suggesting that Ọ̀ṣun is someone who does something

difficult with grace and ease. The elision *ṣàgbá* suggests this play on words. *Aṣàdé* means one who sculpts brass and *ṣagbá* means to sculpt a calabash. The prefix, *a*, indicates that one who sculpts. Thus, one who sculpts a hard substance, brass, and who also sculpts a pliable substance, calabash, is one who accomplishes tasks great and small with similar ease and grace. *Aṣa* and *ṣa* are derived from the same morpheme, *ṣa,* and this adds literary and stylistic beauty to the imagery in this line.

18. *Olórò* refers to the first *Ọ̀ṣun* crown that was worn according to Chief Jákùtà of Ọ̀yọ́. It also means "a confidante, the owner of words".

19. *Ìjẹ̀ṣà* is an *Ọ̀ṣun* town, an ancient town of the people of Ilẹṣa in Òyó State. According to Chief Jákùtà, the farmers of this town produce more kolanuts than any other town.

20. *nìyá Ònì:* *ni ìyá Ònì* is a celebratory phrase signifying that *Ọ̀ṣun* is "the Great Mother who we are celebrating today." This can refer to her festival day or every fifth ritual day.

21. *t'Èfọ̀n: ti Èfọn* meaning "from Ẹfọn." According to Chief Jákùta, the full name is Èfọn-Aláaye. It is surrounded by hills and valleys near Òkẹ̀-Ìmẹ̀sí in Ekìtí-land.

22. *t'Ànkẹ́:* *ti Ànké* from Ànkẹ́, possibly Àyìnkẹ́, a female cognomen or pet name, meaning "one (we) praise (in order) to pet."

23. *t'ónílẹ̀-obi: tí oni-ilẹ-obì* means "from the owner of the land of kolanuts." A reference to Ìjẹ̀ṣa (see note 19 above).

24. *ilẹ̀kẹ́* are coral beads, especially those signifying an *Ọ̀ṣun* devotee.

25. *Èfòntẹ́,* used together as *ìlẹ̀kẹ́ Èfòntẹ́,* suggests that these coral beads are spread throughout Èfọn. It may also suggest that the special coral beads of *Ọ̀ṣun* come from Èfọn region.

26. *bá wọn:* "with them (others)." Women who worship *Ọ̀ṣun* form an *ẹgbẹ́* (society) which empowers them. See

note 28 below for another stylistic variation of this phrase.

27. gúngùn means "very long." Compare the whole phrase ba wọn l'orun gùngùn with a similar phrase bọ'nọn l'ọwọ́ gbọgbọọgbọ in note 29 below. Notice the poetic stylistics used between bá wọn and bọ́nọn in conjunction with the paralleling anatomical references, ọrùn (neck) and ọwọ́ (hand).

28. bọ́nọn: bá wọn meaning "with them." See note 27 above.

29. gbọgbọọgbọ means "very long." The whole phrase bọ́nọn l'ọwọ́ gbọgbọọgbọ means "like them (others) one grows very long hands." Both images of growing a very long neck to receive ìlèkẹ̀ (Ọ̀ṣun's coral beads) and of having very long hands to receive Ọ̀ṣun's blessings symbolize the abundant fulfillment and benefits derived from respecting and worshipping YèYé, the Good Mother Ọ̀ṣun.

30. Èjìgbà ìlèkẹ̀: According to Abrahams, these beads are placed around the neck of the Áláàfín on the day of his coronation which takes place at Kòso where Ṣàngó's shrine is located. The Ìyá kékeré (junior mother of the palace) places both the crown and the beads on him. Èjìgbà is also a town in Òṣogbo District.

31. Ìjùmú another important Ọ̀ṣun town called Ọ̀ṣun Ìjùmú. According to Babaláwo Ẹlẹ́bùruîbọn, there are many different Ọ̀ṣun and Ọ̀ṣun towns, each having a different mythology. See Chapter Two for further discussion.

32. eré abọ́: abọ́ is a medicinal infusion, and perhaps a reference to a type of medicinal herb which is plentiful and hangs downward throughout the Ọ̀ṣun Grove.

33. òkè Èfòn the hills of Èfòn. The imagery here suggests that the Ọ̀ṣun devotee is exceedingly happy to receive the Èfòn coral beads, and therefore revels also in the blessings from this town.

34. sòde: so idẹ means "hangs down with brass" (or "bears

brass like fruit hanging down from a tree").

35. *sò lèkè: so ilèkè* means "hangs down with *ìlèkè* beads" (or "bears *ìlèkè* beads like fruit hanging down from a tree").

36. *sàkò iyùn hàti: so àkò iyùn ha ẹ́ti* means "hangs down heavily with beads in the ear lobes." *Iyùn* is a synonym for *ìlèkè*.

37. *Ajá ṣe tań ajá ṣe b' éégun ni* means "the dog finishes; the dog thinks it is bones." It seems that the allusion here is to those who doǹt know either the religious or economic value of coral beads.

38. *Ìléerée mi abọn* is untranslatable.

39. *Jólóye:* Chief Jàkútá notes that it is a special type of Ijèṣà dance requiring a special type of dress or cloth.

40. *'Bòkun: Obòkun.* According to Abrahams, the name of an ancestor and *òrìṣà* in Ìléṣà. Awọlayẹ notes, however, that it is the official name of Ìléṣà, and Chief Jàkútá says that it refers to the title of the ruler of Ìjèṣà.

41. *epo* means "palm oil." Note that each of the towns or districts mentioned here highlights a particularly important market and ritual item. It seems that Ìjèṣà, like *Òṣun*, is abundantly rich.

42. *jólóye dùn'yáà mi:* "jólóyé (dance) is sweet to my mother (*Òṣun*)." Compare lines 32 and 33 which intimate that *jólóye* is sweet to me and to my Mother (*Òṣun*).

43. *ọmọ ilẹ̀ obì*: "offspring of the land of kolanuts." According to Òṣun's cosmology, she is from Ìjèṣà, the land of kolanuts.

44. *Ẹ ẹ jẹ́ a rèlé: Òṣun Òṣogbo, Ẹ̀ jòwó, jẹ kí àwá lọ sí ilé Òṣun* Òṣogbo means "Please, let us go with goodness to the house of *Òṣun* Òṣogbo." This key phrase signals that Òṣun is now properly introduced, and the praise-singer is about to proceed with the rest of the *oríkì*.

45. *Awọ́mọ̀ọ̀da: Awo-ọmọ́ọ̀-dá* means "the secret child is created." In the context of this praise-poem, this appellation hints at the spiritual mystery of procreation.

The latter suggestion is strengthened by the subsequent appellation in line 37, and annotated in note 17 above.

46. **Aṣádẹ-bí-ẹ-ń-ṣágba:** This is the same as note 17 above, but notice the stylistic differences.

47. Lines 38 through 42 repeat lines 1 and 5 while incorporating lines 11, 17, and 18, bringing this section of the praise-poem full circle, signaling movement to the next section of the *oríkì*. Lines 1 through 42 represent the introduction or overview of the elegant deity, *Ọ̀ṣun Ṣẹ̀ẹ̀gẹ̀sí*, her prowess, characteristics, and a few townships where she is worshipped or through which her river flows. The next section focuses specifically on her power as a woman, healer, and divinity.

48. **Òwọ̀rùrù-f'ara-l'ako!** *is Ò-wọ́-rùrù-fi-ara-lu-àkó!* means "one who flows along majestically hitting (her) body against the grass." The banks of the Ọ̀ṣun River are lined with tall grasses, shrubs, trees, and various plants.

49. **Òwọ̀rùrù-f'ara-l'àpáta!** *is Ò-wọ́-rùrù-fi-ara-lu-àpáta!* means "one who flows along majestically hitting (her) body against the rocks." In addition to note 48, there are several rocks and assorted stones which are more visible during the dry season. Here, *Ọ̀ṣun's* status as a river goddess is personified, and references in note 48 and note 49 together suggest *Ọ̀ṣun's* beauty, power, and sensuality.

50. **Oníkíí Awoyègúnlẹ̀:** *oníkí* is the owner of the praise, *àwọ-yè-gún-lẹ* means "the secret of being alive (that) settles at the bottom (of the water)." At the climax of the annual *Ọ̀ṣun* festival after the offering has been accepted, the waters of the Ọ̀ṣun River are said to carry medicinal properties. Women without children are especially encouraged to collect the river water and use it as either an infusion, tea, or bath throughout the year to encourage fertility and heal female troubles.

51. **Mo tún kóre Yèyé Ọ̀ṣun:** I turn (return) again to greet the Great Mother *Ọ̀ṣun*. The chanter indicates that she is

continuing with the same poem. However, note that she has already opened this section of the poem with greetings to Ọ̀ṣun before she utters the acknowledgment.

52. **mọ̀mọ̀**: "please," used for special imploring, emphasis.
53. **mọ̀gba**: *mọ̀mọ̀ gba*, "please help." Notice the stylistic variation in morphemic tonality.
54. **Mo ké mọ̀gbà lọ́dọ̀ omí** means "I cried for deliverance through the water." Several meanings are implied here. Water ushers in the life of a child during the birthing process, thus water is an agent of deliverance. Water is a symbol of Ọ̀ṣun to whom one cries for deliverance. Water as an agent in the preparation of *àgbo*, a medicinal infusion for childhood illnesses, infertility, and birthing. Also notice the poetic variations between line 52 and line 54.
55. **Mo ké mọ̀gbà lọ́dọ̀ rẹ o!** "I cried for deliverance to you!" This literal translation is a direct plea to the Good Mother, Ọ̀ṣun. The poetic variations are evident also between lines 54 and 56.
56. **àkùkọ** means "cock." One of several masculine terms associated with Ọ̀ṣun.
57. **ganganran** means "giant." The symbol of Ọ̀ṣun as a giant cock suggests her prominence among women and men.
58. **Tó rorí ọpẹ rèé kọ́lé sí: Tí ó re orí ọpẹ rèé kọ́ ilẹ́ sí** means "one who climbs (goes) on top of the oil palm tree (literally, in order) to build a house." Since there are different kinds of palm trees in western Africa, a distinction is made between palm nut and palm wine trees. Palm oil is the term used to refer to the actual oil from the palm nut kernels. According to Abrahams, the oil palm tree *(elaeis guineensis)* has both the female spadices and male inflorescences needed for self-fertilization. However, the female and male components of the oil palm tree appear during different cycles. Ọ̀ṣun perches atop this tree and serves as the unifying image of fertility. This image also replicates the *ọ̀pá ọba* (staff of

authority) used by the Àtáọ́ja to confirm his right to rule.
The staff is about five feet high and the *ẹlẹyẹ* (type of
bird) is carved on top of it. As mentioned above, birds
symbolize the *àjẹ́* whom *Ọ̀ṣun* leads.

59. *wọ́n* means "they." A plural personal pronoun used when
     addressing or referring to an elder to signify respect and
     honor. Here, it is an honorific reference to *Ọ̀ṣun*.

60. *p'Alára*: *pé Alárá,* "to call Alára," title for the ruler of
     Ará."

61. *Mo dúró ọwọ́ ò tó ò!* means "I stand, my hands cannot
     reach it!" The blessings from the worship of *Ọ̀ṣun*
     Òṣogbo are infinite.

62. *Ọ̀ṣun Òṣogbo Òròkí*: In Abrahams Yorùbá dictionary,
     Òṣogbo Òròkí meaning "greetings, you Òṣogbo person."
     He also notes that *Òròkí* refers to a famous woman,
     probably from Òṣogbo. It may be the name of a former
     Ọ̀ṣun priestess.

63. *mo tẹ́ 'ṣo: mo tẹ́ ṣọ,* meaning "I spread my clothes," that
     is, to receive or carry *Ọ̀ṣun*'s blessings.

64. *Èmí ó gbà si o* means "I will certainly receive more."
     Taken together with lines 61 through 64, this image
     compares well with the image of *Ọ̀ṣun* as the
     everflowing, here the ever-giving. These lines also
     remind the listeners that *sùúrù* (patience) brings success,
     hence one waits, *mo dúró*. In *Ìrẹtẹ̀ Àlàó*, an *odù Ifá* cited
     in chapter three, impatience costs *Ọ̀jìyàòmèfún, Ọ̀ṣun's*
     first priest, to forfeit the gifts and money she wanted to
     give him. Accordingly, he called together two other
     babaláwo to help *Ọ̀ṣun* cast *Ifá* to help her to have a
     child. Their divination and recommended offering are
     successful, but when she gives birth, *Ọ̀jìyàòmèfún* has
     gone elsewhere to earn a living. The other *babaláwọ,*
     Dúró and *Èfín,* share in *Ọ̀ṣun's* generosity without him.

65. *òwayarìn-wayanrìn-kówó-sí* equals *ò-wa-yánrìn-wa-*
     yanrìn-kó-ówó-sí, which means "one who scoops sand

and gathers yanrin to hide money." The compression of images here is wonderful! The roots of *yanrin* (bot. *lactuca taraxicofolia*, or wild lettuce) also contains healing properties. It is very tasty, especially when served with fish. The healing of women who give birth to children as well as the children themselves are a source of wealth. As a water divinity, *Ọ̀ṣun's* riverbanks are of course sandy. Fish and cowrie shells are plentiful in her waters. Although the Ọ̀ṣun Grove is a protected area, the poetic image here evokes *Ọ̀ṣun's* fertility (fish who are symbolically as abundant as children) and wealth (cowrie sea shells).

66. *Ẹ̀ wáá ẁ Ọ̀ṣun Òṣogbo! È-wá-wo-Ọ̀ṣun-Òṣogbo* means "You (all) come and see *Ọ̀ṣun Òṣogbo!*" The invitation to join in the admiration of *Ọ̀ṣun Òṣogbo* parallels the invitation to the other *òrìṣà* (divinities) to join *Ọ̀ṣun* in celebrating her festival.

67. *abíyamọ: a-bí-ya-ọmọ* means "one who gives birth to children, a nursing mother." Notice that a similar phrase, *ayamọ*, is used as a greeting for the bereaved meaning, "the dead will be born to you as a child" – a clear reference to reincarnation of one's ancestors. *Àbíkú* children are said to be born repeatedly to the same mother only to die (return to the ancestors) again. Thus, women who have several miscarriages are advised to perform certain rites. *Ọ̀ṣun* is known for curing such female ailments with special healing waters in *Àìwẹ́, Ọ̀ṣun's* pot for medicinal preparations. As part of their training, *Ìyálòṣà Ọ̀ṣun, Ọ̀ṣun* priestesses, learn to prepare the *àìwẹ́* and other medicines.

68. *tí i retí igbee!* means "who listens to noise!" *Abíyamọ* (nursing mother) usually sleeps lightly so she can hear the cries of her child in the night. Also notice the alliteration with *ì* (pronounced *EE*) produced here.

69. *Ṣàwẹ̀lolú* is another *oríkì* (praise-name) for *Ọ̀ṣun*

meaning, "one-who-makes-the-special-decorated-small-pot-of-*Ọ̀ṣun*-great." The small pot refers to the pot used for storing *àïwẹ́*, the generic name for the medicine that is used for female ailments, especially those pertaining to fertility problems, and ailing children.

70. *Ọlọ́rọ̀ Ọba Ìjẹ̀ṣà* is the title for the confidante and friend of the ruler of Ìjẹ̀ṣà. This entire line summarizes *Ọ̀ṣun*'s attributes and roles in Yorùbá cosmology, and establishes the close relationship between *Ọ̀ṣun* and Ìjẹ̀ṣà. Compare to line 14 above.

71. *Ibunnu má sùn!* means "In the dead of night, please do not sleep!" This phrase complements note 68 above. Notes 68 through 71 celebrate *Ọ̀ṣun*'s multiple roles including motherhood, ancestor, and leader of the *àjẹ́*. Nursing mothers sleep very lightly, and are very protective of their newborn infants during the middle of the night. The *àjẹ́* (powerful beings), the *l'ééégun* (ancestors), and the *ajogun* (malevolent forces) are especially active during this time of night as well.

72. *Iwin Adénlé*: the spirit of Adénlé, a former *Atáójá*.

73. *Iwin Látọ̀nà Àjàdi*: the spirit of Látọ̀nà Àjàdì, another former *Atáójá*.

74. *Èèyàn tó bá tètè*: "Human beings who quickly (greet or pay respect to the Good Mother *Ọ̀ṣun* receive abundant blessings.)"

75. *Èmi mọ tètè*: meaning "I most certainly will quickly (greet or pay respect to the Good Mother *Ọ̀ṣun*) acknowledges that *Ọ̀ṣun* is receptive to anyone who appeals to her properly. Most assuredly, this worshipper intends to partake of *Ọ̀ṣun*'s generosity.

76. *Mo yá gbowo*: "I gather money." As a wealthy woman, *Ọ̀ṣun* gives wealth as well as children who themselves symbolize wealth.

77. *Mo yá gbọmọ*: "I gather children." The use of *yá* ("to scoop or dig") in both phrases mirrors the image of *Ọ̀ṣun*

in note 65 as one who scoops vegetables, a source of nourishment, then hides her treasures therein for later distribution.

78.   *Iwin Oyèwálé:* the spirit of Oyèwálé, the present Atáọja reigning in Ọ̀ṣogbo.

79.   *Gbogbaara Ọ̀kèya,* "All the people of Ọ̀kèya" refers to the people north of the River Niger *(Ọya).* Ọ̀kèya means "top of *Ọya* [or Niger] River." According to her cosmology, *Ọ̀ṣun* saved the people of Ọ̀ṣogbo from conquest during the Fulani slave-raiding Wars. The Fulani raided the savanna and forests regions which lie south of their territory across the Niger River. This line suggests that even those north of the River Niger should likewise respect *Ọ̀ṣun.*

80.   *mọ̀ mọ̀:* "doesn't know."

81.   *Taá ni ò mọ̀ mọ̀ p̀ Ọ̀ṣun Oṣogbo, nìí b' ó baá ṣèlú Ọ̀ṣogbo o?"* means "who does not know that it is *Ọ̀ṣun Ọ̀ṣogbo* who helps the *ọba* rule Ọ̀ṣogbo?" Again, there are several meanings suggested here. The line implies the co-rulership between female representing *Ọ̀ṣun* through *Ìyá Ọ̀ṣun* and male representing *Olùtimihin* and *Laróye* through *Atáọja.* It also suggests the interrelationship of spiritual and political rule as well as the pact that *Ọ̀ṣun* as primordial ruler of Ọ̀ṣogbo made with *Olùtimihin* and *Laróye,* the predecessor of the present *Atáọja.*

82.   *mọmọ:* "certainly." Notice the word play between notes 80 and 82. *Mọ̀ mọ̀* in line 81, note 80 above means "doesn't know," while *mọmọ* in line 85, note 82 means "certainly." Although these morphemes are contradictory, stylistically they enrich the sound and meaning of the *oríkì.*

83.   *fi í retí igbe* is similar to note 68 above. In this section the word *nítori,* meaning "because," indicates the basis for *Ọ̀ṣun's* actions as a wife of *Ṣàngó,* and a nurturing mother.

84.   *torí àmàlà* means "because of *amàlà,*" *Ṣàngó's* favorite food.

85.   *Ṣàngó* is one of the major *òriṣà,* husband to *Ọ̀ṣun, Ọya,*

and Ọba, all of whom are river deities. As a divinity of thunder and lightning, Ṣàngó hearlds the rains which swell the rivers. This clearly indicates fertility and nourishment since cyclical droughts bring about famine, destitution, and migration to new water sources. As a human being, he was the fourth ruler of Ọ̀yọ́, and it is believed that his mother, Yẹmọja, hailed from Nupe (Tápá).

86.   **Baálèè mí,** Babá ile mí means "father (man) in my house."

87.   **ọkọọ mí** my husband. Line 89 refers to Ṣàngó's role as ruler of Ọ̀yọ̀ and husband to Ọ̀ṣun.

88.   **fi í gbàyánrìn,** fi rí gbà yánrìn literally means "one uses sight to locate vegetable." Yánrìn is a favorite spinach-like vegetable of Ọ̀ṣun. Lines 87 through 90 allude to Ọ̀ṣun's role as wife and mother.

89.   **Iwin Adénlé** refers to the spirit of Adénlé as a previous caretaker of Ọ̀ṣun.

90.   **Iwin Àdùnni** refers to Adúnní as a present caretaker of Ọ̀ṣun.

91.   Note that the opening lines of this third phase of the chant differs from the first and second phases. Here, there are no additional praise-names for Ọ̀ṣun, instead the chanter opens by acknowledging her predecessors. Doing anything without acknowledging one's predecessors is prohibited.

92.   **Ìbà** means "homage" which indicates paying respect to one's predecessors.

93.   **mo ríbà orìn mí** means "using homage to pay for the privilege of learning and reciting the Ọ̀ṣun chants." In some West African cultures, offering acknowledgment by direct reference or a gift is courteousness and indicates good manners and proper respect.

94.   **Adétayùn:** Adé-ta-iyùn literally means "royalty purchases beads," figuratively speaking, a source from which beads are purchased. She is one of the earliest Ọ̀ṣun priestesses of Òṣogbo. Because of its context,

Adétayùn may also be a cognomen for Ọ̀ṣun herself. The name Adéta in line 105 below may be a shortened form of Adétayùn.

95. *abiyamọ:* see note 67 above.
96. *làhàholo* refers to suffering for the sake of her child, emphasizing that the nursing mother suffers for the sake of her child through all the phases of pregnancy, childbirth, nursing, and the child's adolescence. It also refers to the tall grass which lines the banks of the Ọ̀ṣun River, possibly lemon grass.
97. *gbàgọ̀ nínú* means "wiggles inside." This image suggests the flowing sensual beauty of the Ọ̀ṣun River.
98. *olóbò-tújẹ̀* is also a plant which grows inside of the Ọ̀ṣun Grove in Ọ̀ṣogbo. From its description, it may be similar to *aloe vera.* According to Abraham's dictionary, it is also known as *ẹwẹ ayaba,* and is frequently called ringworm because the oil is known to irritate children's skin. However, the leaves are used for treating dysentry. The term *olóbò-tújẹ̀* sometimes refers to the female genitals (*òbò*).
99. *ẹgbìn* is a gazelle, a very beautiful animal used here to symbolize Ọ̀ṣun's beauty. The gazelle, a member of the antelope family, is often found hidden among tall grass eating leaves and shrubs.
100. *rére* is a green plant that grows in the Ọ̀ṣun Grove.
101. *Mo mọ̀ sì b'ọlọ́mọ ṣọ̀ṣọ́ ròdé: Mo mọ̀ bá ọlọ́mọ ṣe ọ̀ṣọ́ re òde* means "And it is I (emphatic) who certainly follows the owner of children go on an outing in adornment." Here, the praise connotes Ọ̀ṣun's love of fine jewelry, clothing, oils, and other forms of adornment and beautification. Her worshippers, too, emulate her in order to associate with and honor her. An outdooring occurs forty days after the birth of a child when the mother and extended family women and women friends escort mother and child throughout an area of the township to introduce the newborn to the community.

102.   **Adéta** is one of the earliest priestesses of *Ọ̀ṣun Ọ̀ṣogbo*. See also note 94 above.

103.   **gilọ̀gilọ̀** is one of several ideophones referring to a very radiant beauty.

104.   **Tí î paráà 'wó l'ádiẹ jẹẹ!** *tí ó ń pa ará Ìwó ní ádiẹ jẹ ẹ!* means one who kills the chickens which belong to the people of Ìwô. In other praise poems, songs, and references to *Ọ̀ṣun*, it is noted that with her status as an *àjẹ́* and leader of the *àjẹ́*, she must be properly supplicated in order to avoid confusion in one's life. Chickens are a ritual food.

105.   **Egbẹ́róngbé** is another very early priestess of *Ọ̀ṣun Ọ̀ṣogbo*.

106.   **tijú ẹfuń:** *tí ojú ẹfun* means "coyness, alluring, to shut the eye because of white powder." *Efun*, white powder, is often used in *òrìṣà* worship, especially that of *Ọ̀rìṣànlá*, the divinity who shapes human forms that are held in the womb.

107.   **Ọ̀bàrà-gẹsin-làlú,** According to Chief Jákùtà, *Ọ̀bàrà* is from *Mẹ́rìndínlógún* (sixteen cowries divination). It is the sixth one and an important *odù* about a great one who rode a horse through the town in promise of *Ọ̀ṣun's* dignitÿ honor.

108.   **èniyàn jú òwò:** *èniyàn ó jú òwò* means "people are greater than money." This refers to *Ọ̀ṣun's* reputation as an astute business woman who esteems the value of human beings.

109.   **èniyàn jú abíkù:** *èniyàn o jú abiku* means the living child is greater than the *abíkù* child. *Abíkù* literally means one who is born to die, which refers to the children of women who have had several miscarriages or whose children repeatedly die in early childhood. *Ọṣun*, as the giver of children, is the best one to handle such children whose repeated cycles of birth and death torment their mothers. *Àìwẹ́* is a medicinal application used to treat such women

and children. This line emphasizes her power to heal children who are considered a source of wealth because of their added productivity to collective family life.

110. **Arúgbó** means elder. This line intimates that Ọ̀sun's powers as a healer and giver of children are so great that she can even give children to elder women.

111. **Ènìyànjúù mí**: *ènìyàn jú ù mí* means "one who is greater than I," symbolizing the faith with which worshippers submit themselves to the meaning and power of Ọ̀sun. Together, the three lines beginning with *ènìyàn jú* affirm Ọ̀sun's attributes as a wealthy woman who gives and protects children as well as forms a sisterhood with other women like herself.

112. The seven lines from 113 to 119 form a chorus that repeats earlier lines throughout the poem, echoing the concepts of Ọ̀sun as a graceful, powerful woman. These lines summarize and remind the audience that Ọ̀sun's greatness complements her femininity and her motherliness and indicate a shift to another theme. These are sensual, consummate images here which segway into the concept of paying homage.

113. **júbá**: *jú ìbà* means "to make or pay homage" (as to an elder, an authority figure or *òrìṣà*).

114. **alaré** is a title meaning "the owner(s) of *aré*." *Aré* is entertainment of the *òrìṣà*. This class of professional (usually guild) performing artists include all performers whose poetry, song, drumming, and dance are meant to entertain both divine and human audiences. Although the different genres in this class draw their images and references from the cosmology, such material may not always be sacred, in fact, it is frequently quite secular.

115. **huǹmọ́**: *hun ọmọ* means "suffers the child (offspring)," suggesting that the offspring suffers for the solo actions or violations of the elders.

116. **gbọ́dọ̀ huǹmọ́**: must do homage (so that) the offspring do

not suffer.

117. **Ṣẹbọra** is a collective term which refers to the divinities. *Ọmọ l'ójú ṣẹbọra* means "an offspring, a child who is the eye of the divinities."

118. *mo ribà orin mi,* meaning "I find homage in my song" symbolizes that singing the *oríki* itself is a form of homage.

119. *Ìbà nì n ó f'ọjọ̀ òní jú: Ìbà nì n ó fi ojọ̀ òní jú* means "it is homage (that) I am using today for elevation (as payment for my songs)."

120. *t'òsùn* refers to beautification. One who deals in red camwood powder, a locally manufactured cosmetic used by young women to beautify the body, and to pray for children. *T'òsùn* also refers to the camwood tree (African rosewood), whose bark produces a red dye and whose flowers are a conspicuously bright yellow, *Ọ̀ṣun's* favorite color and the color of brass.

121. *t'àìwẹ́:* of medicinal waters referring obliquely to the small decorated pot that *Ọ̀ṣun* uses to retain water for those in need of children. After the blessing of the Ọ̀ṣun River during the annual festival, her waters are deemed sacred and medicinal, in other words, the whole river is holy water.

122. *Ọmọ Àṣẹkúnlá* is another name for *Ọ̀ṣun. Àṣẹ-kún-ọlá* means creative power (of the universe) enhances wealth. The word *ọmọ,* "child," reinforces the belief that children are wealth, and wealth is power. *Ọ̀ṣun* and all powerful women like her are able to enhance their innate power by using the *àṣẹ* given to them by *Olódùmarè.* That *àṣẹ* is used to obtain the necessary wealth to empower themselves and properly care for their children. According to *Yorùbá* cosmology and religious philosophy, *Olódùmarè* used *àṣẹ* to create the universe. Everything in the universe, thus, has its own *àṣẹ* that it uses variously. The key to the fulfillment of any

potentiality is initiation, which contains secret knowledge, *áwo*. *Èṣù* is the guardian of the *àṣẹ* that *Olódùmarè* used to create the universe and its diverse life forms.

123. *L'óreé Àgbọ̀nmọ* means "goodness of obedient children." Compare line 134 and line 137 for variations in musical and literary style.

124. *ọmọọ jẹ́ bí yọ̀*: *ọmọ jẹ́ bí iyọ̀* is an *oríkì* for a lineage meaning "one who is as effective as salt." This *oríkì* suggests the potency of *Ọ̀sun's* medicinal powers, especially those related to childbirth.

125. *'Gbà tá i jẹbí yọ̀*: *igbà tí àwá ò jẹ́ bí iyọ̀* meaning when we are effective as salt. The line is an extension of *ọmọọ-jẹ-bí-yọ̀*, and suggests that women who are as powerful as *Ọ̀sun*, and/or are *Ọ̀sun* priestesses strive to emulate *Ọ̀sun's* potency.

126. *l'Àìwẹ́* "at *Àìwẹ́*" refers again to *Ọ̀sun's* pot which is used for healing infertile women and sick children. The pot symbolizes the power of the *àjẹ́* and the effectiveness of *Ọ̀sun's* healing powers.

127. *Ìgbà tí n ó jẹ bí yọ̀*: *Ìgbà tí n ó maa jẹ́ bí iyọ̀* meaning "I will be as effective as salt." Remember that *Ọ̀sun* was given *àṣẹ* by *Olódùmarè*, and she is *àjẹ́*. *Ọ̀sun* priestesses who are trained as healers also become *àjẹ́* and are as effective as salt.

128. *Mo gb'ọ̀wọ́ ijó gẹngẹ* "I grow long hands (arms) for dancing." The movement dance for *Ọ̀sun* requires gently swaying of extended arms while the dancer holds a calabash (a symbol of *àìwẹ́*) in her hands. This indicates that the dancer will redouble her praise to *Ọ̀sun*.

129. *Ọ̀sun l'Àìwẹ́* is an *oríkì* (praise name) for *Ọ̀sun* used to unify her divinity with her sacred, curative medicinal pot of medicinal waters, *Àìwé*.

130. *L'óóreé àìgbọ̀n mọ́* equals *óló óóre àìgbọ̀n ọmọ*, meaning "for the goodness of a disobedient child." Children

irrespective of occasional, behavior are still a blessing.
131.   *Irúlá* refers to the seeds of the okra vegetable used for planting. The image here clearly suggests the multiple children, the seeds, by which humanity perpetuates itself.
132.   *ọ̀jẹ̀* is a title for *Egúngún*. To become an ancestor completes the life cycle. Thus, the *Ọ̀sun* worshipper, as a giver and receiver of children, represents total human fulfillment. As a woman, *Ọ̀sun* and her worshippers form a bridge between pre-living and afterlife. Moreover, *Ọ̀sun* herself is a human and divine ancestor.
133.   *Ta ní ó mọ̀mọ̀ bá mi dẹ̀lẹ̀ Ìyáà mi ó* This is an invitation to follow the chanter to *Ọ̀sun*'s house (shrine) and an invitation to share in the blessings and rewards of *Ọ̀sun* worship. As noted in chapter three, *Ọ̀sun* demanded that innately powerful women like her should also have the right to initiation into the secrets (keys) to divination, healing, and infinite knowledge.
134.   *Ará t'Ọlọ́rọ̀ ẹdùn* meaning the one who is the confidante or mouthpiece of twins, *ibéjì*, which are revered in Yorùbá society. This complex image intimates the reverence with which *ìyá ibéjì*, "the mother of twins" is accorded as the vehicle for their entry into the world. *Bàbá ibéjì*, "the father of twins" is similarly honored.
135.   *Ibú alẹ́ o!* "Dead of night!" This is the time when both the *àjẹ́* (powerful beings) and *égun* (ancestors) are most accessible.
136.   *mo ṣiwọ́ tán.* Having delivered twins, the parents̀ role, especially the mother as giver of children, is viewed as having reached perfection.
137.   *Mo yáa m̀ojú le koko!* "To take on an austere countenance is to signify self-mastery!" This is especially true with respect to childbirth when Yorùbá women are cautioned against crying out loudly in pain.
138.   *mo ṣáwó* "I practice (do) the secrets." The chanter acknowledges that she is an initiate into the secret and

sacred knowledge (*àwo*) of Ọ̀ṣun worship.

139. *mo ṣè ṣègùn*: "I practice (do) medicine." The chanter here acknowledges that she also knows and practices as a healer.

140. *Mo ṣàigbọ́dọ̀-ràn*: The power that one has gained from practicing the secret knowledge and healing arts has allowed the worshipper to do that which she could not previously do.

141. *Ọ̀tún-ùn mí, ìmú-ń-kele*: On the right is *kele*, the beads which signify initiation as well as worship of Ṣàngó and Ọya. *Ọ̀tún* is often used as a title indicating the deputy or second in rank. See photo on page 15.

142. *òsìi mí ń fa bàbà*: "on the left is *bàbà*," that is, copper, which is part of Ọ̀ṣun's iconography. *Òsì* is often used as a title for the next in rank to *Òtún*, therefore, the third in command. *Òtún* and *òsì* are military positions. See photo on page 15.

143. *Agbedeméjì mí ń mú ṣẹ́rẹ́ lọ́wọ́*: From my very centre, I carry the rattle in my hands. According to Professor Abímbọ́lá, the *ṣẹ́rẹ́* is a gourd with a very long neck used as a rattle for Ṣàngó, one of Ọ̀ṣun's husbands. (See Wándé Abímbọ́lá. *Ifá Divination Poetry*. New York: (Nok Publishers, 1977). *Ọya*, the favorite wife of Ṣàngó, also symbolizes the Niger River.

144. *È bá mọ̀ sì yáa báa mí, Kóree Yèyé f' Ọ̀ṣun*: "You (the listeners) should hurriedly help me to praise the Good Mother Ọ̀ṣun." Having indicated Ọṣun's attributes which underscore her perpetuation and protection of humanity, the listeners should rush to praise, that is, to thank Ọ̀ṣun for her blessings. This could also be an invitation to become an Ọ̀ṣun worshipper.

145. *Mo kóree Yèyé f'Ọ̀ṣun*. This praise-poem ends here. The *oríkì* begins with this greeting to Ọ̀ṣun, the Good Mother, and so ends with it. The song and its function are complete.

Sanctuary in Ọ̀ṣun Grove   Photo by author

Courtesy of Y. Ẹlẹbùrúîbọn

Babaláwo Yẹmi Ẹlẹbùrúîbọn

Chapter Two

THE *ÒRÌṢÀ* SYSTEM: AN OVERVIEW OF YORÙBÁ COSMOLOGY

The Yorùbá worldview is a complex network of interdependent relationships among *eníyàn* (human beings) and *òrìṣa* (deities). It is a worldview that accepts the extraordinary as an integral part of the nature of existence. It is a worldview that acknowledges — indeed, knows — the *àṣẹ* (life-force) that permeates *òrun* (heaven), *ilẹ́* (earth), and *eníyàn* (humanity). It is a worldview that maintains an intimate knowledge of *àṣẹ* as it becomes manifest in spirit, nature, and human existence. It is a worldview that, simultaneously, reflects the polarities and analogies within the oral, performing, and plastic arts. The Yorùbá worldview is pervasive in that it embraces antithesis and synthesis as interdependent concepts by holding positive and negative forces always in balance. It is a way of knowing, as my great-grandmother did, that too much of anything is not good, even too much good is bad.

Yorùbá cosmology imparts a complex religious philosophy which locates itself in Ilé-Ifẹ̀ cited as the center of the world. For centuries, Ilé-Ifẹ̀ has remained the spiritual center of the Yorùbá world while other towns and regencies have become noted political, economic, or artistic centers. Even during the political reign of the Old Ọ̀yọ́ Empire from the fifteenth to the eighteenth centuries, Ilé-Ifẹ̀ remained the spiritual power behind major Yorùbá thrones. Consequently, Ilẹ́-Ifẹ̀'s quintessential spiritual role not only spread outside of Ilè-Ifẹ́ but also legitimized the political authority, conferred by the Ọ̀ọni-Ifẹ̀, the supreme Yorùbá religio-political ruler, among the major crowns throughout Yorùbá-speaking western Africa.

As demonstrated by the religious and political organization of the Ọ̀ṣun festival, religious and political functions of the Yorùbá social order are juxtaposed rather than superimposed over one another. Today this remains true, despite the economic and intellectual prominence of such modern cities as Lagos, Ilorin, and Ibadan. For most Yorùbá people, true political, social, and economic authority still evolves from and is confirmed by the Ọ̀ọni-Ifẹ̀. I am told by my Yorùbá colleagues and informants[1] that a religious observance occurs in Ilé-Ifẹ̀ every day of the year except one when they take a holiday. It is indisputable then that Ilé-Ifẹ̀ is the spiritual center of the Yorùbá from which authority and social status evolve.

What is less evident but quite revealing about the relationship between Ilé-Ifẹ̀ and the rest of Yorùbá territory is its oral historiography[2] and philosophy found in the *Ifá* Divination Corpus. In the corpus, we find an elaborate body of knowledge in which mythology, philosophy, and history exists along with other fields of knowledge. Analysis of the *Ifá* corpus in conjunction with other Yorùbá oral genres is a challenging experience that can illuminate otherwise obscure cosmological and historical data, as well as sometimes obscuring otherwise obvious data. Significantly, as Professor Wándé Abímbọ́lá states, "The Yorùbá regard *Ifá* as the repository of their beliefs and moral values."[3] And what holds the *Ifá* corpus together and makes this belief system so fascinating and complex is its *òrìṣà* system or network of deities. Each of the 401 *òrìṣà*, or deities, has her and his own mythology, history, and *oríkì* (or praise poetry), which disclose origin, status, and location of a central shrine. Between the *Ifá* corpus and the diverse oral genres celebrating the *ọrìṣà* themselves, we learn whether a given *òrìṣà* is purely a spiritual entity, a deified being, a personified natural or human characteristic, or a life force. Within this elaborate system of orature, we learn the history of migrations, the founding of towns, the indigenous view of some historical events and, most importantly, we learn what the Yorùbá people themselves thought, and still think, about the art of living. I am emphasizing these seemingly mundane aspects of Yorùbá cosmology because, like the religious structure, the cosmic ethos parallels rather than objectifies Yorùbá social order.

Before introducing some of the deities who comprise the Yorùbá cosmic structure, I would like to introduce a few key words and concepts. These are *orí* or head, *oríkì* which, depending on the context, means either praise name or praise poetry, *òrìṣà* or deity, *iwa* or character, and *ẹbo* or sacrifice. These concepts and key *òrìṣà* indicate that free will and destiny coexist in Yorùbá cosmology, unlike in Western thought where they are in opposition. For example, according to Yorùbá thought, one "chooses" a head (*orí*) prior to gestation. That head contains a destiny or life-path. One's *ori*, the *Ifá* corpus states, follows a person throughout life, while one's *òrìṣà*, or deity, is restricted by more provincial, communal demands, and can be abandoned or changed.[4] For this reason among others, the head or life-path (*orí*), is praised (*kì*), by means of the oral literary genre known as *oríkì* (literally, "to praise the head.") Both *ori* and *òrìṣà* are influenced by a person's willingness to provide the necessary *ẹbọ* or sacrifice to achieve the desired results. *Ẹbọ* then is a medium of exchange to achieve a goal, change an event, or improve a situation. Its mystery aside, human beings make sacrifices constantly.

The concept and function of *orí* in Yorùbá cosmology also implies a deep sense of responsibility for an individual's behavior. It further connotes that human beings are interdependent with the divine order rather than completely at its mercy. This explains the belief that the *òrìṣà* behave in *òrun* ("heaven") as human beings behave *n'ayé* ("on earth"). In fact, the Yorùbá proverb, *ẹ̀nìyàn kò sí, kò sí Mọlẹ̀*, reinforces that concept. However, the ability to choose an *orí* is determined by one's *ìwà* or character, and it is uncertain whether *ìwà* precedes, accompanies or follows *orí*. Like all other Yorùbá activities, *orí* is chosen by the unborn in heaven through consultation. Failure to select an amicable head results in a difficult life, which can only be conquered by a great deal of sacrifice. Conversely, while selection of a good head insures fewer obstacles, it does not guarantee a flawless life. In both cases, however, the deities are present to assist human beings in overcoming adversity, and living personally and communally fulfilling lives.

In interviews with *babaláwo* Yẹmi Ẹlẹ̀búrúibọn, an *Ifá* priest in Òṣogbo, he narrates an *odù Ifá* which explains that the *òrìṣà* are sent by *Olódùmarè*, the Supreme Deity, to organize the world and assist humanity to live successful lives.[7] To receive this assistance, human beings are required to offer a designated *ẹbọ*, or sacrifice, which acknowledges the reciprocity and bonds between the spiritual and secular elements of life. *Ẹbọ* culminates in ritual which allows the person or persons involved to transform themselves and momentarily to transcend the confines of a problematic situation. While engaged in a ritual mode, an individual or community as supplicant becomes a conduit for spiritual communication. This state occurs when the *òrìṣà* "ride" their human hosts who, in turn, speak for them. The *òrìṣà* speak by means of *aṣẹ*, the quintessential power of *Olódùmarè*, and their vision and messages are interpreted through the specifics of iconography, movement, and vocabulary. As the essence and symbol of Supreme Creative Power, *Olódùmarè* influences every particle of life and dust with life-force (*àṣẹ*), eternally binding all life together. It is this common telepathic thread, *àṣẹ*, through which spirit, humanity, and nature communicate.

Despite this rather complex relationship among choice, free will, and restitution, *Olódùmarè*, as the Supreme Deity, remains at the pinnacle of Yorùbá cosmology. The *òrìṣà* are

Olódùmarè's ministers whose talents and tasks are assigned by the Supradeity.[8] Yet the oftentimes androgynous *Olódùmarè* is *not* the focus of Yorùbá religious practice. Ìdowu points out that *Olódùmarè* is irrefutable, omniscient, and inscrutable. Unlike the other *òrìṣà*, there are neither shrines nor rituals established for *Olódùmarè*.[9] Rather, it is the 401 *òrìṣà* who minister to human needs and implorations who are accessible, finite, and intelligible. These other deities are penetrable through a network of human and artistic means: (1) *babaláwo* or "fathers of the secrets"; (2) *babalóṣà* and *iyalóṣà* or "fathers" and "mothers" of the deities (or chief priests and priestesses); respectively, and (3) participation in rituals, festivals, and secular ceremonies that occupy every aspect of Yorùbá life. Among the major *òrìṣà* are *Òrúnmìlà*, the *òrìṣà* of wisdom and knowledge; *Èṣù*, the guardian of the crossroads and keeper of the *àṣẹ*;[10] *Òṣun*, the *òrìṣà* of fertility and leader of the *àjẹ́*; *Òbatálá*, the *òrìṣà* who shapes human forms; and *Ògún*, the *òrìṣà* of war, iron, and creativity. Obviously, these few *òrìṣà* barely represent the breadth of the Yorùbá pantheon, but their names and identities are key to penetrating Yorùbá cosmology.

The *Ifá* corpus provides two similar narratives that explain the multiplicity of *òrìṣà*. In both narratives the protagonist *òrìṣà* is shattered in an act of vengefulness from which the other *òrìṣà* arise. This simple explanation of the dispersal of the singular Deity obscures more probable explanations about the complexity of the Yorùbá pantheon. However, as the presence of *Ṣàngo* and *Jàkúta* in the pantheon demonstrates, some of the *òrìṣà* are deified heroines and heroes, while others are retained from the religious structure of aboriginal as well as migrant people.[11] The constant reference to warfare, relocation, covenants, droughts, and similar events indicate a dynamic and evolving social order. Seemingly, over several centuries, the present-day Yorùbá people were in the process of "becoming," and during that process, conquest and cultural affinity among diverse ethnic groups played a major role in their evolution. The plethora of *ọrìṣà*, their histories and mythologies, and the location of their major shrines contribute to this perspective. Moreover, the historical tension among such townships and regencies as *Ilé-Ifẹ̀*, Modakeke, Ọ̀yó, Ìjẹ̀bu-Ọ̀de, and Ondo suggest transition and fusion. These shifts in locale, references to wars and treaties, dialectical differences, and an extensive oral literature containing these allusions corroborate this notion of cultural evolution and syncretism. While this may seem tenuous and speculative, if valid these transitional phases help to explain some of the contradictions in the composite *ọrìṣà* presence as well as the adaptability of those Yorùbá who survived Western captivity in Cuba, Brazil, Haiti, the United States, and elsewhere.

The following diagrams (pp. 53 - 59) illustrate some of the more prominent *ọrìṣà* and their roles in the cosmology. Diagram A provides an overview irrespective of their mode of incorporation into the pantheon. Diagram B identifies some deified ancestors, and Diagram C names the natural forces known as *ọrìṣà*. Some of the *ọrìṣà* from Diagram A are repeated in Diagrams B and C because the latter illustrations are intended to differentiate the modes of incorporation mentioned above. By mode of incorporation, I mean the manner in which an *ọrìṣà* becomes part of the pantheon. Those *ọrìṣà* who enter the pantheon from *ọrun*, or heaven, are considered the principal deities; those who enter as deified ancestors from *ayé*, or earth, represent a second major mode of incorporation; and those personified forces such as wind (often represent by *ọrìṣà* such as Ọyá) are the third major mode of incorporation. In addition, many major *ọrìṣà* travel with migrating communities, and become part of the indigenous lore such as with *Odùduwà*, or they are invested by those communities as a founding or heroic *ọrìṣà* with another cognomen. This regenerative process allowing for the growth of the pantheon provides key allusions which are found in the oral literature itself. For example, *Ọṣun Òṣogbo*, according to the *Ifá* corpus, is a major *ọrìṣà* from *ọrun*. However, we also learn from *odù Ifá* about *Ọṣun Ápáránìrà* or *Yẹmẹsẹ* from Ido Ẹ̀kìti and *Ọṣun*

Ìjùmú from `Ìjùmú township who become secondary *òrìṣà* and/ or deified ancestors from other locations usually cited along the course of the river.[12]

All *òrìṣà* are distinguished by their respective mythologies. For example, *Òṣun Òṣogbo* is considered the real *Òṣun* as will be demonstrated throughout this book. But since *Òṣun* means *to* "seep out" or "a source from which something seeps out," a deity whose mythology narrates an act of bravery in which the hero/ heroine "falls down and becomes a river" or "a source" may be called *Òṣun* so-and-so. These different *Òṣun* also allude to the word *Òṣun* as a female rulership title. Despite these complexities the principal *òrìṣà* can be distinguished by their longevity. With the exception of the major *òrìṣà* from the first three catagories mentioned above, *òrìṣà* are vulnerable because they must remain efficacious or people abandon them or replace them with more useful ones. This may help to explain the resilience of such *òrìṣà* as *Ògún, Èṣù, Yẹmọja, Òṣun, Egúngún,* and *Ṣàngó* in the Western hemisphere. In this regard, greater familiarity with Yorùbá language, culture, and oral literature in the West may disclose both their ancestral townships and clues to their resilience in captivity. What these modes of incorporation and the longevity of the *òrìṣà* reveal are operative lifestyles and patterns of religious survival that pre-date Western enslavement and captivity.

Festival Drama as an Expression of Cultural Literacy

Festival drama provides the context for examining the *òrìṣà* mythologies and engaging Yorùbá cosmology. This spiritual sojourn is often intertwined with the political history of a specific area or with the Yorùbá people in general. The *Ifá* corpus provides the organizing principle by which the *òrìṣà* festival calendar is maintained. In my interviews and discussions with several Yorùbá priests, priestesses, and scholars, I learned the signifi-

cance of festivals in Yorùbá belief systems. They pointed out that
the festival calendar follows an established order, but the specific
date on which a particular ọ̀rìṣà celebration begins is determined
only by consultation with *Ifá*. The *Ifá* festival, for example, precedes the *Ọ̀ṣun* festival sometime in June, while the *Ògún* festival follows in October as determined by *Ifá* divination.[21]

This ongoing calendar allows for constant interaction between the society at large and its cultural caretakers. Two elements of festival drama suggest its efficacy in promoting cultural
literacy: (1) the specificity of the ọ̀rìṣà celebrant, and (2) the collective ọ̀rìṣà participation. As indicated, knowledge of the ọ̀rìṣà
is encoded in several oral literary genres. *Ìyẹ̀rẹ̀ Ifá, oríkì, orin,
Ṣàngó-pípè, Ìjàlà*, and *efo* among others are distinguished by literary and performance styles, subject matter, and structure. For
example, during an annual *Ifá* festival, *ìyẹ̀rẹ̀ Ifá* will certainly
dominate the event with other oral genres performed to enhance
the celebration.[22] On a social level, repeated exposure to diverse
oral genres would reinforce symbols, images, themes, and linguistic conventions that pertain to a specific literary form. The
festival context, then, provides the forum for exposure to and
renewal of these forms and relevant themes.

With respect to the participation of the collective ọ̀rìṣà,
as demonstrated in chapter five, the celebrant ọ̀rìṣà and representatives invite full ọ̀rìṣà and human participation. During the *Ọ̀ṣun*
festival, the *babaláwo* call *Ọ̀rúnmìlà* and the other *IrúnMọlẹ̀* to
join in celebrating the *Ọ̀ṣun* festival. The *àyàn* drum ensemble
evokes the ọ̀rìṣà, enticing them to obfuscate the boundaries between the sacred and the secular. Such an invitation is tantamount
to total immersion in Yorùbá cultural philosophy. It engages both
the spiritual and human worlds, merging them as a collective unit
and thereby regenerating the efficacy of *àṣẹ*. As such, the common language of festival, the repetition of ideals, the reinforce-
ment of *orìṣa* symbols, and contextualizing of contemporary issues reinforce the premise upon which a social vision critiques
and maintains itself. In terms of Yorùbá cultural literacy, this

suggests that the circularity of existence is maintained by a delicate respect for the power of *aṣe* manifested by natural, human, and spiritual forces. It suggests that human beings penetrate the sacred world through the pathway of a particular *orìṣa*, thereby engaging and evolving within the dictates of cultural knowledge.

Here, the relationship between oral literature and language is organic and pervasive. It is organic because knowledge of diverse sacred meanings of a given *orìṣa* are replicated in diverse secular contexts. It is pervasive because intrinsic proverbial meanings, family and personal *oríkì*, and other forms of social discourse are validated by the cosmology and the *orìṣa* who give it substance. In this regard, festival drama sets the stage for the performance of myriad oral literary genres, relevant dances, and spectacle. Together, the orature and festival drama contain the means through which sociocultural bonds are renewed and consensus maintained. Nevertheless, it is not my intention to suggest the existence of a monomorphic *orìṣa* system. On the contrary, as Idowú points out, a study of the mythology, symbolism, and iconography of the *orìṣa* reveals contradictions that as noted earlier suggest various stages in the evolution of Yorùbá culture and cosmology. This is certainly true of *Oṣun's* mythology. Given that, both the *orìṣa* system and its contradistinctions imply an engaging venue for Yorùbá cosmological and social discourse.

Viewing the *Òrìṣà* System

Diagram A illustrates some of the principle *orìṣa* whose origins are basically of pure spiritual essence. These deities have their primary interaction with *Olódùmare* as they are frequently mentioned in the *Ifá* and other oral literary genres in direct relationship to the Supreme Creator Essence. These spiritual beings either reside permanently in *ọrun* or have descended from there to *aye* or earth. In the latter capacity, most are *Olọrun's* emissaries. With the exception of *Olódùmare*, their order of appearance here represents neither a hierarchy nor a general concensus among all Yorùbá people regarding the significance of specific *òrìṣa* in their regions.

DIAGRAM A:
OVERVIEW OF *ÒRÌṢÀ* SYSTEM

OLÓDÙMARÈ or ỌLÓRUN[13]
(The Supreme Creator Essence)

ORÍ
(First and most important *òrìṣa* in *ọrun*)

ÒRÚNMÌLÀ	*ÈṢÙ*
Source of wisdom and knowledge; *òrìṣa* of the *Ifá* divination corpus	Keeper of the *àṣẹ*, guardian of the crossroads; inspector of all sacrifices

ÒGÚN
Deity of war and iron; patron of hunters, warriors, and other users of metals

ỌBÀTÁLÁ
Shaper of human form, patron of the plastic arts

ÒṢANYÌN	*ÒṢÚMARÈ*
God of medicine, an herbalist	Rainbow deity

ÒṢUN
Giver of children, leader of *àjẹ́;* owner of the beaded comb

OLÓKUN	*AMAKISI*
Goddess of the oceans and seas	Deity who lights the world from the east

---

Diagram A is an abbreviated representation of some principal *òrìṣa* whose origins are basically of pure spirit essence. These are emissaries of the Supreme Creator Essence, some of whom descended from *ọrun* to *ayé* with a specific charge or duty, while others (like *Amakisi)* remain in *ọrun*.

DIAGRAM B:
DEIFIED ANCESTORS
Most are from Ilé-Ifẹ̀ or descendants of royal (political) and
mythical (spiritual) parentage.

ODÙDÙWÀ
Progenitor of the Yorùbá

ỌKÁNBÍ
Eldest son of *Odùdùwa*

ṢÀNGÓ
Deity of thunder and lightning;
the fourth ruler of Òyó; son of
Ọ̀rányàn and Yemọja

ÒRÁNYÀN
Grandson of *Odùdùwà*, King of
Ilá; progenitor of the Òyọ́
people

MỌREMI
Heroine of Ilé-Ifẹ̀, wife of *Òranyàn*

ÀJÀKÁ
Son of *Oranyan*

OBÁLUFỌN
Grandson of *Oduduwa*

As their category implies, these *òrìṣà* are considered deified
human beings because of some heroic or significant deed as well
as their relationship to Odùdùwà. Unlike the *òrìṣà* in Diagram A,
they *ascend* from *ayé* to *ọrun*. This category of deified ancestors
is also significant because it illustrates how the divine rulership
and hierarchies of Ilé-Ifẹ̀ (the spiritual center) and Òyọ́ (the political center) are legitimized. As Agiri suggests, the blood line
seems tenuous at best, and the terms son and grandson more than
likely suggest histories of migration and conquest rather then inheritance.[14] Consequently, like many of the *òrìṣà* in Diagram C below, these *òrìṣà* seem to inhabit the world more than the heavens.

DIAGRAM C:
SOME OTHER IMPORTANT ÒRÌṢÀ[15]

YEMỌJA
Goddess of rivers, streams. and
mother of several *òrìṣà* including
Ṣàngó and *Àjàká*

ÒYÁ
(River Niger), goddess of the
wind; favorite wife of *Ṣàngó*

ỌBÀ
River goddess and
mythical wife of *Ṣàngó*

ODÙ
(*Ifá* Chapter) also wife of
Òrúnmìlà

ÒṢÓ̀ÒSÌ
Androgynous hunter deity

ERINLÈ̟
River hunter deity often referred to as either the wife or bro-
ther of *Ògún*

ÒRÌṢÀ-OKO
Diety of the hill

ORÒ
Spirit

JÀKÚTA (Ọ̀yọ́)
Thunder deity

ÒRÀŃFÈ̟ (Ifè̟)
Lighting deity

AGẸMỌ
`Ìjẹbú ancestral deity

Here we find other important *òrìṣà* who either evolve from
natural phenomena such as *Ọya* or are mates to some of the major *òrìṣà* mentioned in Diagram A, such as *odù*. Many have dual
or conflicting mythologies, like *Ọya*, and some are androgynous
like *Ọṣọ̀sì*. As previously mentioned, I believe that the patterns
of migration and a primordial presence, including primordial female rulers such as *Ọṣun*, may account for some of these discrep-
ancies. *Ọṣun's* presence in *òrun* and on *ayé* certainly is an example. Again, I refer to Agiri's essay on Ọ̀yọ́ history which
names several female *obá*, and also suggests the presence of a
pre-*Odùdùwà* aboriginal population.[16]

Diagram D outlines some of the most frequently mentioned *òrìṣà* in the Yorùbá pantheon. These *òrìṣà* flourish throughout the oral literature in connection with each other. Many of those listed here survived the Middle Passage and its subsequent religious, economic, political, and social oppression. These *òrìṣà* seem to dominate *òrìṣà* concepts and worship irrespective of their origins and domains.

DIAGRAM D:
SOME MAJOR ÒRÌṢÀ

ẸṢÙ
Keeper of the *àṣẹ*, guardian of the crossroads

ÒRÚNMÌLÀ Deity of Wisdom and Knowledge	**OBÁTÁLÁ** One who shapes human forms
ÒṢUN Power, femininity, and fecundity	**ṢÀNGÓ** Deity of thunder and lightning; fourth ruler of Òyọ́
ÒGÚN Deity of war and iron	**ÒYÁ** Favorite wife of Ṣàngó; associated with the River Niger, wind, and tornadoes.
YEMỌJA Goddess of the rivers and the seas	**OLÓKUN** Goddess of the oceans
ÒSANYÌN Deity of herbs and herbal medicine	**ÒRÒ** Spirit

OBÁLUAYÉ
Smallpox deity

In Diagram E are listed those major forces which influence human and spiritual endeavors. *Àṣẹ*, the quintessential power; *Àjẹ́*, powerful beings; *Osó*, transformative powers; and the *Ajogun*, the purely malevolent forces such as death, curses, and disease.

DIAGRAM E:
OTHER FORCES[17]

ÀṢẸ
Quintessential power of *Olódùmarè* used to create all things;
spiritual and/ or human power

ÀJẸ́	*OSÓ*
Powerful beings	Transformative powers

AJOGUN
Malevolent forces such as illness, death, and curses

These diverse forces infuse the universe in all its manifestations with its kinetic, synergistic energy.

According to Professor Wánde Abímbọla, the sixteen major *odù (Ifá* Chapters) are also considered *òrìṣa*, and carry importance as such.[18] The other 240 *odù* are also *òrìṣa*. The names of *odù* are:

1.	Ogbè	9.	Ògúndá
2.	Ọ̀yẹ̀kú	10.	Ọ̀sá
3.	Ìwòrì	11.	Ìká
4.	Òdí	12.	Òtúúrúpọ̀n
5.	Ìrosùn	13.	Òtúá
6.	Ọ̀wọ́nrín	14.	Ìrẹ̀tẹ̀
7.	Ọ̀bàrà	15.	Ọ̀sẹ́
8.	Ọ̀kànràn	16.	Òfún

The other 240 *odù* are known as the *Ọmọ odù*, children of the *odù* or *Àmúlù*, mixed patterns. The signatures for the *Ojú odù* are formed by doubling the pattern for each one, hence, *èjì* or *mèjì* added to the name meaning two patterns. Although the *odù* are considered *òrìṣà*, like *Olódumarè* there are no shrines or specific festival days set aside in their honor.

The *Ifá* Divination Corpus is the organizing principle of Yorùbá thought, cosmology, and philosophy. Professor Wándé Abímbọ́lá's definitive works on *Ifá* clearly illustrate the essential role of this "encyclopedia of Yorùbá knowledge." Diagram F outlines some of the major disciplines and interconnections within the corpus in which a senior *babaláwo* may specialize.

DIAGRAM F:
IFÁ DIVINATION CORPUS OF YORÙBÁ KNOWLEDGE

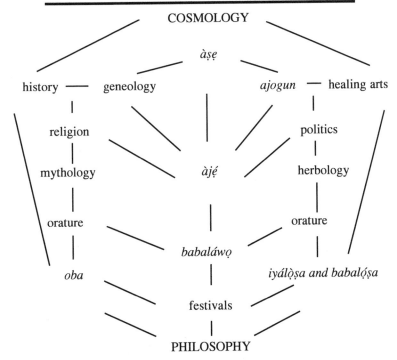

Diagram F is my attempt to visualize the extensive knowledge and organization of the *Ifá* corpus. The schema is divided into eight lines to simplify this explanation. Let us assume that the cosmology dominates the organizational structure of *Ifá*, while its philosophy lays the foundation roughly creating a diamond shape, with history and the healing arts at left and right extremes. In the vertical from cosmology to philosophy are the core of *Ifá* organization. *Áṣẹ* (the quintessential power), *àjẹ́* (the powerful beings), the *babaláwo* (fathers of the secrets). The festivals are the context for reenactment of the *òrìṣa* presence, the cosmological ideal, and is the "glue" that maintains the whole philosophical system.

Power (*áṣẹ*) is disseminated and held through religious and political systems. The mythology and medicinal knowledge explain the origin, *raison d'etre*, and uses of human and spiritual power. The entire network is based upon an extensive oral literary corpus. The *babaláwo*, as priest-scholars, legitimize and authorize the actions of the political and religious leadership along with the regulation of the festivals and other ritual duties. On either side of the schema, the movement from religion to *obá* (left) and from political to *iyalòṣà* and *babalòṣà* (right) reconfirm the circularity of Yorùbá belief systems.

These charts present to readers a sense of both the structure of oral discourse and literary knowledge as well as an appreciation for the complexity of the system itself. The latter point is particularly important because oral, literary, and historical studies are too often viewed as a simplistic, rather sexist operation in which information is "passed down solely from father to son." On the contrary, oral systems of education impart order, discipline, and knowledge which is disseminated by learned members of a society to those who have been chosen by demonstrated talents, oracular selection, or family stewardship to learn and maintain a given sociocultural legacy. For the Yorùbá, the *Ifá* Divination corpus and the *òrìṣa* system contain an extensive oral literary repository of myths, symbols, and icons that form the basis for Yorùbá cultural literacy.

Yorùbá Social Discourse in Ritual and Festival Drama

The *Òṣun* festival exemplifies a context for social discourse in ritual and festival drama. This discourse occurs variously as a forum for contemporary issues as well as a celebration of Yorùbá cosmological belief systems and sociopolitical history. The *Òṣun* festival with its rituals and its drama creates an environment wherein communal, spiritual, and personal discourse occurs at a most crucial philosophical juncture of Yorùbá thought. That philosophical juncture is *orita* or the crossroads, the purview of *Èṣù*, the *òrìṣà* who guards the *àṣẹ*, the quintessential creative power. In the context of the festival, personal, spiritual, and communal empowerment is renewed. In the discourse among *enìyàn* and *òrìṣà* at the crossroads of ritual and festival drama, *ẹbọ* or sacrifice seals the covenant between them and binds human beings to communal and personal fulfillment. Personal fulfillment is both communal and spiritual when it seeks health, wealth, cleansing, safe and healthy childbearing, individual female health, personal and communal achievement. These social issues are especially relevant to the meaning of the *Òṣun* festival given the high infant and maternal mortality rates. A woman's prayer for the safe delivery of her infant and her own recovery is certainly suggested in the *orin Òṣun* — *Òṣun* songs — which praise her knowledge and medicinal use of *Ãìwẹ*, a special medicine for childbearing women referred to in the *oríkì Òṣun* in the first chapter.[23]

Festival discourse itself is communal and spiritual. It is the existence of the community which insulates and supports the individual who in turn contributes to the maintenance and growth of that community, its traditions, and its historical relevance. The structure and meaning of the *Òṣun* festival attests to this. The *ìba fegùn* or homage to the ancestors confirms the strong testimony that the community is only as strong as its individual members.

Moreover, *ìbà l'egùn* recall spiritual (*òrìṣà*) and human (*ènìyàn*) images which then serve as models for contemporary human aspiration. Such recall through the *oríkì orin*, and *iwi* further bind the community and its individual members to their spiritual source.

However, it is the exuberance of the spiritual elixir that embraces the *Ọ̀ṣun* Grove during the festival which empowers and elevates this community of individuals. The calling of *Ọ̀ṣun, Òrúnmìlà*, and the other *òrìṣà* to join their earthly counterparts at the *olójùmẹ̀rìndínlógún*, or lighting of the sixteen candles, serves to acknowledge the potency and potential of the crossroads. It images the juncture between *ọrun* and *ilè* as both stage and altar for the dialogue among human beings as well as between human beings and divinities. This juncture communicates and, with the assistance of *Òrúnmìlà*, interprets the aspirations and the will of both the sacred and the mundane. Such social discourse, then, fulfills the philosophical objectives of Yorùbá cosmic vision.

Notes

1.   During the past decade as a doctoral candidate, professor, and researcher in Yorùbá literature and language, I have benefitted from ongoing correspondence and discussions with several Yorùbá scholars, informants and researchers. Among these are Professors Wándé Abímbọ́lá, Rowland Abíọdun, Jacob Kẹ́hìndé Olúpọ̀nà, Ọlábiyi Babalọlá Yáì, Yíwọlá Áwolayé and Andrea Benton Rushing whose works, conversations, and friendships have been an invaluable resource and inspiration, for this chapter especially and for the work entirely.

2.   David Henige, *Oral Historiography* (London: Longman, 1982.) This is a very useful tool for researching this category of oral literature.

3. Wándé Abímbọ́lá, *Ifá Divination Poetry* (New York: Nok Publishers, Ltd., 1977.)

4. Wándé Abímbọ́lá, *Sixteen Great Poems of Ifá* (UNESCO, 1975, 158-173). See also: Rowland Abiodun, "Verbal and Visual Metaphors: Mythical Allusions in Yorùbá Ritualistic Art of Orí," In *Word and Image: A Journal of Verbal Visual Inquiry*, 1987: 3(3) 252-270.

5. E. Bọ́lájí Idòwú, *Olódùmarè: God in Yorùbá Belief* (London: Longmans, 1962): 63. See also; Wọlé Ṣóyínká, *Myth, Literature and the African World* (Cambridge; Cambridge University Press, 1977).

6. Abímbọ́lá, *Sixteen Great Poems of Ifá;* and Abíọ́dún, "Verbal and Visual Metaphors."

7. Babaláwọ Yẹmí Ẹlẹbùrùibọn. Personal interviews, Òṣogbo, Òyó State, Nigeria, 1981.

8. Idowu, pp. 38-70.

9. *Ibid.*

10. Abíọ́dún, pp. 255-257.

11. Samuel Johnson, *The History of the Yorubas: From the Earliest Times to the Beginning of the British Protectorate* (rpt) (Westport, Connecticut: Negro Universities Press, 1970): 26-78. See also: Babatúndé A. Agiri, "Yorùbá Oral Tradition with Special reference to the Early History of the Òyó Kingdom," In Wándé Abímbọ́lá (ed), Yorùbá *Oral Tradition* (University of Ilé-Ifè, Nigeria Department of African Languages and Literatures, 1975): 152-197.

12. Ẹlẹbùrùibọn, *op. cit.*

13. The configuration for Diagram A results, especially from the pioneering work of Professor Rowland Abíọ́dún cited in note 4 above, along with the other works cited here.

14. Agiri, *op. cit.* Johnson, *op. cit.*

15. Johnson, *op. cit.* Abímbọ́lá, *Ifá* and *Sixteen Great Poems of Ifá, op. cit* Abíọ́dún, *op. cit.* S.A. Babalọlá, *The Content and Form of* Yorùbá *Ìjálá* (London: Oxford University Press, 1976).

16.   Agiri, *op. cit.*
17.   Abímbọ́lá, *op cit.* See also J.O. Ṣọ́dípọ̀ and B. Hallen, *Witchcraft, Magic, and Religion* (London Ethnographica Ltd., 1986).
18.   W. Abímbọ́lá, *Ifá Divination Poetry,* 15.
19.   *Ibid.*
20.   Abímbọ́lá, *Ifá Divination Poetry, op. cit.* and *Sixteen Great Poems of Ifá, op. cit.*
21.   Elẹ́bùrùibọn, *op. cit.* Abímbọ́lá, *Ifá.* Peter Bádéjọ, *Àṣà Ìbílẹ̀* Yorùbá (University of California at Los Angeles, 1980).
22.   Ọlátundé O. Ọlátúnji, University of Ilé-Ifẹ̀, Nigeria "Ìyẹ̀rẹ̀ Ifá: Yorùbá Oracle Chants" *African Notes,* 7, 2.
23.   Diedre L. Bádéjọ, *A Goddess of Our Own: An Annotation of Ọ̀ṣun Oral Literature* (work in progress).

Chapter Three

ÒṢUN IN YORÙBÁ COSMOLOGY

Cosmology explores the metaphysical nature of the universe. It offers an ethnocultural view of the original organization of the world and of the objective relationships between human beings and nature, between human beings and divinities, and among human beings themselves. Cosmology usually attempts a philosophical approach — a rationale — for the inexplicable as well as the explicable nature of the world. Cosmology, then, embraces humanity's attempt to come to terms with its very existence in a wonderful yet mysterious world. As Mazizi Kunene demonstrates, without this cosmic perspective, individual societies are victimized by the capriciousness of others.[1]

Various scholars have written about aspects of Yorùbá cosmology and its very elaborate cosmic perspective. Some have defined and described its intricate structure.[2] Abíódún and others have focused on its role in the arts and folklore.[3] Scholars such as Bíobáku and Olúpònà have pointed out the historical allusions from its oral literature.[4] Still others like Abímbólá and Babalolá have provided the data and classification of the various oral literary genres themselves.[5] Together these studies allow us to reconstruct the synergistic elements that constitute this Yorùbá cosmic perspective and *Òṣun*'s place in it.

In *Myth, Literature and the African World*, Wole Ṣóyínká emphasizes the "temporal concepts in the Yorùbá worldview."[6]

Here, he demonstrates the cyclical nature of àṣẹ, the life-force which the Yorùbá acknowledge as existing within all phenomena. Those life-forces are expressed in the eternal cycle of (1) the ancestors, (2) the living, and (3) the unborn. Ọ̀ṣun, as the goddess of fertility, plays a crucial role in the perpetuation of that cycle. Earthly women parallel Ọ̀ṣun's spiritual role in the cosmological organization of the world order, signifying that without female participation, the whole life cycle is arrested.

Also, Yorùbá cosmology proposes that innumerable challenges exist within each of these cycles and that those challenges are mediated by offering a prescribed sacrifice, or ẹbọ. Since balance within and between the cosmic and human realms is a primary cosmological objective, a breach or imbalance within or among those realms violates the Yorùbá concept of order. Immorality results from imbalance, and restoration to a moral state can only occur with the proper sacrifice. Good and evil become relative terms dependent on each other for definition and value. For example, àìkú (longevity) and ikú (death) represent positive and negative life forces, respectively. However, ascendancy into the venerated position of ancestor can only be obtained after a long and productive life hence the cosmic or spiritual benefits of ikú are dependent upon àìkú. To further illustrate this point, the repeated death of a child (àbíkú) cannot of itself elevate the child to the status of ancestor. Rather, the child's troublesome spirit must be made to remain with its mother (Dúrósimí) so that it may complete its life cycle properly. Through consultation with Ifá, the beleaguered parents are asked to make a specific offering, or sacrifice, so that the child may become old (àgbàlagbà). Premature death, that is death before reaching the status of elder, creates an imbalance or immorality.

Morality in Yorùbá cosmology creates harmony in the cosmos. Immorality, on the other hand, creates disharmony which ruptures the individual and/or communal psyche. This disharmony or rupture exacts from the human and spiritual will something greater than mere propitiation. It demands the deeper thought and healing found in dynamic change. It demands the creative action that evolves from negative circumstances that is signified and consumed by collecting items for *ẹbọ*. Healing the rupture is the charge of the *òrìṣà*, and followed properly, the recommended treatment, *ẹbọ*, leads its constituency closer to the concept of divine order. Thus good and evil are not measured merely in terms of offenses against the individual or even against the physical community. Instead, the deeper wisdom invested within the corpus of *Ifá* oracle presupposes that a rupture is often simply one aspect of the destructive-creative synergy of the universe. Hence, offenses by or against nature are part of the exacting ethos that alone can release profound human and spiritual rejuvenation. Humanity, nature, and spirit each demonstrates its own *àṣẹ* or power, and such acts of hubris compel the cosmos to delve deeper into its own essence. Each benefits from these ruptures through their rendezvous at the crossroads when *Èṣù* inspects the contents of *ẹbọ*, or sacrifice. Spiritual will and the will of nature are juxtaposed against human will which *chooses* to accept or reject the challenge and/or the remedy. Penance and retribution, therefore, are not always aspects of punishment for crime, but can be the first acts of a resumed awareness, *jí*, and an appeal to the axiom of cosmic adjustment, or restoration.[7]

In the oral literary sources cited below, the performance and consequences of sacrifice greatly affect the affairs of *òrìṣà* such as *Òṣun* and human beings. Sacrifice becomes a key concept in Yorùbá cosmology and, as Ṣóyínká explains in his work, an act of "cosmic adjustment." An example of one such breach of morality occurs when the male *òrìṣà* violate the principle of balance between themselves and *Òṣun*. The balance maintained by the male-female principle is skewed by this "disjuncture" and, as the *odù Ifá* tells us, sacrifice must be performed to restore it. Ṣóyínká's essay on the "Fourth Stage" suggests the setting for the tensions that lead to that restoration. In defining and discussing the "fourth stage," that is, the "abyss of transition," Ṣóyínká presents, perhaps, the most significant insight into Yorùbá cosmo-

logical thought, especially as it relates to dramatic ritual enactment. According to the playwright, the "fourth stage" is the
"metaphysical abyss both of god and man."[8] It represents not
only the stage where ritual drama is enacted, but also a matrix
where antinomies, generally speaking, are mediated.[9] The
"fourth stage" provides the contextual framework for the ritual
aspects of festival drama and identifies the mythopoetic and
musical nature of Yorùbá language as its means of communication. The praise poetry and festival songs of Ọ̀ṣun exemplify
this.[10]

The "fourth stage" then embodies the spectrum of creativity. It communicates with and meditates upon the dichotomy
expressed by the constructive/ destructive forces of humanity,
spirit, and nature. Through the mythopoetic symbolism found in
the oral poetry and songs, the "fourth stage" propitiates those
forces and antinomies that can be mitigated but rarely destroyed.
It is an objective stage of cosmic reality that recognizes a necessary balance of power between differing forces. Such forces become catalysts for both "human challenge" and "cosmic adjustment." With respect to the festival drama of the Yorùbá goddess
Ọ̀ṣun, that cosmic adjustment means that the female principle
must engage the male principle, which cannot proceed without
her. In terms of its human challenge, it means acknowledging her
ability to arrest humanity by merely refusing to release its inhabitants from within her. In short, both the cosmic adjustment and
human challenge demonstrate her ability to suspend the future.

In this chapter, the Ifá Divination oral literary corpus provides examples of that cosmic adjustment and human challenge
with specific reference to Ọ̀ṣun. As the source and authority on
Yorùbá cosmology and mythology, the Ifá corpus establishes her
role in the pantheon. In the preface to his work, Ifá Divination
Poetry, Professor Wándé Abímbọ́lá stated,

> In Yorubaland where Ifá is a major divinity, this fascinating
> system of divination has been closely identified with

Yorùbá history, mythology, religion, and folk-medicine. The Yorùbá regard *Ifá* as the repository of their beliefs and moral values. The *Ifá* divination system and the extensive poetic chants associated with it are used by the Yorùbá to validate important aspects of their culture. In traditional Yorùbá society, the authority of *Ifá* permeated every aspect of life because the Yorùbá regard *Ifá* as the voice of the divinities and the wisdom of the ancestors. [11]

This central authority of *Ifá* is observed at several junctures during the *Ọ̀ṣun* Festival. Its significance is most pronounced when the babaláwọ (*Ifá* priest) comes to the palace to cast the ọ̀pẹ̀lẹ̀ (divining chain) at the end of the *Ifá* Festival. At this time, the date and other requirements for that year's festival are confirmed through the *Mẹ̀rìndínlógún* of *Ọ̀ṣun* in conjunction with the odù *Ifá* of *Òrúnmìlà*. Another important example of the role of *Ifá* in the *Ọ̀ṣun* Festival occurs during the *Olójùmẹ̀rìndínlógún*, the lighting of the sixteen lamps which are themselves symbolic of the sixteen major *odù Ifá*, the *ÌrùnMọlẹ̀*, the sixteen major Yorùbá crowns (*adé*), and *Ọ̀ṣun's* quintessential relationship to each and all of them. During the evening on the fourth day of the festival, the chief political and religious leadership, the major traditional *dramatis personae*, the people of Òṣogbo township create a unique interplay between themselves and the *òrìṣà*. The *babaláwọ* play the *ilù àyàn*, the drum ensemble of *Ifá*, which summon all the *òrìṣà* to join the township in celebrating *Ọ̀ṣun* and her festival (see photo on p. 125).

Given the prominence of *Ifá* in Yorùbá life and cosmology, I began to explore the *Ifá* oral literature to understand the nature of the Yorùbá goddess *Ọ̀ṣun*, her mythology, and her place in the Yorùbá pantheon. What emerges is the picture of an exceptional goddess whose presence at the organization of the world placed her in a pivotal position as a woman of power. The *odù Ifá* which narrates the mythology of *Ọ̀ṣun*, in themselves challenge certain gender constructs. Several narratives debate the view of women as subordinates to male political, social, or economic control. According to her mythology, reciprocity and balance operate as essential motifs of the male-female principle. The ẹsẹ, or narrative poems of the Ifá corpus, demonstrate the crucial role of women in planning, maintaining, and directing socio-political and religious interactions. Exploring the nuances of Ọ̀ṣun in the Ifá opens the way to understanding the significance of the festival in its broadest social context, and to explaining the interaction among the major dramatis personae in this communal ritual drama.

Although many scholars such as Reverend Johnson, S. A. Fádípẹ̀, and Wándé Abímbọ́la have noted the intricacy of Yorùbá religion, its enactment in ritual and festival drama clearly articulates the axioms which guide the cosmological structure. Whether there are 201 or 401 òrìṣà, most writers concur that all the òrìṣà serve complex roles that reflect both natural and super-natural phenomena. Principles of balance and reciprocity dominate both the premise and the complexity of the òrìṣà system. Such principles are found in the nature of the òrìṣà and the role of sacrifice in human and divine interaction. One can safely suggest that the objective here is to maintain harmony between and within spiritual and physical planes. In short, Yorùbá cosmology is driven by attempts through sacrifice to rectify any disharmony or imbalance and successfully accomplish any tasks that support Divine Order. Restitution occurs between humanity and the òrìṣà, between women and men, among the òrìṣà themselves, within families and between clans, lineages and towns. Because plant and animal life constitute an organic part of the Yorùbá cosmic sensibility, restitution between humanity and nature is both a symbolic and a pragmatic recognition of their interdependency. The important concept here is that social and spiritual harmony requires constant vigilance and sacrifice. If we agree that harmony is the objective, then reciprocity through sacrifice is the vehicle or process through which harmony is obtained. Let us consider how these two factors, harmony and sacrifice, are revealed in the following odù Ifá, Ọ̀ṣẹTúrá.

A Woman of Power

Who exactly is the goddess Ọ̀ṣun? What are her qualities, and what makes her significant? Yorùbá oral literature defines Ọ̀ṣun as one of the original deities, or IrúnMọlẹ̀ who followed Ògún through the "transitional gulf" to maintain the world. She is, according to both the Ifá literary corpus and her own praise poetry, the oríkì Ọ̀ṣun, a very powerful and beautiful woman. Ọ̀ṣun is the giver of children, wealth, and power to women; she is the leader of àjẹ́ (powerful beings), a ruler, and a protectress of Òṣogbo township. As such, she is a woman of power and femininity who, in the words of Filomena Steady, exemplifies the meaning of "original feminist."[12] She is, in the words of Alice Walker, "outrageous, audacious, courageous or willful" as well as "responsible, in charge, serious."[13] According to Ọ̀ṣẹTúrá, an odù Ifá,

Ọ̀ṣun is a very great woman. She is the wife of Ṣàngó and the wife of Ọ̀rúnmìlà. Ọ̀ṣun is the principal and the leader of àjẹ́. Ọ̀ṣun is a great woman according to ỌṣẹTura in Odù Ifá. When Olódùmarè sent all the IrúnMọlẹ̀ to come to organize the world, Ògún, Ṣàngó, Ọ̀rúnmìlà, Ọbátálá, and all the other deities, Ọ̀ṣun was the only woman among them. They came down to arrange everything. They put everything in order. When they assembled, when they had their meetings, they did not invite Ọ̀ṣun. Being an àjẹ́, Ọ̀ṣun destroyed their plans. They were not successful with any of their programs. They had to return back to Olódùmarè. They reported everything, and Olódùmarè asked them, How about Ọ̀ṣun? They said that because she is a woman they did not invite her to their meetings. Olódùmarè asked them to go and beg Ọ̀ṣun. So all the IrúnMọlẹ came back. They apologized and they made a sacrifice to Ọ̀ṣun. And Ọ̀ṣun said that she wanted all the initiation of the ritual they perform for men which they used to keep women behind, she wanted it. And she wanted every woman who is powerful like her to be initiated. So they called Ọ̀ṣun, and they showed her everything.

The events narrated here occur after Ògún has penetrated the chthonic realm that separates the òrìṣà from humanity.[14] Having landed at Ilé-Ifẹ the cradle of Yorùbá civilization, the divinities then face the task of organizing and maintaining the world. As Abímbọlá demonstrates, Olódùmarè sent each one with a specific task and talent to fulfill that mission.[15] Ògún, the god of war and iron, functions as a creative/destructive force. Ọrúnmìlà, the god of divination, provides humanity with wisdom and knowledge necessary to resolve its difficulties. Ṣàngó, the god of thunder and lightning, exemplifies the vagaries of rulership and nature. Èṣù, guardian of the crossroads, provides the element of chance. And Ọṣun, the goddess of fertility, ensures continuity of and balance within humanity.

We glean a cosmological vision of order where Ọ̀rìṣà-ńlá creates human form and Olódùmarè gives it life-breath, Ọṣun expels the breathing human form through her womb thus forcing it to live.[16] In forcing the human form to experience the trauma and joy of birth, she also offers to protect it against its own frailties as well as the capriciousness of other forces. As a woman who knows the agony of birthing humanity, she bonds with other women who share this painful responsibility to maintain the world. Like other òrìṣà, she experiences what humanity experiences. As a woman, she empowers other women with whom she shares that specifically female identity and responsibility. As a female deity, she possesses the power to withhold the life-force which activates humanity through the male principle. That singular power emphasizes that without the female principle, the male principle is rendered impotent. In a word, she possesses what Steady calls "real power."

The theme of the ese Ifá above in ỌṣẹTúrá confirms Ọṣun's greatness. She is, we are told, a very great woman in and of herself. Three elements in the narrative elaborate upon this theme. First, Ọṣun marries two very powerful major òrìṣà; second, she is the principle and leader of àjẹ́; and, third, she is the only female òrìṣà among the ÌrúnMọlẹ̀ who were sent to organize the world. In this *odù Ifá*, we also learn that the source of her power, like that of the other *òrìṣà*, evolves from *Olódùmarè*, the Supreme Creative Essence. Her marriages to *Ọ̀rúnmìlà* and *Ṣàngó* attest to her own intrinsic power. The former alludes to both her acquired and inherent knowledge of divination, while the latter alludes to her rulership and her role as a river goddess. As demonstrated in other *odù Ifá*, both marriages reflect balance and reciprocity. With respect to the male/female principle discussed above, her marriage to *Ọ̀rúnmìlà* suggests that wisdom and knowledge are qualities shared by male and female. This belief is confirmed by a proverb which states that a woman and a man see a snake simultaneously, and the woman kills the snake. There is no problem; it only matters that the snake is dead.

In the two *odù Ifá* given below, *Ọ̀ṣun* demonstrates her innate ability to divine. Despite this talent, she lacks the full knowledge of the art of divination that *Ọ̀rúnmìlà* possesses. So, his knowledge of divination is juxtaposed against her knowledge of kinetic spiritual power. Because kinetic spiritual power is given to her by *Olódùmarè*, it is not a manifestation of evil, but simply a form of power to be used at her discretion. Indeed, in *Yorùbá* cosmology, seemingly diametrically opposed forces propose parity or balance of power rather than a simplistic concept of good and evil. This is borne out by the presence of the *ajogun* (malevolent or negative forces) in *Yorùbá* cosmology. Abímbọ́la points out that it is they rather than the *òrìṣà* who oppose the well-being of humanity.

How this complex perspective of benevolent and malevolent forces operates is dramatically illustrated in the mythology of *Ọ̀ṣun*. Her role as a benevolent force complements her role as leader of the *àjẹ́*, who according to the *babaláwo*, are "powerful beings."[17] Although frequently translated as "witches" in English, the negative connotation of that word misses the essence of the *àjẹ́* in *Yorùbá* cosmology. My informant explained that everyone has her/his own power that can be used for good or for evil. So it is with the *àjẹ́* who are an embodiment of power and an expression of the matrix of potentiality from which that power emanates. *Ọ̀ṣun* as *òrìṣà* remains a benefactor to humanity; as leader of the *àjẹ́*, she protects the covenants that seal the positive and/ or negative actions of the *àjẹ́*. Her role is "to know and keep" the secret of the covenants and to provide, through *Ifá* and/or *mẹ̀rìndìnlógún* divination, the requisite material offering that release those seals. Rather than confront she facilitates the reversal of negative power. As will be illustrated later in this chapter, she fulfills the role assigned to her by *Olódùmarè*.

In keeping with the organic nature of *Yorùbá* cosmic thought, *Ọ̀rúnmìlà* maintains the wisdom to unveil the forces at work against an entity or individual, and the knowledge of a requisite sacrifice to placate those forces. Again, as the *odù Ifá* below demonstrates, *Ọ̀ṣun* maintains the power to bind or loosen the covenant of those forces represented by the *àjẹ́*.[18] Her marriage to Ọ̀rúnmìlà, in part, signifies balance between vision and control of powerful forces which interact with humanity and the *òrìṣà*. In addition, their marriage signals reciprocity between knowledge and mastery of knowledge as they are mediated through sacrifice. Reciprocity occurs both at the moment when sacrifice is accepted as well as offered. *Ọ̀ṣun's* acceptance of the sacrifice offered to her by the male *ÌrúnMọ̀lẹ̀*, for example, confirms this point.

Her marriage to *Ṣàngó* imparts an elegant mythopoetic image of *Ọ̀ṣun* as a force within nature and humanity. *Ṣàngó*, too, as the god of thunder and lightning, represents a force within nature. Together they illustrate the cycle of fertility that occurs during the rainy season. The thunder and lightning of *Ṣàngó* announces the rain that fills the rivers, represented by his wives, *Ọ̀ṣun* and *Ọbà*. *Ọya*, *Ṣàngó's* favorite wife, symbolizes the wind who resonates with the sound of his thunder. As in nature, *Ṣàngó* draws strength and power from them, thereby commanding the skies with his thunderous voice and his fiery spirit. *Ọ̀ṣun*, as goddess of fertility, enriches the soil that must bear both human and natural fruits. In addition, her marriage to *Ṣàngó* parallels her co-rulership of Òṣogbo. Several appellations in her *oríkì* in chapter one, and in other sources refer to her as *ọba*, "my lord," and "one who wears a big chieftaincy title."[19] More importantly, we find in her praise poetry this very revealing line, "Who does not know that it is the *Ọṣun* Òṣogbo, who helps the *Ọba* manage/rule Òṣogbo?"[20] Such mythopoetic symbolism compares well to her capacity as the wife of a deity whose fiery temper and commanding presence is legend. For *Ọṣun* not only reciprocates his power with her own abilities, but she also balances his fiery spirit with her cooling waters. As ruler of Òyó, *Ṣàngó* 's life among human beings parallels *Ọṣun's* presence among the townspeople of Òṣogbo.

Ọṣun — Leader of the *Àjẹ́*

In his *Sixteen Great Poems of Ifá*, Wándé Abímbọ́lá notes that the *Yorùbá* believe that supernatural powers manifest both benevolent and malevolent forces. He states that the *òrìṣà* (divinities) are the benevolent forces, while the *ajogun* (warriors against humanity) are the malevolent forces. The *ajogun* include the:

> *àjẹ́* (powerful beings), *ikú* (death), *àrùn* (disease), *òfò* (loss), *ẹ̀gbà* (paralysis), *ọ̀ràn* (trouble), *èpè* (curse), *ẹ̀wọ̀n* (imprisonment), and *èse* (any other evil thing that affects human beings).[21]

Although Abímbọ́lá includes *àjẹ́* here, *Ọṣun's* oral literature and the *odù Ifá* cited here suggest that *Ọṣun* is guardian of the *àjẹ́* covenants similar to *Èṣù's* guardianship of *àṣẹ*. Further, as Abímbọ́lá quote and *Ọṣun's* oral literature indicate, *àjẹ́* includes the spectrum of positive and negative powers. Abímbọ́lá notes that the conflict that arises out of the dichotomous interests as well as actions of benevolent and malevolent supernatural forces are grounded in the constant struggle of these opposing powers

for the "regulation of human life."[22] Again, sacrifice demonstrates to the òrìṣà that their assistance is recognized and re-
spected. Such tensions and invocations further explain Ọ̀ṣun's
role as leader of àjẹ́, or powerful beings.

According to *odù Ifá, Ọ̀sẹ̀Túrá* (cited above), and *Ọ̀kànràn
Sòdẹ̀* (cited below), *Olódùmarè* assigns each of the principle
òrìṣà a specific task, giving each a particular talent or power. The
òrìṣà, including *Ọ̀ṣun*, were collectively sent to "put everything
in order," to prepare the world for the challenges presented by
human habitation. The assembly of the *IrúnMọlẹ̀* represents some
of those challenges to human endeavors, including creativity,
war, leadership, wisdom, artistry, fate, death, and spirituality. If,
as Abímbọ́lá points out, these characteristics of the divinities
symbolize the benevolent challenges to humanity, then *Ọ̀ṣun's* kinetic spiritual power must also be benevolent. Three factors also
support this view. First, as mentioned earlier, *Olódùmarè* empowers *Ọ̀ṣun*. Second, *Olódùmarè* reprimands the male *IrúnMọlẹ̀*
for offending her. And third, *Ọ̀ṣun* as well as other women "like
her" who possess innate kinetic power reap benefits from her
actions. Indeed, these three factors confirm *Babaláwò
Ẹlẹ́bùrúîbọn's* contention that the *àjẹ́* are powerful beings who
use that power both positively and negatively.

Ọ̀ṣun symbolizes woman power as the "principal and leader
of *àjẹ́* who suspends the plans of the male divinities because their
actions have caused an imbalance at the very foundation of the
universe. This *odù Ifá* implies that any attempt to organize the
world without the female principle leads to inertia. Moreover,
Ọ̀sẹ̀Túrá infers that gender imbalance violates the laws of the
universe envisioned by *Olódùmarè*. Additionally, it suggests that
"real power" resides in the feminine principle because it ushers
in life. The ability to reproduce not only herself, that is the female form, but also the male form remains a cosmic mystery,
which to some, is tantamount to sorcery. *Ọ̀ṣun*, we must remember, is not only the principal and leader of *àjẹ́*, she is also the
giver of children, a fertility goddess. As such, she protects that
which she births. Those birth pains insure human continuity,

without which the *òrìṣà* cannot exist.[23] It also invests the female with a special knowledge of and interest in human perpetuation. *Ọ̀ṣun*'s praise poetry notes that she is "the nursing mother who eagerly listens to noise."[24] How then can the male *òrìṣà*, without consultation with *Ọ̀ṣun*, plan for the human inhabitation of a world?

However, while actual birthing weakens the female, the ability to reproduce empowers her. Similarly, while the moment of impregnation weakens the male, the ability to impregnate empowers him, thus creating reciprocity and balance of sexual powers. Yet, for males it is a momentary power that demands separation from the actual process of human creation. For the female, it is a long term commitment which demands the sacrifice of her innermost sustenance and being. While the period of gestation renders her vulnerable, her ability to suspend humanity makes the male vulnerable. The reciprocity and balance here sustains the universal order. Hence, *Olódùmarè*'s inquiry "What about *Ọ̀ṣun*?" subtly questions the male *òrìṣà*'s denial of *Ọ̀ṣun*'s role in the cosmic order, and their affront to the Supreme Being who has designated her role as critical to the human and spiritual order. The *odù Ifá* acknowledges the presence of sexism but does not condone it. By their actions, the male *òrìṣà* undermine the decision of *Olódùmarè* to empower *Ọ̀ṣun* in the first place, and *Olódùmarè* humbles them before her.

Like *Ọ̀ṣun*, the *IrúnMọlẹ̀* derive their power from *Olódùmarè*, or *Olórun*, the other cognomen for the Supreme Being.[25] Like *Ọ̀ṣun*, they are assigned specific characteristics. These male *òrìṣà* represent tangible, definable forces. Although it is intangible, even wisdom, *ọgbọ́n*, is accessible and defineable through *Ifá*. Not so with the unborn human form. *Ọ̀ṣun* holds a mystery in her body that is both intangible and undefinable. Thus, the unborn human form remains mysterious until its entry into the physical world through the birth canal. The child ushered into the world is knowable only after it has been observed by the living for eight days, when it is named, claimed, and transferred to the human community.

Thus, the "naming ceremony" defines the human form, tags it, so to speak, makes it tangible and identifiable in the physical world. Prior to birth, the unborn remains a mysterious force in the protective waters of the womb. The female principle then, must guard the mystery that forms within her. This image of the unborn human form floating in the watery womb is found in bold relief on the walls of the *Ọ̀ṣun* grove (see photo). Such safeguarding of the unborn reflects *Ọ̀ṣun's* protection of the covenant she maintains with the mysterious powers of the *àjé*. As kinetic spiritual power, she protects that which she nurtures. In other words, she protects that to which *Olódùmarè* gives life. Here, the relationship between the giver of life and the giver of children becomes clear. Perhaps *Olódùmarè* empowers *Ọ̀ṣun* as leader of *àjẹ́* in recognition of her role as giver of children.

As *àjẹ́*, leader of the *àjẹ́*, and giver of children, *Ọ̀ṣun* proposes an intriguingly complex image of women's "real power." As *àjẹ́*, *Ọ̀ṣun* has her own innate power; as leader of the *àjẹ́*, she has the "knowledge" of, and is the source of, their manifested powers; and as giver of children, she has the power to withhold as well as protect her progeny. Consequently, *Yèyé*, the Good Mother, is a tapestry: (1) kinetic spiritual energy, (2) warrior-woman, (3) giver and sustainer of life, and (4) a beautiful, wealthy woman, indeed.

Like *Ògún* who symbolizes a flash-point between creative and destructive forces, *Ọ̀ṣun* symbolizes a flash-point between benevolent and malevolent forces. As an *òrìṣà* of power and fertility, *Ọ̀ṣun's* iconography images the womb as a powerful matrix, nurturing myriad possibilities. Inside, it secrets the primordial moment where spirit and flesh coagulate, where *àṣẹ* (life-force) enters *ara* (body).

Fertility, Power, and Cosmic Harmony

The mythologies and intertwining relationships among *Olódùmarè*, *Ọbàtálá*, *Ọ̀ṣun*, *Ọ̀rúnmìlà*, *Èṣù*, and *Ṣàngó*, further weave fascinating concepts regarding *Òṣun*'s role in Yorùbá cosmology. As mentioned earlier, the *òrìṣà* maintain a vested interest in humanity that is explained by the proverb, *Ènìyàn kò sí, kò sí 'Imọ̀lẹ̀,* explained earlier.[26] We begin, as does Ìdowú with *Òrìṣà-ńlá* or *Ọbàtálá*, the sculptor of the human form, whose job is simply to shape that form. He does not give it life, nor does he participate in its development or birthing. His sole responsibility is to sculpt human beings, and lock them in a special place where *Olódùmarè* will come to give them life.[27] However, the oral literature also tells us that *Òrìṣà-ńlá* favors *ẹmu* or palm wine. Ṣóyínká notes that *Èṣù*, the provocative deity of chance tempts *Ọbàtálá* with palm wine. *Ọbàtálá* becomes a little tipsy, his hands slips, and he creates albinos, hunchbacks, and other handicapped people. As a result, palm wine is taboo to *Òrìṣà-ńlá* and his worshippers, while the handicapped are sacred to him. *Ọbàtálá*, not *Èṣù*, is totally responsible for his own actions and the human forms that he creates. In spite of *Ọbàtálá*'s mishap in creating some human forms, *Òṣun* gives them birth.

Aside from the specific role *Ṣàngó* played in Ọ̀yọ́, according to the orature he is the god of thunder and lightning and one of *Òṣun*'s husbands. As noted earlier, *Ṣàngó*'s rulership of Ọ̀yọ́ parallels *Òṣun*'s co-rulership with the Atáója, the traditional ruler of Òṣogbo a point to which I will return later. Although the demise of his rulership of Ọ̀yọ́ has been wonderfully dramatized in Dúró Ládípọ̀'s *Ọbá KòSò*, this discussion focuses on the images and themes found only in his relationship with *Òṣun*.

Several oral literary and written sources demonstrate that migration and resettlement were constant factors in Yorùbá history. Various *òrìṣà* mythologies corroborate this. As the people moved, resettled, and conquered new territories, so did the *òrìṣà* whose mythologies illustrate that they often reigned over territories far beyond their mythic places of origin. In this respect, *Ṣàngó* and *Òṣun* share a common mythic history. His mother reportedly came from Nupe and conquered Ọ̀yọ́ while *Òṣun* came from Ìjùmú and eventually settled in Òṣogbo.[28] During his reign in *Ọ̀yọ́*, *Ṣàngó* had two other wives, *Ọbà*, the goddess of the Obà River, and *Ọya*, goddess of the wind and the Niger River.[29] Metaphorically, his personification as thunder and lightning, and their personification as wind and river forge powerful images of nature. These mythical images reflect the tropical cycles where thunder and lightning announce that rainfall has swollen the river. The potent flash of the thunderbolt shakes and zigzags across the heavens, lightning sears the earth, and together they give the clarion call that the insemination of the soil has begun. These images are efficacious for people whose lives in the tropics oscillate between dry and rainy seasons. The *Ọ̀ṣun* Festival is celebrated during the rainy season when the river is fullest.

But despite this rich and powerful image, *Ṣàngó* remained childless while he was married to the goddess of fertility.[30] Nonetheless, he is not entirely to blame. In the spirit of balance and reciprocity, another *odù Ifá* narrates a time when *Ọ̀ṣun* too was infertile. In the *odù Ifá* that follows, *Ọ̀ṣun* consults *Ifá* to remedy her own childlessness:

> *Ọ̀ṣun* is a wealthy woman who has a golden (brass) mortar, or *odò idẹ*. But she has no children. She wanted children at that time. So she called three *babaláwo*, *Èfín*, *Dúró* and *Ọ̀jìyàòmèfún* who was the first *babaláwọ* to divinate for *Ọ̀ṣun* every five, five days. But as this *babaláwọ* had two other friends, *Èfín* and *Dúró*, he called them to the house of *Ọ̀ṣun*. They divinated together for *Ọ̀ṣun*. *Ọ̀ṣun* made a promise that if she can have a baby before the end of the year, she will reward them.
>
> *Èfín* stayed at the town. *Dúró* stayed too. But *Ojíyàòmèfún* who was the first *babaláwọ* of *Ọ̀ṣun* became tired of waiting. He was unsuccessful in the town. He travelled from place to place. The other *babaláwo* warned him to stay in town so he could get his own reward. But he could not stay in one place. He used to travel from here to there. So, when *Ọ̀ṣun* had children, she wanted to reward all three *babaláwo*.

She sent for *Èfin* and *Dúró*. *Òjíyàòmèfún* was nowhere to be found. So the other *babaláwọ* sang:

Òrìṣànfin áwọ odè ̀Idò ò!
Òjìyàòmèfún l'orìtá l'ogbéṛè kèṛè
Òrìṣà Dúró, awọ̀ ilèè 'Kítí
Òjìyàòmèfún l'orìtá l'ogbéṛè kiri.

Òrìṣànfin, the priest of ̀Idò
Òjìyàòmèfún at the crossroads kept wandering about,
Òrìṣà Dúró, the priest of Ẹ̀kítí land.
Òjìyàòmèfún at the crossroads kept wandering about.

So that was *Ìrẹtè Àlàó*. *Ọ̀ṣun* gave all this to the two *babaláwo*. She gave them money, servants, and all of what she had. And *Òjìyàòmèfún* was nowhere to be found."[31]

Fertility is central to Yorùbá thought and cultural praxis. It is the medium through which the meaning of life is expressed and realized. Fertility is spiritual, natural, and corporeal. Within this construct woman is earth-deep, firm, and fertile. She is water ever-flowing and regenerative. Woman is the custodian of fire and wood, icons of metamorphosis and synthesis culminating in the preparation of life-sustaining food. Woman's fertility is changed by these images. She is the giver and protectress of physical life through which *àṣẹ* is known and knowable. Thus, fertility, in general, and woman's fertility, in particular, is highly prized and valued; infertility, or childlessness symbolizes disaster, stinginess, a non-productive life, the dissolution of *àṣẹ*.

We can further appreciate the critical role of fertility and impotency in Yorùbá thought and cultural praxis when we consider (1) the high maternal and infant mortality rates, and (2) the unbroken cycle of life that unifies the ancestors, the living, and the unborn. For a highly structured, settled, and agricultural people who occupy some of the richest lands in western Africa, fertility is an omnipotent icon set in eternal contrast to the ravages of human and natural barrenness.

This *odù Ifá* then contextualizes these images in the cosmology and confirms the reciprocity between *òrìṣà* and *ènìyàn*, first by portraying *Ọṣun* as an infertile woman and second by reaffirming that consultation with *Ifá* and the proper sacrifice are indices to sociocultural as well as personal fulfillment. In the cosmic order, *Ọṣun* suffers the agony of childlessness before she can perform her duties as giver of children to other childless women. *Ìrẹtẹ̀ Àlàó*, cited above, notes that she is wealthy, but like her human counterparts in Yorùbá society, wealth alone is an insufficient measure of a productive, successful life.

Furthermore, *Ọṣun*, as a model for childless women, makes her accessible to other childless women by offering them a compassionate and dignified goddess. Like her human counterparts, she must employ the healing powers of *Àgbo,* medicinal waters, to counteract the weakening of *àṣẹ* represented by the state of infertility. Although *Ọṣun* is *àjẹ́* and a wealthy divinity, she follows the cultural guidelines which dictate the process for problem solving in Yorùbá society. *Ifá* is key to addressing these problems. *Ifá* is more than a mechanism for problem solving. We know that *Òjìyàòmẹ̀fún* was the "first *babaláwọ* of *Ọṣun.*" The five-day pattern conforms to the traditional market week of five days. This literally means that she consulted with *Òjìyàòmẹ̀fún* weekly. Hence, her actions formalize the ritual actions for other women by following the cultural practice of weekly divination. In this respect, *Ọṣun* joins the other *òrìṣà,* such as *Ọrúnmìlà,* who also consult *Ifá. Ifá* consultation is an habitual practice irrespective of status or circumstances, and the *òrìṣà,* as well as human beings, consult it. From this *odù Ifá, Ọṣun* is also a model because she must endure the normal gestation period of pregnancy. During this interim, her *babaláwo, Òjìyàòmẹ̀fún,* becomes frustrated because he fails to acquire a sufficient clientele for *Ifá* consultation. As a result, he migrates from place to place in search of his livelihood. And his impatience causes him to relinquish his share of *Ọṣun's* wealth.

Although the narrative given here is not explicit, we can deduce that Ọ̀ṣun sacrificed her wealth to have children. It confirms the Yorùbá worldview emphasizing that children are greater than material wealth, and reinforced by the female name, Ọmọlára," meaning children are my body. Ọ̀ṣun performs sacrifice like other childless women to ensure motherhood. Simultaneously, she responds to the interdependency of the Yorùbá life cycle, which includes the unborn, the living, and the ancestors. A break in the chain weakens and eventually destroys the cycle, for the ancestors as well as the divinities are dependent upon the living for their own existence while the unborn depend upon the living and the divinities for their birth. Hence, Ọ̀ṣun's immortality as an òrìṣà depends upon her ability to produce offspring who will continue to worship her. Moreover, as an empathetic goddess of fertility, she ensures her own immortality by giving children to other women who, along with their children, worship her (see photos). Wealth in Ìrẹtẹ̀ Àlàó then is temporal, and insignificant, compared to the benefits of motherhood. In a cosmic sense, she sacrifices or invests that wealth to reap those benefits. In a cosmic and mundane sense, children replenish her material as well as spiritual wealth.

Ọ̀ṣun — Leader of Women

In Ìrẹtẹ̀ Àlàó (cited above), Ọ̀ṣun uses her wealth to restore harmony, reciprocity, and balance in her life by having children. These are major objectives for Yorùbá women and men as consultation with Ifá and the preparation of sacrifice demonstrate. Associated with this concept of harmony, reciprocity, and balance is motherhood because it alone creates a tapestry of human and divine benefits by providing the conduit for the ultimate position of elder and ancestor. Women's power is unequivocal because, like the womb itself, women are a mysterious matrix of internal synergism where spirit and body first meet. To defeat women is to defeat the awesome power of life itself; for women to remain childless is selfish, inhuman, cynical, and finite. As a leader of women, *Ọ̀ṣun*'s wealth, power, beauty, femininity, and nurturing elevate those qualities that Yorùbá women and men alike esteem. Women are the symbols of continuity, round like the earth and the womb, protective of the life they give. Where *Ọ̀ṣun* and women like her are empowered to arrest male sexism, they are also responsible for the immortality of males as well as females. The human family consisting of both genders are the concern of *YèYé, the Good Mother*. For *Ọ̀ṣun*, then, leadership of women means modelling independence as well as interdependence. As a "good mother," she wisely settles the disputes of her children. Rejection of men, like the rejection of women, causes cosmic rupture, an imbalance, a threat to human and divine continuity.

In *Ọ̀ṣẹ́*, an *ẹsẹ* from the *mẹ́rìndínlógún* collected by William Bascom, the women move away from the men to live atop a hillside. The king calls together the *babaláwo* who divinate and prescribe a sacrifice which proves ineffective. In frustration, the king calls the *IrúnMọlẹ̀* to return the women to him. The women's separation exposes the vulnerability and potential annihilation of humanity and deity alike, and again illuminates their interdependency. The future of rulership and mankind are threatened by the womeṇs self-imposed isolation, and the deities face extinction without future generations to remember them. Women's intrinsic power is demonstrated here by their ability to defend themselves against the men of the township they left behind, against the male *òrìṣà*, and against the wisdom of *Ifá*. This excerpt from the Town of Women in William Bascom's *Sixteen Cowries* is a divination poem from the *ọsẹ́* catagory that narrates how *Ọ̀ṣun* led the rebellious women back into the township.

> Diviners are the ones who behave
>   Like cowards,
> Medicine men are the ones who behave
>   Like those who do not heed advice,

If war enters a town,
Wise men are the ones we consult.
They were the ones who cast for the
Four Hundred and One Deities.
They were making war on the Town of Women,
An unsuccessful war that they could not win.

(repetition of lines 1-4)

Wise men are the ones we ask.
They are the ones who cast for *My Mother,*
        Otolo Efon,
Oshun was making war on the Town of Women.
The king said that the Sixteen Spirits
He said that they should go and capture
The Town of Women for him.
They said they would go.
Shango went, he failed.
Shopona went, he failed.
Egungun went, he failed.
Ogun, went, he failed.
They tried, they all did,
And they failed.
"Shall we consult the women?
Ha! Women, Never!
The war that we failed to win!"
They said let's consult them.
They called Yemoja,
They called Oshun,
They called Yemoja,
They called Oshun Eleyo,
They called all of them,
They called Oya.
"Yemoja, you are the one to go to this war."
"Ha!" she said, "Before I go Oshun should go."

Oshun said, "Let me go.
If I should fight and fail to capture it, then
you others can go."
Oya said she would go first.
Oya went, and they drove her back.
Oshun said she should go,
And Oshun went.
Oshun said, "This war that I am going to,
What should I do to win it?"

Through the *Ifá* oracle, *Ọ̀sun* divinates, and offers a sacrifice. She
is told to tie a calabash around her neck. She plays the calabash
like an instrument, and sings

Sewele, sewele,
Oshun is coming to play,
Oshun does not know how to fight
Sewele, sewele.

The women see her, and join her singing.They dropped their
weapons, and began to follow her back down the hillside. This
was how the whole town began serving Oshun.

Oshun was the one who brought them.

(Repetition of lines 1-4)

Oshun was making war on the Town of Women.
She sang, "We have brought them,
Long, long, long rope."
This how they took power
And gave it to women until today,
And that women became the husbands,
And have more power than men
In the presence of the king.

Since a woman won the war for him
They are
The ones who live with him.
This is why men must stay away from the wives
    of the king,
And his wives must not approach them,
As orisha has spoken.[32]

In *òṣè*, the collective power of the Town of Women is undaunted. The women defeat rulers symbolized by *Ṣàngó*, they defeat disease symbolized by *Ṣòpònò*, they defeat ancestors symbolized by *Egúngún* and they defeat the epitome of male prowess symbolized by *Ògún*. When the male *IrúnMọlè* fail, the king sends for the female deities. Among them, *Òṣun* is the victor. She cajoles them into playing with her, and leads them back to the township where they rejoin the king.

Leadership entails responsibility. As an *òrìṣà* and *IrúnMọlè*, *Òṣun* is responsible for protecting the vehicle through which humanity perpetuates and nurtures itself, women. As a giver of children, she is responsible for the protection and health of the awesome power of the womb. As *YèYé, the Good Mother* of women and men, she is responsible for the continuous engagement of both women and men. Here, the war is a peaceful one, and conquest is by appeasement, perhaps suggesting that women's power itself must be placated and cajoled, like the *Gèlèdé*, into such continuous engagement. The king we are told gives power to women because they won the war, and have become the "husbands." Because of *Òṣun*'s leadership, the threat to human and divine existence is abated.

Òṣun and the Art of Divination

Chapter five defines and examines various aspects and preparations for the *Òṣun* Festival. One of the major events is the *Olójùmérìndínlógún*, the lighting of the sixteen lamps, which signals the second major phase of the festival. Babalọlà points out in *Folklore Forum* that sixteen is a particularly important number in Yorùbá thought.[33] There are the sixteen major *odù*, which are senior to the other 240 *odù* in the *Ifá* corpus.[34] The formulation for the corpus itself rests upon 16 times 16 or 256 *odù*. More important for our discussion of *Ọ̀ṣun* is the correlation between the *olójùmẹ́rìndálógún* and the sixteen-cowrie divination system that she learned from *Ọ̀rúnmìlà*, one of her husbands. Another *odù Ifá* states,

> At one time, *Ọ̀rúnmìlà* was not at home. *Ọ̀ṣun* was his wife. Many people used to come to have a reading, and *Ọrúnmìlà* was not at home. *Ọ̀ṣun* was vigilant when *Ọ̀rúnmìlà* was doing everything. She had some knowledge of *Ifá*, so she started to divine. She even took people into the grove to initiate them.
>
> *Ọ̀rúnmìlà* was coming back from his journey, and he heard *Ọ̀ṣun* singing in the forest in the grove. And *Ọ̀rúnmìlà* asked, "Who is there?" And she replied, "It is *Ọ̀ṣun*." She explained to him that many people used to come in his absence (for consultation), so she took them into the grove with the little knowledge she had. And *Ọ̀rúnmìlà* said alright. He gave her the sixteen cowrie to use for divination.

Babaláwo Yẹmí Ẹlẹ́bùrúîbọ̀n continued,

> In that divination, we hear people say, *òdí, ogbè, òyẹkú, ọsá.* But it is not a complete set of *odù*, it has only one leg (meaning one side): *òdí, ogbè, òyẹkú, ọbàrà, ọsá.* Like *odù Ifá* says, *ọbàrà mẹ́jì, ọbàrà ogbè, ogbè 'dí,* it (*ẹ́ẹ́rìndìnlògùn* or sixteen cowrie divination) doesn't have that. It just has *ogbè, ọsá, òyẹkú,* and so on like that. It has *Ifá* in it, and it was *Ọ̀rúnmìlà* who gave that to *Ọ̀ṣun*.[35]

In the first *odù* presented on pages 123–124, *Ọ̀ṣun* agrees to accept the sacrifice offered by the male divinities on the condition

that they gave her "all the initiation of the ritual they perform for
men by which they keep women behind." Her introduction to the
secret knowledge paves the way to greater knowledge. From this
odù, we notice her talent for acquiring the art of divination.
Armed with the codes of initiation, Ọ̀ṣun observes Ọ̀rúnmìlà
while he divinates for his clients, and thereby begins to acquire
the art and knowledge of the oracle. As a result, Ọ̀rúnmìlà
teaches her the "assistant cowrie" or the mẹ́rìndìnlògùn, known
in Nigeria and the Western Hemisphere as the Sixteen Cowrie
Divination System. As Bascom explains, "The signatures of the
sixteen cowrie divination is simpler than that of the complete Ifá
system."³⁶

When I asked Babaláwọ Ẹlébùrūîbọn why Ọ̀ṣun was given
this particular system he said it is because she is a woman.
Pressed further, he said that the training for complete knowledge
of the Ifá system requires decades of study with various master
Ifá priests in different parts of Yorùbáland. He claimed that
women can study Ifá if they wish, after which they are called ̀Iyá
nIfá. But he noted that the demands of training young girls in this
specialized study continues into what would ordinarily be the
childbearing years of women.³⁷ In further interviews, I was in-
formed that a woman's power is most potent during her menstru-
ating years. Indeed, in a spiritually charged environment, menses
is a manifestation of àṣẹ. Perhaps this explains the exclusion of
women in some male-dominated secret societies until after
menopause. Consequently, Ọ̀ṣun, goddess of power and fertility,
accepts the mẹ́rìndìnlògùn, and remains an awesome force in
Yorùbá cosmic structure.

Nonetheless, the odù Ifá demonstrates some reservation
about Ọ̀ṣun acquiring the full measure of Ifá divination along
with her power as àjẹ́ and leadership of the àjẹ́. Consider this
odù:

Ọ̀kànràn Sọdẹ̀ is the odù Ifá that narrates how Ọ̀ṣun among
all other òrìṣà, Ọ̀rúnmìlà Ẹlẹ́gbàrà, Ògún, Ṣàngó was the

one who was to receive knowledge from *Olódùmarè*.
Olódùmarè, the Supreme Being, sent a message to the earth
that he would throw knowledge to them, and that whoever
picked it up would be rewarded. He did not name the
specific day or say what it would look like. But he told them
that he was going to send knowledge to them. So they all
began to wander and search for it. *Ọ̀ṣun*, as a woman,
consulted *Ifá* divination, *Ọ̀rúnmìlà*. And *Ifá* told her that she
was going to be among the successful people who would
find the knowledge. But she should make a sacrifice of the
gown she was wearing. In olden days, this type of long
gown, like the men's *bàbá rìgá*, was worn by women.

Ọ̀rúnmìlà told her to make a sacrifice with that gown, a
rat, and money. And she refused to make the sacrifice of
that gown. On the day that everyone was looking for the
knowledge, she was the first person to discover it, although
she did not know what it meant or what it looked like. *Ọ̀ṣun*
picked it up and put it into her pocket. Unfortunately, the
thing fell down. *Ọ̀rúnmìlà* was behind her. He saw it, picked
it up and kept it.

Because *Ọ̀ṣun* refused to make the sacrifice, *Ẹlẹ́gbàrà*
tore the inside of her clothes and made holes in her pockets.
So it was *Ẹlẹ́gbàrà* who punished *Ọ̀ṣun* for disobeying by
not making the proper sacrifice. As a result, automatically
there was a hole in her pocket. And the knowledge fell out.

When they were all tired of searching, they gathered
together and asked each other what they'd found and what
they saw. Then *Ọ̀rúnmìlà* said "I only found this." And
Ọ̀ṣun was digging her hands into her pockets to bring out
what she found, but it was not there. Then, she said to
Ọ̀rúnmìlà. "I saw that before you. I was the first person who
saw this today." *Ọ̀rúnmìlà* replied, "A man took it from your
pocket. I saw it on the ground." And so it was *Ọ̀rúnmìlà* who
became more knowledgeable than the other *òrìṣà*. He became
the person who gave the *òrìṣà* the knowledge and power.

So that is how Ẹlẹ́gbàrà punishes those who refuse to make the sacrifice and rewards those who perform the sacrifice.[38]

Although sexism plays a role in this *odù Ifá*, that theme alone obscures the dominant views and objectives of harmony in Yorùbá cosmology. Consider that if *Ọ̀ṣun* had both the power of *àjẹ́* and the full power of divination, a mythical imbalance as well as a possible functional conflict could occur. As an *ÌrúnMọ̀lẹ̀*, she is a benevolent *òrìṣà* who mediates the positive and negative powers of the *àjẹ́* on behalf of humanity. Since the *Ifá* peers into the nature of humanity's position and the forces working for or against it, *Ọ̀ṣun's* control of the *Ifá* could place her in conflict with the *àjẹ́*, humanity, or herself. Her marriage to *Ọ̀rúnmìlà* mitigates against yet another possible imbalance, while simultaneously acknowledging her ability to perform divination. Perhaps, the *òrìṣà* wish to avoid making the same error twice by excluding her altogether thus reinforcing an ideal state of balance and harmony as the cornerstone of Yorùbá cosmological thought.

Given the three *odù* cited above, I believe that Yorùbá cosmology clearly delineates tasks among the *òrìṣà* which are meant to maintain harmonic relationships among them more than to establish any gender-based patterns of behavior or hegemony. Recognition of *Ọ̀ṣun's* role as giver of children and leader of the *àjẹ́* empowers her. Where she knows the activities of the *àjẹ́*, as demonstrated below, she doesn't know the object of or the reasons for those activities. That knowledge remains in the domain of *Ọ̀rúnmìlà*. Meanwhile, her possession of the *mẹ̀rìndínlógún* parallels the different systems of divination possessed by the other major *òrìṣà*.[39] Moreover, *Ọ̀rúnmìlà's* willingness to teach *Ọ̀ṣun* the assistant *Ifá* divination system acknowledges her capacity to learn it and her comparable role in disseminating wisdom and knowledge. The following extensive *odù Ifá* gives greater insight into the relationship between *Ọ̀ṣun* and *Ọ̀rúnmìlà* as the gods of the *àjẹ́* (powerful beings) and *ọgbọ́n* (wisdom) respectively.

They (*àjẹ́*) were all trainees of *Ọrúnmìlà*. *Ọrúnmìlà* taught them the art and practice of *Ifá*. He asked them to go to perform divination and when they returned they should reward him. But these people went, they performed successfully, but they did not come to greet (reward) *Ọrúnmìlà*. So *Ọrúnmìlà* became angry, and he brought out his sword and killed all of them.

Ẹ̀gànrẹ̀fẹ́fẹ́ arrived at Ẹfun. He transformed himself into *Ọ̀*yo, the bird of *àjẹ́*. *Edídágẹ̀rẹ̀gẹ́rẹ́* went to heaven and became Ogbígbò. *Bọyẹ* became Kòwẹ́. They were all birds of *àjẹ́*, and they started to fight *Ọrúnmìlà*. They said to him, "We have problems. We will give you problems." *Ọrúnmìlà* could not sleep. He could not eat. He called his priests to come and divine. They divined. They made a sacrifice. The sacrifice was not accepted. *Ọrúnmìlà* asked another priest, the first student of *Ọrúnmìlà*. His name is *Odánílòjùwẹ̀rẹ̀wẹ́rẹ̀*. Then he told *Ọrúnmìlà* that these *àjẹ́* have a fowl in front of their leader. Unless *Ọrúnmìlà* can break this fowl, he will not have peace.

Odánílòjùwẹ̀rẹ̀wẹ́rẹ́ asked *Ọrúnmìlà* to go to the lake of the river *Ọ̀ṣun*. *Ọ̀ṣun* was their leader. And *Ọrúnmìlà* went there. They asked *Ọrúnmìlà* to make a sacrifice of 200 parrots, 200 fish, 200 rats, 2 goats, and the money, and all the rest of the materials of the leaf of *Ifá*. *Ọrúnmìlà* found everything. It remained parrot feathers. He could not find them.

Ọrúnmìlà as looking for parrot feathers, and somebody said, "It was *Ọ̀ṣun* who has a lot of parrot feathers. She used to decorate her house with parrot feathers." Then *Ọrúnmìlà* went to the river *Ọ̀ṣun*, and he knocked on the door. *Ọ̀ṣun* said, "Who's that?" *Ọrúnmìlà* said, "It is me, *Ọrúnmìlà*. *Ọ̀ṣun* said, "I don't know you." *Ọrúnmìlà* said, "You forget that I was the one who initiated you. You forget we made our vows together. You stood in one eave, and I stood in the other eave. We were sitting together, and we made this vow." *Ọ̀ṣun* said, "Yes, I remember. Come in." *Ọ̀rúnmìlà* entered. *Ọ̀rúnmìlà* said, "I want 200 parrot feathers." Then, *Ọ̀ṣun* said for what purpose. And *Ọ̀rúnmìlà* said that he was in trouble with the *àjẹ́*, *Ẹ̀gànrẹ̀fẹ́fẹ́*, *Awọ̀rì Ògún*, *Bọyẹ Ajáìyẹ́*. Then *Ọ̀ṣun* said "Ah, it was this place where they made the fowl." And if he had not gone there in search of parrot feathers in order to complete the sacrificial offering, *Ọ̀rúnmìlà* could never have known that they made and kept the fowl that gave him problems at *Ọ̀ṣun's* house.

So *Ọ̀rúnmìlà* begged *Ọ̀ṣun* to forgive him. *Ọ̀ṣun* went inside and brought out 200 parrot feathers. *Ọ̀rúnmìlà* went back, made the sacrifice, and they forgave him. And so whatever this society of *àjẹ́* makes, they have a meeting, and they make a vow that this is what they will do, and it may be so. This is the odù which explains the role that *Ọ̀ṣun* plays among the *àjẹ́*.[40]

In this *odù Ifá*, first, *Ọ̀rúnmìlà*, the god of wisdom and knowledge, must also follow the cultural practice of divination and sacrifice to ameliorate his difficulties. Second, *Ọ̀ṣun*, the leader of the *àjẹ́*, cannot accept sacrifice directly, so in her coyness she pretends not to know *Ọ̀rúnmìlà*. *Ẹbọ* or sacrifice must proceed through the proper channels which means that *Ẹ̀ṣù* must inspect and approve of its contents. Third, the mythical marriage of *Ọ̀ṣun* and *Ọ̀rúnmìlà* respectively mirrors the balance and reciprocity between power to control good and evil, and the wisdom and knowledge to comprehend its depths. This construct establishes the archetypal cosmic pattern that drives the social order.

Consider also, in the previous discussion of the *odù Ifá*, *ỌseTùrá*, that the *IrúnMọlẹ̀* were directed by *Olódùmarè* to beg *Ọ̀ṣun* for forgiveness. Their culturally defined method for approaching the goddess resembles that of human beings, with a noticeable exception. Since *Ọ̀rúnmìlà* participated in her exclusion, it seems inconceivable that he alone could perform divination for himself. Divination is the acquisition of knowledge about

the origin and nature of a problem, while sacrifice demonstrates
the wisdom to accept resolution to it. The òrìṣà of divination
must humble himself, seek his own student to divinate for him,
and prepare the requisite sacrifice. Olódùmarè seems unequivocal in providing problem-solving direction to human beings as
well as to òrìṣà and underscoring the mirror images of both. The
established pattern is unwavering, that is, to seek knowledge, to
make a sacrifice, and to accept the resolution. The veracity of this
pattern is underpinned by these odù Ifá primarily because it emanates from its own ethos, that is, the Ifá itself. But, it suggests
parity among the òrìṣà, human beings, and forces of nature with
respect to the process and structure of restitution for transgres-
sions of any magnitude or dimension.

The last-cited odù Ifá confirms that the òrìṣà of wisdom and
knowledge is fallible; consequently, he too must follow the acknowledged pathway toward restitution. When Ọ̀rúnmìlà mur-
ders the àjẹ́ in anger, he creates havoc. The disrespect and defi-
ance of the àjẹ́ as well as his actions are unjustifiable. Because
he is the deity of wisdom and knowledge, the crime violates the
intent of ọgbọ́n which suggests reasonableness, and a rational
resolution to offenses and problems. Furthermore, his wisdom
and knowledge is not omniscient because he does not fully know
or comprehend Ọ̀ṣun's full powers until he goes in search of the
parrot feathers which she symbolically "owns."

At first, Ọ̀rúnmìlà's sacrifice is rejected, and Ọ̀ṣun, his pro-
tege and his wife, repudiates him. Both Èṣù and the oracle he represents punish his irrationality. Ọ̀rúnmìlà's failure to consult Ifá
regarding the action to be taken against the offending àjẹ́ results
in his humiliation. Like most of his clients, Ọ̀rúnmìlà gets himself into trouble before he consults the oracle. As such, his punishment seems the greater. Like Ọ̀ṣun, he commissions another
babaláwo to divinate for him. And like the goddess, he must wait
before the resolution of the problem occurs. These factors ensure
reciprocity among the òrìṣà since, with the exception of Èṣù, they
all operate with some constraint.

The cosmic archetype confirms another pattern of behavior. Having negotiated with *Ọ̀ṣun*, *Ọ̀rúnmìlà* receives the 200 parrot feathers that he needs for the appropriate sacrifice. Although she will accept or reject the offering eventually, neither *Ọ̀ṣun* nor *Ọ̀rúnmìlà* can resolve the issue themselves. *Ọ̀ṣun* is the leader of the *àjẹ́* but she cannot accept the sacrifice directly from *Ọ̀rúnmìlà*. Cosmological proscriptions enforce this. She maintains the covenant that binds *Ọ̀rúnmìlà* to his tormentors, but *Èṣù* must be the first to judge the acceptability of the sacrifice before it passes to her. Symbolically, the marriage of *Ọ̀ṣun* and *Ọ̀rúnmìlà* holds the most fascination here because it represents the binding of internal creative power to knowledge on one hand, and the combined force of insight and productivity on the other.

Ọ̀ṣun and the Settling of Òṣogbo

Both the *odù Ifá* and the *oríkì*, or praise-poetry, of *Ọ̀ṣun* narrate her role in the settling and rulership of Òṣogbo and her protection of the township during the Fulani Wars of 1843.[41] According to the *odù Ifá* that follows, Olútímíyìn of Ọ̀yọ́ and Èlàáróyì, written variously as Làáróyì and Èlàáró, of Ìpólé near Ìlẹ̀ṣà were the co-founders of present-day Òṣogbo. As noted in chapter four, traditional history states that Òṣogbo as a settlement is about 350 years old.

Olútímíyìn was a hunter who tracked elephants. During one of his expeditions, he discovered the cool, everflowing Ọ̀ṣun River. According to the *odù*, he killed a mother elephant near the banks of the Ọ̀ṣun River, and led the baby elephant to the place where the market stands today. There, he built a shrine to Ògun, the divinity of iron and war, which still stands. Because he knew of the drought in Ìpólé in Ìjẹ̀ṣàland, Olútímíyìn informs Láàróyè who ruled Ìpólé that he had discovered the river and its luscious grove. Láàróyè led the people of Ìpólé to the shores of the Ọ̀ṣun River where he and Olútímíyìn built their new homes. Babaláwo Ẹlébùrúìbọn continued the narrative as follows,

Ọ̀ṣun was already there, by the time that they built their
tents at the side of the river. But as there were many big
trees in the grove, they wanted to cut one of them. They put
fire under the tree and it fell into the river, and they all
heard the noise inside the river say, Ọ̀ṣogbo, all my pots of
indigo dye[42] have been broken. So that is how they started
to greet her. Because of the disturbance, Ọ̀ṣun asked the
settlers to move away from her river banks.[43]

In compliance, they moved to the marketplace where the palace
stands today (see diagrams and photos). We are told that Olútìmíyìn
built his house where the palace stands, and that Láàróyè built
his house in front of the palace where they keep the images of
Ọ̀ṣun.[44] The diagrams illustrate the relationship among these
various locations. During the Ọ̀ṣun Festival, the celebration follows the course described in this narrative. As will become clear
in the following chapters, the ritual path reenacts the history as
well as the mythology of Ọ̀ṣun and Òṣogbo township. Although
this history is an important part of her mythology, Ọ̀ṣun is especially revered because of her protection of the settlers and the
giving of children to childless women.

Ọ̀ṣun, Yorùbá Cosmology, and Festival Drama

Obviously, the mythology of the goddess Ọ̀ṣun is a key construct
in Yorùbá cosmology that recalls cultural history and philosophical perspectives. As will become evident in the following chapters, mythology, cultural history, and philosophy shape the context and the content of the Ọ̀ṣun Festival. The diverse roles of the
goddess reflect the roles of the women who participate in the
festival. The concept of balance recurs in the roles of the priests,
in the worship of the goddess, in the relationship between humanity and divinity, and in the sacred and secular reenactment
of the myths of Ọ̀ṣun and the history of Òṣogbo. To fully appre-

ciate these components, the following chapter explores the complexity of the *Ọ̀ṣun* Festival.

Notes

1. Mazizi Kunene, "The Relevance of African Cosmological Systems to African Literature Today," *African Literature Today*, 11 (1980):190-205.

2. S. A. Fádípè, *The Sociology of the Yorùbá* (Ìbàdàn: Ìbàdàn University Press, 1970). See also, S.A. Johnson, *History of the Yorubas: From the Earliest Times to the Beginning of the British Protectorate* (Westport, Connecticut: Negro Universities Press, rpt, 1970).

3. Rowland Abíọ́dún, "Verbal and Visual Metaphors: Mythical Allusions in Yorùbá Ritualistic Art of Ori,"*Word and Image, A Journal of Verbal and Visual Inquiry* (1987), 3(3): 252 - 270; Rowland Abíọ́dún, "Woman In Yorùbá Religious Images," *African Languages and Cultures* 2,1 (1989): 1-18; Wande Abímbọ́lá, *African Art Studies: The State of the Discipline* (Washington, D.C.: Smithsonian Institution, National Museum of African Art, 1987); J.K. Olupona, *Kingship, Religion, and Rituals in a Nigerian Community* (Stockholm/Almqvist: Wiksell International, 1991); J.K. Olúpọ̀nà, *Religion and Society in Nigeria: Historical and Sociological Perspectives* (Ìbàdàn: Spectrum Books Limited, 1991); William Bascom, *Sixteen Cowries: Yorùbá Divination from Africa to the New World* (Bloomington and London: Indiana University Press, 1980); Robert Farris Thompson, *Flash of the Spirit: African and Afro-American Art and Philosophy* (New York: Vintage Books, 1984).

4. S.O. Bìòbákú, *Sources of Yorùbá History* (Oxford: Clarendon Press, 1973).

5. Wándé Abímbọlá, *Ifá Divination Poetry* (New York: Nok Publishers, Ltd, 1977), 1-36: S.A. Babalọlá, *The Content and Form of Yorùbá Íjàlà* (Ìbàdàn, Nigeria: Oxford University Press, rpt 1976): 1-84.
6. Wọlé Ṣóyìnka, *Myth, Literature, and the African World* (Cambridge: Cambridge University Press, 1976).
7. Ṣóyìnká, *ibid.*
8. *Ibid.*
9. Houston Baker, *Blues, Ideology and Afro-American Literature* (Chicago: Chicago University Press, 1984).
10. Diedre L. Bádéjọ, *A Goddess of Our Own* (work in progress).
11. Abímbọlá, *op. cit.*, v.
12. Filomena Steady, *Black Women Cross-Culturally* (Cambridge, Massachusetts: Schenkman Publishing Company, 1981).
13. Alice Walker, *In Search of Our Mother's Garden* (Orlando, Florida: Harcourt, Brace, Jovanovich, 1983).
14. Ẹlẹbùrúbọn, Personal interviews, 1982.
15. Abímbọlá, *Ifá Divination Poetry:* 1-4.
16. E. Bọlájí Idòwú, *Olódùmarè: God in Yorùbá Belief* (London: Longmans Ltd, 1962): 63. Ṣóyínká, *op. cit.*: 15. See also Abímbọlá, *op. cit.*
17. Ẹlẹbùrú̃ibọn, interviews, 1982.
18. *Ibid.*
19. Bádéjo, *op. cit.*
20. *Ibid.* See also chapter one of the present work.
21. Wande Abímbọla, *Sixteen Great Poems of Ifá* (UNESCO, 1975):35.
22. *Ibid.*
23. Bádéjọ, "The Goddess Ọ̀ṣun as a Paradigm for African Feminist Criticism." *Sage: A Scholarly Journal on Black Women*, VI, 1 (Summer 1989): 27-32.
24. Bádéjọ, *A Goddess of Our Own.* See also chapter one of the present work.

25. Thompson, *Flash of the Spirit, op. cit.*: 5.
26. Idòwú, *Olódùmarè, op. cit.*
27. *Ibid.*
28. Johnson, *History of the Yorubas*. See also, Babatúnde Agiri, "Yorùbá Oral Tradition with Special Reference to the Early History of the Ọ̀yọ́ Kingdom," in Wándé Abímbọ́la (ed), *Yorùbá Oral Tradition* (Ilé-Ifẹ̀, Nigeria: Department of African Languages and Literatures, University of Ifẹ̀, 1975): 157-197.
29. Agiri, *ibid.*
30. *Ibid.*
31. Babaláwọ Yẹ́mí Ẹlẹ́bùrûïbọn, Personal interviews, 1983.
32. Bascom, *Sixteen Cowries:* 413-419.
33. S.A. Babalọlá, Interview with Gerald Cashion: "Studies in Yoruba Folklore" in *Folklore Forum* (Indiana University Folklore Institute; Bibliographic Special Series, 11, 1973, 63-70).
34. Babalọlá, Interview, See also Bascom, *Sixteen Cowries*.
35. Ẹlẹ́bùrûïbọn, 1982.
36. Bascom, *Sixteen Cowries*.
37. Ẹlẹ́bùrûïbọn, 1982.
38. *Ibid.*
39. *Ibid.*
40. *Ibid.*
41. Ẹlẹ́bùrúïbọn, 1982. See also "*Òṣogbo*" in "*Ọ̀yọ́ Town Series*" (Ibadan: Ministry of Local Government and Information. January 1977): 12-14.
42. Among her other attributes, *Ọ̀ṣun* was a noted dyer. Also the *Ọ̀ṣun* Grove is filled with trees and plants which produce the colors for tye dying such as the *pèrègùn* tree.
43. Ẹlẹ́bùrûïbọn, 1982. See also photographs and illustrations.
44. *Ibid.* See also photographs and illustrations.

Chapter Four

THE *ÒṢUN* FESTIVAL: STRUCTURE AND MEANING

The *Òṣun* Festival is ritual, it is drama, and it is festival. It is ritual because it seeks (1) to reengage the community's own cosmic ethos and ethnic consciousness, (2) to reaffirm the religious prowess of the *òrìṣà Òṣun*, (3) to pay homage to her benevolence, (4) and to seek her protection and blessings in the forthcoming year. The *Òṣun* festival is drama because it is *staged* before an audience with a particular plot that builds toward a climax followed by its denouement. As drama, it entertains, informs, and communicates emotionally and socially with initiates and non-initiates alike. Distinctions are clearly established between the former participants who engage in the exclusively sacrosanct rituals and the uninitiated who are invited to share in the resulting affective communal rites. Finally, it is festival because those who attend expect to be entertained as well as to participate in a communal celebration of Yorùbá history and culture. The audience along with other participants, entertainers, and dignitaries anticipate the feasting as well as the music, song, dance, and camaraderie of others.

Ritual, drama, and festival are reflected variously throughout the sixteen days of celebration. First, the religious and traditional political hierarchy play specific roles mainly in its ritual and drama. Second, the *Òṣun* worshippers along with other *òrìṣà* worshippers enhance the ambience of ritual, contribute to its drama, and participate in its festivity. Third, the presence of visitors, vendors, and entertainers creates a festive climate. The demarcations among these various roles and functions are reflected in the *space* each segment of the community occupies. The fluid creation of stage and stage positions results in intrinsic social control and culturally prescribed knowledge. As I will illustrate below, the *Ọ̀ṣun* Festival is clearly staged. The *Atáója* (ruler of Òṣogbo), *Ìyá Ọ̀ṣun* (chief priestess of *Ọ̀ṣun*), *Àwòrò* (chief priest of *Ọ̀ṣun*), *Arugbá* (sacrifice carrier), and the *Ìyálàṣẹ* (caretaker of the *àṣẹ*) perform specific movements and actions that are meant to signal sequential stages of the *Ọ̀ṣun* festival and to move its action closer to the climax. Dance, body gestures, and song can indicate a specific movement in the ritual and festival drama. Action, such as the changing of crowns and attire, the entry of a particular musical ensemble, or the *ọlọṣẹ* (whipping boys) signal the beginning of a new scene and, simultaneously, the completion of another ritual and/or festival segment. Consequently, events and interactions from the first day of the annual festival flow throughout each sequence progressively towards the completion of an action. This ebb and flow of ritual and festival movements are controlled, indeed choreographed, by that religious, political, and social hierarchy. As the central performers, their ritual reenactments of the mythical and political history of *Òṣogbo* gives structure and meaning to the sixteen-day festival. The following discussion highlights four events, including the festival day itself, which demonstrate how ritual, drama, and festival intertwine.

The Preparation and Paraphernalia for the *Ọ̀ṣun* Festival

I attended the *Ọ̀ṣun* Festival in Òṣogbo township, then part of *Ọ̀yọ́* State, Nigeria, during late August and early September in 1982. While there, I visited the palace of the *Atáója*, the *Ọ̀ṣun* shrine in the Grove, and the house of the Ìyá Ọ̀ṣun. I also interviewed Babaláwo Yẹ́mi Ẹlẹ́bùrúîbọ̀n, the Ìyá Ọ̀ṣun, and the Ọ̀ṣun priests and priestesses including Mrs. Ṣàngó Tundun Àsàbĭ at the palace, shrine, and elsewhere. Between 1981 and 1983, I took several photographs and slides, recorded many oral narratives, praise poems, and festival songs as well as odù Ifá which refer specifically to Ọ̀ṣun. Some of these odù Ifá, oríkì, and orin Ọ̀ṣun are included in this book.

Preparation for the Ọ̀ṣun Festival begins with ritual. According to informants cited in this book, the Atáója, Ìyá Ọ̀ṣun, Àwòrò, and Babaláwo are the vicars of this primary ritual observation. Atáója means "the one who uses his hands to feed the fish," one of Ọ̀ṣun's images. As ruler of Òṣogbo, he mediates between his earthly charge and his spiritual obligation. He "feeds" the contents of the sacrifice (ẹbọ) to the divinity of the Ọ̀ṣun River on the appointed day. Clearly, he bridges both worlds. Ìyá Ọ̀ṣun is the mother of all Ọ̀ṣun worshippers or chief priestess. The Àwòrò helps the Ìyá Ọ̀ṣun and Arugbá carry the ẹbọ (sacrifice) to the Ọ̀ṣun River. The babaláwo, or father of the secrets, attends to the casting of the ọ̀pẹ̀lẹ̀ which reveals the thoughts and desires of Ifá who mediates between the òrìṣà and ènìyàn. At an appointed time, the Atáója summons the babaláwo to the palace to perform divination. According to Babaláwo Yẹ́mi Ẹlébùrúîbọ̀n, the Ọ̀ṣun Festival in Òṣogbo follows that of her husband Ọ̀rúnmìlà. However, Ifá consultation provides the specific date and particular sacrificial requirements for each annual celebration. This specific Ifá consultation is restricted to the religious and political hierarchy of Òṣogbo and Ọ̀ṣun worship. After the date and sacrifice are disclosed, the Atáója prepares to make public the wishes of the goddess Ọ̀ṣun. As the representative of the goddess, his official announcement marks the beginning of the festival.[1]

The Atáója's position in the festival reflects both mythical and historical accounts of the founding of Òṣogbo.[2] The oral literary sources suggest that Ọ̀ṣun ruled Òṣogbo at the same time that *Ṣàngó* ruled Ọ̀yọ́ around the early 1600s. Local government records indicate that modern Ọ̀ṣogbo was founded in the late eighteenth century. Unlike the mythical account, these records indicate that the followers of both Òlútímíhìn and Láróòyè were fleeing drought conditions in their respective areas. The records further note that Láróòyè was also the seventh Owa of Ìpọ̀lè, an Ìjẹ̀ṣà town about eight kilometers from Ọ̀ṣogbo. Frequent historical and mythical references to Ìpọ̀lè, Ọ̀yọ́, and Ìjẹ̀ṣà are found in the praise-poetry, and songs of *Ọ̀ṣun* cited in chapter one.[3] These latter sources corroborate both the narratives of the *odù Ifá* and the local government documents found in Ìbàdàn. Consequently, it is possible to suggest that female rulership was prevalent during the two hundred or so years between *Ọ̀ṣun's* rulership of Ọ̀ṣogbo in the early 1600's to the late 1800's when Òlútímíhìn and Láróòyè made a treaty with her to begin a settlement in Ọ̀ṣogbo. It is also possible to suggest that since *Ọ̀ṣun* means "a source" or "to seep out," that her name itself may be a title for female rulership. This may explain as well the proliferation of *"Ọ̀ṣun"* -related titles throughout Ìjẹ̀ṣà territory. The fact that some of the *Ọ̀ṣun* titles now refer to males may signal the transition from female to male rulership as a result of increasing warfare and slave-raiding. Consider here the debate over the gender of *Odùdùwa*, the progenitor of modern Yorùbá people as an example of the ambiguity surrounding gender and rulership in modern Yorùbá discourse.

In addition, Robin Law's book, *The Ọ̀yọ́ Empire c1600-1836*, documents the significance of Ọ̀ṣogbo as an outpost of the Ọ̀yọ́ Empire during the eighteenth century and as a sanctuary against the Fulani slave-raiding wars.[4] This data further corroborates the existence of nineteenth-century female rulership with which Olútímíhìn and Láróòyè negotiate. It substantiates the role that the *Atáója* plays in Ọ̀ṣogbo as well as in the *Ọ̀ṣun* Festival. These historical and cosmological references verify that the *Atáója* as a descendant of Láróòyè and his co-founder, Olútímíhìn, and *Ọ̀ṣun* as ruler of a preexisting township are co-rulers of modern Òṣogbo. The presentation of gifts, food, and entertainment renews the bond between ruler and ruled, between human and spiritual communities. This exchange occurs on the first day of the sixteen-day festival when the *Atáója* announces the date and requirements for the communal offering to *Òṣun*. This announcement is presented as a formal event *staged* at the center of town, situated at the Òṣogbo market where the *Ògún* shrine is located (see illustration on page 112). In this manner, the bond is complete.

This first major public event of the *Òṣun* Festival fills the streets of Òṣogbo with pageantry and communal spirit. The *Atáója* leaves the palace surrounded by his wives, attendants, musicians, and guards. The royal horn-blowers lead the way through Òṣogbo announcing the approach of the *Atáója* with their instruments. The royal party walks down the streets displaying the *Òpá Ọba*, the staff of political and religious authority. He arrives at the designated spot and is seated along with his wives and courtly entourage. The *Atáója* accepts these communal gifts of food and drink noted above on behalf of the goddess *Òṣun*. In honor of her festival, these offerings are shared among the many visitors to the palace later that day. The procession with its music and pageantry establishes a format that occurs throughout the celebration.[5]

Those who come to pay homage (*júbà*) to the *Atáója* enhance the festive nature of the occasion while honoring their patron goddess, *Òṣun*. The *Ìyá Òṣun*, *Àwòrò*, and *Ìyálàṣẹ* are among the first and most significant of those who gather at the center of Òṣogbo. As cited in chapter five, the covenant that Olútímíhìn and Láróòyè made with *Òṣun Òṣogbo* reaffirms the sanctity of her Grove. The procession reminds its inhabitants of the bond between them and *Òṣun* as ruler and divinity. Their procession also reminds Òṣogbo people of the spiritual bond with *Òṣun* as a giver of children and as a warrior-woman who protected them against the devastations of war and drought. Moreover, the bonding between the religious and political leadership of Òṣogbo reminds the township of its unifying history. Local rulers who owe allegiance to the *Atáọ́ja* along with other important families and organizations within the community also participate in the opening celebration. Each makes a contribution to the success of the festival and praises the *Atáọ́ja* for his role as tutelary ruler of the town. Because he co-rules Ọ̀ṣogbo with *Ọ̀ṣun*, local officials also pay their respects to his dual spiritual and historical position.[6] Many offer monetary gifts, which contribute to the resources necessary for feeding a large number of visitors. The contributions in food and beverage may be reserved for the goddess and her devotees, (a responsibility of the *Ìyálàṣẹ*), for the Atáọ́ja's family and attendants, or for general consumption by visitors and guests. Women who have given birth during the intervening year between festivals also contribute to and participate in the procession. With their babies tied to their backs or in utero, these women pay homage to the *Atáọ́ja* as the guardian of the *òrìṣà* who has blessed them with children. They also donate food and beverage to the *Atáọ́ja* as well as sing his praises and the praises of the goddess in thanksgiving. *Ọmọde Ọ̀ṣun*, children of *Ọ̀ṣun*, are also quite visible during the opening ceremonies of the festival. Some children, as apprentices to priests, priestesses, and musicians, play accompaniment on drums and *sẹ̀kẹrẹ̀* as they proceed towards the *Atáọ́ja* to pay their respect. Other children who come to pay homage are devoted to *Ọ̀ṣun* because she has blessed their mothers with them, or called upon them through the *Mẹ́rìndínlógún* or Sixteen Cowries Divination oracle to worship her.[7] Children from the town also join in the celebration by singing and following the musicians and inhabitants during the event (see p. 112). The high visibility of children demonstrates *Ọ̀ṣun's* role as a fertility goddess and the spiritual mother of Ọ̀ṣogbo.

   This communal celebration of *Ọ̀ṣun* is also apparent in the array of colors, especially gold, yellow, and amber — symbols of authority, and other paraphernalia that symbolize the *òrìṣà Ọ̀ṣun*. Her golden colors are found among the clothing of the women and children. The *Ìyá Ọ̀ṣun* and other priestesses wear the coiffures associated with her. Women, men, and children alike adorn themselves in brass and coral beads. The *òpá ọba*, the staff of the *Atáọ́ja's* authority, stands before him next to his seat in the center of town. Musicians play the *dùndùn* drums and the *ṣẹ̀kẹ̀rẹ̀*, which are instruments used by *Ọ̀ṣun* worshippers and praise singers. Even in this synergized atmosphere, the *Atáọ́ja* remains the most significant symbol of the goddess on this first day of the festival, for as her co-ruler, he speaks on her behalf. Indeed, without the presence of the *Atáọ́ja* and the *Ìyá Ọ̀ṣun*, the worship and celebration of *Ọ̀ṣun* cannot occur.[8] However, townspeople attend this preliminary activity not just to pay homage to the *Atáọ́ja* as the representative head of the community but also to receive his blessings as the protector of the society. As noted earlier, he represents the first *Atáọ́ja* of Ọ̀ṣogbo, who sealed a treaty with *Ọ̀ṣun* that led to its peaceful and successful settlement. The *Atáọ́ja's* procession is only the prelude to the actual ceremonial beginning of the *Ọ̀ṣun* Festival. For it is not until the *Olójùmẹ̀rìndínlógún*, the lighting of the sixteen lamps, that the festival is declared opened officially.

Olójùmẹ̀rìndínlógún: The Lighting of the Sixteen Lamps

Another pre-festival event is the lighting of the sixteen lamps (*olójùmẹ̀rìndínlógún*), which occurs four days after the *Atáọ́ja* announces the commencement of the festival.[9] The palace courtyard is the setting for this ceremony. This event corresponds, symbolically, with the sixteen-cowrie divination that *Ọ̀ṣun* received from her husband *Ọ̀rúnmìlà*. In addition, the sixteen lamps represent the sixteen major *òrìṣà* who organized the world, the sixteen major *odù Ifá*, and the sixteen palm nuts used in *Ifá* divination.[10] When I attended the ceremony, *olójùmẹ̀rìndínlógún* began around 7 p.m. and lasted until daybreak, when the lamps are extinguished. Olójùmẹ́rdĩnlógún itself is a brass column that holds sixteen tray-like receptacles. Cotton and palm-oil are placed in each of the receptacles and kept ablaze throughout the night-long ceremony (see p. 124). The metal candleholder stands toward the center of the courtyard close to the palace. Huge cans of palm oil and baskets of local cotton are alternately placed in each tier and set ablaze, a process which continues until morning when the lamps are extinguished.

The illustration on page 113 outlines the staging of this ceremony. There are three main entrances to the central area of the courtyard. The first entrance is for the Ọ̀ṣun priestesses and other initiates of Ọ̀ṣun, the Atáója and his entourage use the second entrance, and the third entrance is used by followers and initiates of other òrìṣà as well as other musicians. The àwọn ìlù àyàn (Ifá drummers) occupy a designated area. They are responsible for invoking the spirit of Ọ̀ṣun and other òrìṣà to join in the official opening of the festival. The Ìyá Ọ̀ṣun, Àwòrò, Bálògun Ọ̀ṣun and other major Ọ̀ṣun priestesses and priests offer ritual prayers inside the house of the Ìyá Ọ̀ṣun. These prayers and other rituals that mark this particular sequence in the sixteen-day festival lies beyond the gaze of the general community and other non-initiates. The audience lines the front of local government buildings and the courtyard. The several thousand people who gather in those areas form a natural enclosure to the center stage of activities as well as a backdrop against which the major participants respond (see p. 125). The Ọ̀ṣun priestesses and other drummers with their followers enter from the points noted above but occasionally exit past the sixteen lamps only to reenter as indicated by arrow 4 before returning to their respective points of origin (see illustration, p. 113).

Three major events mark the evening ceremony, (1) the lighting of the sixteen lamps itself, (2) the dances of the Atáója, his wives and attendants, and (3) the music, song, and dance of the Ìyá Ọ̀ṣun and her attendants. Both the Atáója and the Ìyá Ọ̀ṣun enter the courtyard from the front of the palace, dance around the

Òṣun lights and continue back into the palace. Although the crowd dwindles after the first appearance of the *Atáója* and the *Ìyá Òṣun*, many people attempt to remain through the night. The *olójùmẹ̀rìndínlógún* draws the community closer to the ritual aspects of the event by publically calling *Òṣun* to the festival. During this festive occasion, the *Atáója* and the *Ìyá Òṣun* lead the joyous crowd in celebrating her invocation. At three intervals during *olójùmẹ̀rìndínlógún* they enter the courtyard, led by their respective musicians, dance around the lamps and return to their dwellings. Since the house of the *Ìyá Òṣun* is adjacent to the palace, these entrances and exits are readily coordinated. I am told that during their absence from the crowd, the *Ìyá Òṣun*, *Atáója*, and *Òṣun* devotees continue to offer prayers and songs to the goddess. Meanwhile, in the courtyard the *Ifá* drummers continually invoke the spirit of *Òṣun*, *Ifá*, and the other *òrìṣà* to join the festival and commune with humanity.

While the *babaláwo* play the *ìlù àyàn*, the *Ifá* drum ensemble, the worshippers and praise-singers of other *òrìṣà* play music and dance throughout the courtyard (see p. 125). These musicians and singers also invoke the spirit of their respective *òrìṣà* and give praise to *Òṣun*. The drumming is especially significant. As Wole Ṣoyìnká points out, "Music is the intensive language of transition and its communicant means, the catalyst and solvent of its (transition) regenerative hoard."[11] In this setting, *Òṣun* and her companion *òrìṣà* are beckoned to bridge the abyss between themselves and humanity. They are asked to penetrate the "gulf of transition" to reunite with the human community.[12] Through both ritual and dramatic enactment, humanity also attempts to transcend its mundane limitations to reunite with its spiritual ancestors by meeting them half way, so to speak. The drumming, chanting, and prayers create the ambiance and the mechanism for transition as well as the meeting place for communal worship and spiritual restitution.

The myth and history of *Òṣogbo* are dramatically reenacted throughout the lighting of the sixteen lamps. Hunters prepare a path

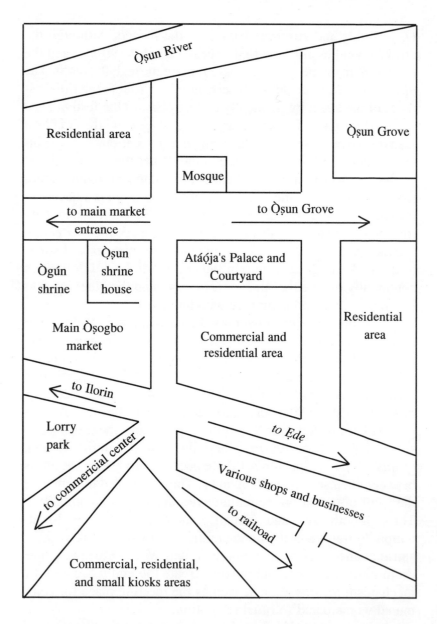

Staging the *Òṣun* Festival in Central Òṣogbo Township

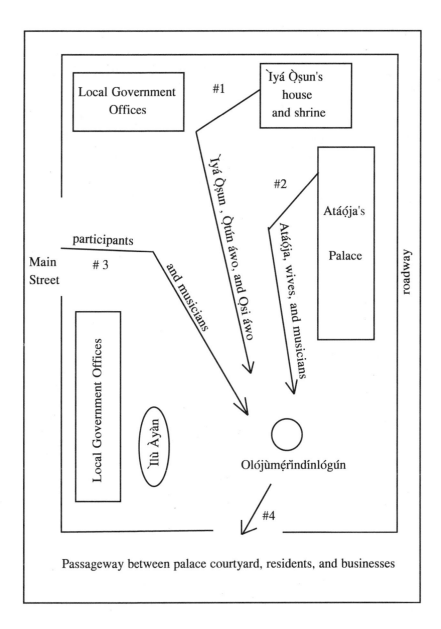

Staging the *Olójùmẹ̀rìndínlógún*

for the *Atáója* and *Ìyá Ọ̀ṣun* from their homes to the courtyard.
These men are reminders of the hunter and co-founder of
Òṣogbo, Olútímíhìn. The hunters fire their rifles into the air announcing their entrance while musicians lead the Atáója, then Ìyá
Ọ̀ṣun, dancing toward the sixteen lamps. This play action reflects
Olútímíhìn's leading of Láróòyè, the first *Atáója*, to the River
Ọ̀ṣun. Like the people of Ìpọ̀lẹ̀, who rejoiced at the founding of
this river, the contemporary *Òṣogbo* townspeople rejoice with
drumming, song, dance, and cheers as the *Atáója* approaches the
olójùmẹ̀rìndínlógún. As ritual mother of the *Atáója* and caretaker
of the goddess,[12] *Ìyá Ọ̀ṣun* reinforces the bond between the sacred and the profane,[13] recalling the pact between the settlers and
the goddess. Together, the olójùmẹ̀rdínlógùn, the Atáója, and the
Ìyá Ọ̀ṣun symbolize the cultural, political, historical, and religious unity of the Yorùbá people of Òṣogbo. Finally, this event
reaffirms *Ọ̀ṣun*'s role in Yorùbá mythology by reenacting her
mythical history as found in both the *Ifá* divination corpus and
her own oral literature.

A Cast of Thousands: The *Ọ̀ṣun* Grove as the Setting for Festival Drama

Eight days after the lighting of the sixteen lamps, the Arugbá
carries the sacrifice from the palace to the Ọ̀ṣun River. This ritual
renews the covenant between the divinity *Ọ̀ṣun*, her religious and
political custodians, and Òṣogbo Township. The *Atáója*,
Atẹ́wógbéja, feeds the contents of the sacrifice to the *òrìṣà* from
the banks of the river to thank her for the blessings of the passing year and to secure another year of her blessings and protection.

The *Ọ̀ṣun* Grove proper is located about a mile from the
palace. Its entrance is on the road that leads from the market established by Olútímíhìn past the palace. Nestled in a deciduous
forest, it is filled with various plant and animal life. Hunting,
fishing, and the felling of trees are forbidden in the sacred grove

itself, commensurate with such restrictions as found in Ọ̀ṣun's oral literature. To this extent, the conservation of the grove is a reminder of the drought that forced the ancestors of Òṣogbo to relocate near the river centuries ago. The power, beauty, and potential of the Ọ̀ṣun River is most evident during the rainy season when the river flows majestically through the grove and the town. Images and statues of *Ọ̀ṣun* and other *òrìṣà* rest at the foot of indigo plants and iroko trees, or hide among the tall lemon grass and other bushes. The *Ọ̀ṣun* Grove is beautiful, serene, and lively. No doubt then, as both oral and written sources concur, the density of the forest and the flow of the river provided ample sustenance as well as a natural barrier against the warring Fulani horsemen.[14]

Obviously, too, the *Ọ̀ṣun* Grove as well as the festival itself offer various meanings for individual worshippers while both remain veritable repositories of Yorùbá cultural and political history. For some women, the blessings of *Ọ̀ṣun* mean a secure place in the marital home with the coming of children. For some women, *Ọ̀ṣun* worship is tied to the legacy of the Sixteen-Cowrie Divination, and the ability to practice an art form that would otherwise be exclusively male. Still other women share the beauty of their voices through *Ọ̀ṣun* chanting and their expressiveness in the creation of new praise-poems. Yet for all women, *Ọ̀ṣun* is the strong mother, sensual, and intelligent, a graceful, feminine leader who, her *oríkì* says, tucked her vagina inside to go and fight.[15] For men and women alike, *Ọ̀ṣun Òṣogbo* symbolizes protection against mortal enemies and the mysterious powers of the *àjẹ́*. These meanings are enhanced by the various songs, dances, music, and paraphernalia of *ẹgbẹ́* or members and groups of actresses and actors who enter the grove dramatically and present themselves before the *Atáója, Ọ̀ṣun's* co-ruler of Òṣogbo.

Ọ̀ṣun's **Representatives**

The following diagram indicates the parallel relationship and structure of the principal caretakers of Òṣogbo and Ọ̀ṣun worship:

Ọ̀ṣun		Atáója
Ìyá Ọ̀ṣun		Àwòrò
Ìyálàṣẹ		Balógun Ọ̀ṣun

Arugbá

As the oríkì in chapter one reminds us, Atáója co-rules with Ọ̀sun.[16] Ọmọ́ṣádé Awolálu also notes that each representative indicated here has a specific function.[17] The Ìyá Ọ̀ṣun and Àwòrò are the administrators of all Ọ̀ṣun worshippers. The Ìyá Ọ̀ṣun is the primary caretaker of the goddess Ọ̀ṣun and the spiritual mother of the Atáója. She is chosen according to seniority, knowledge of Ọ̀ṣun, and the quality of her Ọ̀ṣun worship. Her selection is confirmed through consultation with the sixteen-cowrie divination. Each town that worships Ọ̀ṣun has an Ìyá Ọ̀ṣun who is ultimately responsible to the Ìyá Ọ̀ṣun Òṣogbo.

The Àwòrò is similarly chosen. His major responsibility is to help physically carry the sacrifice to Ọ̀ṣun. The Bálógùn Ọ̀ṣun is a war leader, bodyguard, and leader of the male devotees. She makes the preparations for the festival and is the caretaker of the shrine. The Ìyáláṣẹ is responsible for the food for Ọ̀ṣun and her devotees. She is the first to present food to the Atáója on the first day when the festival is announced. The Arugbá is chosen from the presiding royal family. While an Arugbá, she remains a virgin. She is allowed to marry but she cannot carry the sacrifice afterwards. Age is not a factor, and the sixteen-cowries divination is also consulted to confirm her selection.

Each function parallels or mirrors a particular aspect of Yorùbá political history, religious philosophy, and cultural beliefs. Consequently, the actions and interactions of these functionaries dramatize that history and those beliefs while engaging the ethnocultural and spiritual consciousness of the community. Those performers, artisans, and dignitaries who participate in the festivities enhance the theme of festival drama by their presence and the meaning of their actions. The secondary performers stimulate the senses and the emotions with music, dancing, singing, and chanting. It is then the role of the major performers noted above to sweep the audience into the ritual climax, which culminates in the offering of the sacrifice at the Ọ̀ṣun River. A raised, clasped right arm motion signals that Ọ̀ṣun accepts the sacrifice.

Music: Communication Between Deity and Humanity

In *Myth, Literature, and the African World*, Ṣoyĩnká states that it is "unmusical" to separate Yorùbá musical form from myth and poetry. The nature of Yorùbá music is intensively the nature of its language and poetry — highly charged, symbolic, mythoembryonic.[18] Indeed, it is difficult, if not impossible, to speak of festival drama without speaking of music also. Music is not solely accompaniment but it is also language. With respect to festival drama, music contributes to dialogue and monologue that helps to advance the ritual and festival drama toward a climax. Each interval of the festival music, then, plays a crucial role. It is praise-poetry, evocative drumming, and dance music. More importantly, music is the medium of communication between the deities and humanity. Trumpeters announce the approach of the *Atáója* during his appearances at the center of town, during the *olójùmẹ́rìndìnlógún*, and in the grove. The drummers and horn blowers play his praises or *oríkì*, and advise the crowds to make way for the royal party. The *sèkèrè* players surround the *Ìyá Ọ̀ṣun* on her several appearances. The *Àwòrò* plays the dùndùn drums while the Ọ̀ṣun chanters accompany themselves, their chants, and praise songs with bells, gongs, and other brass instruments. The *Ifá* drummers invoke the spirit of Ọ̀ṣun and the other òrìṣà playing the *ilú àyàn*, while the drummers of other divinities perform similarly on behalf of their own patron *òrìṣà*.

The drumming, singing, and dancing belong to all those present. People who know the sacred non-ritual songs of the festival and *òrìṣà* join freely in singing and dancing along with a favorite musician. In fact, many follow behind a particular drum ensemble or dance troupe, participating in the *oríkì* chants or entertainment as they do so. Such actions enhance the festivity, intensify the emotions, and dramatize the ritual communion of Òṣogbo township and its patron goddess.

The *Ọ̀ṣun* Festival Proper

Early in the morning of the festival day, *Atáója, Ìyá Ọ̀ṣun, Àwòrò, Arugbá,* and other priestesses and priests gather inside the shrine on the palace grounds to offer prayers to *Ọ̀ṣun*. This public prayer meeting mirrors the secluded ritual prayers that are offered on the evening of the *olójùmẹ́rìndínlógún*.

For people who arrive early, the serenity of the grove is engaging. There are several entrances to the central arena where the activities occur; however, the main entrance rests inside the grove at the top of an incline. Walking down the pathway, one notices a sanctuary on the right side. On the left stands a statue of *Ògún*, the *òrìṣà* of war and iron. The *Atáója*'s throne, a table, and several other seats are arranged under a canopy that faces the main entrance. The area in front of the *Atáója* serves as the center stage for the groups of men, women, and children who come to receive the blessings of *Ọ̀ṣun*, and for the many troupes who come to help celebrate the occasion (see p. 126).

Unlike previous days, the many statues of *Ọ̀ṣun* in the grove are draped with palm fronds. The worshippers of other *òrìṣà* leave food for their divinities, while others ask for special blessings during this ritual occasion. During the festival I attended the statue of *Ògún* was tied with the shirt of an accident victim to invoke the *òrìṣà* to help the person recover. As celebrants filled the grove, many gathered near the statue that symbolized their specific deity; others just sought a place from which to view the activities. Musicians representing several different *òrìṣà* set the tone of the festival. Entering the grove from the main gate, they descend onto the pathway toward the canopy where the *Atáója* and his entourage later sit. From there, they move throughout the grove followed by co-worshippers, visitors, and children. *Ṣàngó, Ògún, Ọbàtálá* drummers, chanters, and worshippers enter at various times, move around the grove, stop near the sculptures of their respective *òrìṣà*, and invoke them to come join in the festivities. Since festivals are communal affairs the musicians, with their numerous followers, pay their respects to the statues and symbols of *Òṣun* as well as to the other divinities. In addition, local hunters guilds, swordbearers, occupational and age groups again pay homage to the position of the *Atáója* and the patronage of the goddess *Òṣun*.[19]

Various dance troupes also are represented. The female *Egúngún* dancers put on a spectacle for the audience. Repeating the quick vibrating motions of the *Egúngún* masquerade, the performers are judged for their agility and stamina. The performers are quite titillating as the crowd watches the men on stilts move rhythmically from the entrance of the grove down the sloping pathway into its center. There, they dance and perform acrobatic movements that awe the crowd. Other female dancers from various societies as well as from the *Atáója's* house all enter, dance, and sing accompanied by various drum ensembles. The children's group, *ọmọde Òṣun*, is the most impressive. They are believed to be the children sent by *Òṣun* to their mothers who offered sacrifice to the goddess. When they enter the grove, they raise their voices loudly as they stop to perform in the middle. Wearing *ẹgbẹ* attire, or same patterned cloth, these children are a symbol of their shared blessings and are visible reminders of *Òṣun's* powerful role as a giver of children (see p. 128).

Groups and troupes set the stage for the entrance of the

most important event, the offering of the sacrifice. The palace
trumpeters clear the path for the Atáójá. The royal drummers
play the oríkì of the reigning Atáójá who follows graciously behind them. He enters the grove amid the shouts and praises of a
joyous and emotionally charged audience. Once again, flanked
by his wives, attendants, musicians, and others, the Atáójá
dressed in full regalia, the Most Royal Beaded Crown, and Ọ̀pá
Ọba clearly demonstrates his regal authority as the spiritual, political, and cultural representative of goddess Ọ̀ṣun and
Òṣogbo.[20] He is ceremoniously led down the path from the entrance of the grove to his designated place of honor where he
remains until the time arrives for him to enter the innermost sanctuary of the shrine. Once inside, the Atáójá, along with the Ọ̀ṣun
priestesses and the Arugbá, pray and conduct other religious
rites.

    The Ìyá Ọ̀ṣun, her priestesses, and other attendants enter
the grove and move directly to the river where the path is cleared
for the Arugbá. After they enter the grove, the Arugbá, Ìyá Ọ̀ṣun,
Àwòrò, Bálógùn Ọ̀ṣun and other religious functionaries move
along a specific ritual path through the grove, and eventually
enter the sanctuary. Many babaláwo sit along the sanctuary wall
guarding the sanctity of the ritual occurring inside. Those who
remain outside of these sacred rituals continue in their festive
mood. While the Arugbá, Ìyá Ọ̀ṣun, Bálógùn Ọ̀ṣun, and Àwòrò
remain inside the Ọ̀ṣun sanctuary, other Ọ̀ṣun priestesses, initiates, and worshippers moved toward the center of the grove to
chant, sing, and dance before the Atáójá. These chanters and
singers dressed in white tie their wrappers and wear their hair in
styles that identify them as Ọ̀ṣun devotees. They perform Ọ̀ṣun
Festival songs to the accompaniment of a women's drum-and-
ṣẹ̀kẹ̀rẹ̀ ensemble. As the ritual occurs in seclusion and the festival drama continues in the grove, the crowd becomes more
subdued and anticipatory. Before he joins the Ìyá Ọ̀ṣun and
others in the sanctuary, the Atáójá addresses the people, saluting
them for their participation in the festival and praying for another

year of blessings from *Ọ̀ṣun*. During his 1982 address, he stressed that the *Ọ̀ṣun* festival maintained social, political, economic, and cultural unity for Òṣogbo. He reminded the township of its obligation to register to vote in an upcoming election. The *Atáója* acknowledged the many visitors, including the incumbent governor and deputy governor of the former Ọ̀yọ́ State (now Ọ̀ṣun State), who participated in the *Ọ̀ṣun* Festival. Following his address, shouts of "*Kábíyèsí*" emerged from the crowd. He was then shielded from view by his courtesans, so that he could prepare to enter the *Ọ̀ṣun* sanctuary to fulfill his ritual obligations as cultural-historical custodian of Òṣogbo township.[21]

After completing the rituals inside the sanctuary, the *Arugbá*, along with *Ìyá Ọ̀ṣun* and the *Àwòrò*, carry the sacrifice to a special location on the banks of the Ọ̀ṣun River. There, they invoke the spirit of the *òrìṣà Ọ̀ṣun*, and the *Ìyá Ọ̀ṣun*, *Atáója*, and *Àwòrò* feed the goddess of the river. The acceptance of the offering confirms that the waters of the river are blessed, and people begin to bathe their faces in it, or taste its cool sweetness. Others fill assorted containers with the sacred waters to use it throughout the year for ritual and medicinal purposes. Women, particularly those who desire conception, rejoice in the powerful waters of the goddess *Ọ̀ṣun* to bless them. In the same spiritual recognition of the ritual empowerment of the River Ọ̀ṣun, previously barren women who are blessed with children return to the river and perform special rituals with the *Ìyá Ọ̀ṣun* and the Arugbá.[22] Having bridged the abyss, the ritual and its drama reaches a climax. The audience participates in the festival drama that occurs when the sacrifice is carried and offered to the spirit of the Ọ̀ṣun River. Here ritual (sacrosanct) and festival (secular) drama merge as do the spiritual and mundane cosmos.

In spite of this momentary fusion, the sacred and secular remain secure in their respective domains. Outside the grove, just beyond the walled entrance, people continually gather. Randomly mixed in the crowd along the pathway leading through the grove, the ọlọ̀ṣẹ gather in groups of twos, fours, and sixes to challenge one another with their whips. This act of bravery and endurance symbolically prevents malevolent forces from marring the occasion. The ọlọ̀ṣẹ also serve as crowd controllers who maintain passageways or create them as needed. They, too, are participants in the festival occasion[23].

Food sellers gather in an open area just outside of the entrance to the grove. There, *ákárá, dòdò*, fried fish, and *chin-chin* tempt the festive crowd with their aromas. Refreshments such as palm wine, coke, beer, assorted soft drinks, and wine coolers are also sold. People pose for photographs or stop to dance with a passing ensemble. Women and men laugh, joke, tease, and just talk with one another. They rest along the decorative walls of the grove or seek out friends and relatives. Still others find a space near the crowded riverbank to wade in the water and feel the flow of the sacred waters around their feet. Children splash and play about in the river, and the meaning of the festival is everywhere present in the bosom of the Ọ̀ṣun Grove. The sacrificial rituals are complete, the drama reaches its climax, and the festival winds down toward a calm and joyous evening of celebration at the palace.

Notes

1.   Babaláwo Ifáyẹ́mi Eléburú̃ìbọ̀n, Interviews, 1981-1982.
2.   *Ibid*. See also *"Òṣogbo"* in *Ọ̀yọ́ State Town Series* (Ibadan: Ministry of Local Government and Information, January 1977).
3.   D.L. Bádéjo, *A Goddess of Our Own*. I am presently working on an annotation of these praise songs which identifies these places along with other spiritual and rhetorical references.
4.   Robin C.C. Law, *The Ọ̀yó Empire 1600 – 1836* (Oxford: Clarendon Press, 1977).

5. Mr. Peter A. Bádéjọ, former Senior Cultural Officer, Centre for Nigerian Cultural Studies, Ahmadu Bello University, shared his expertise in festival drama and performance theater. Mr. Bádéjo is presently choreographer/consultant for Bádéjo Arts, London.

6. Bádéjọ, *A Goddess of Our Own*; *Ọ̀yọ́ State Town Series*, *op. cit.*

7. Ẹlẹ́bùrùíbọ̀n. Interviews, 1981-1982. Also *Ìyálọṣa Ọ̀ṣun (Ọ̀ṣun* Priestesses).

8. Ọmọṣádé Awọlálu, *Yorùbá Beliefs and Sacrificial Rites* (London: Longmans Group, Ltd., 1979).

9. D.L. Bádéjo, Field Notes, 1981 -1983.

10. Wande Abímbọla, *Ifá Divination Poetry* (New York: Nok Publishers, 1977). Also, D.L. Bádéjọ, Field Notes.

11. Wọle Ṣoyïnká, *Myth, Literature, and the African World*, (Cambridge: Cambridge University Press, 1976):36.

12. Reverend Samuel Johnson, *The History of the Yorubas: From the Earliest Times to the Beginning of the British Protectorate:* 40-78.

13. Mircea Eliade, *The Sacred and the Profane: The Nature of Religion*. Translated from the French by William R. Trash (New York: Harcourt, Brace, and World, 1959).

14. Law, R.C.C., *op. cit.*

15. Bádéjo, *op. cit.*

16. *Ibid.*

17. Ọmọṣáde Awolálu, *op. cit.*

18. Ṣoyïnká. *Myth, Literature, and the African World*, p. 147.

19. Bádéjọ, Field Notes.

20. *Ibid.*

21. *Ibid.*

22. *Ibid.*

23. Peter A. Bádéjọ, *op. cit.*

Olójùmẹ́r̀ìndínlógún   Photo by author

Photo by author

Atáója celebrating *Olójùmẹ́r̀ìndínlógún*

Photo by author

Ilú Àyàn

Photo by author

Crowd in Palace Courtyard

Photo by author

Ìyá Ọ̀ṣun dancing and greeting *Atáója* in Ọ̀ṣun Grove

Photo by author

Atáója, his wives, beaded crown, and *ọ̀pá ọba*

Atáója's Stage

Praise Singer

Ọmọde Ọ̀ṣun   Photo by author

Women dressed in *aṣo ẹgbẹ*

Photo by author

Female *Egúngún* Dancers

Photo by author

Stilt Dancers

Crowd cheering Ọ̀ṣun's acceptance of the
communal offering

Gathering to collect the sacred waters of the Ọ̀ṣun River

Chapter Five

THE DRAMATIZATION OF THE *ÒṢUN* FESTIVAL

Viewing the *Òṣun* Festival as dramatic art discloses (1) a distinction between sacred ritual and ritual drama, (2) a distinction in form and action between ritual and secular drama, and (3) the symbiotic relationship between them. By sacred ritual, I refer to those religious rites that occur to the exclusion of non-initiates. Sacred ritual is the vortex of any religious practice wherein priestesses and priests conduct those rites which reaffirm the sacred bonds, while reopening the pathway, between supernatural and human beings. Ritual drama usually follows such sacred rituals. Here, the ordained ministers reenact and participate in sacrosanct messages, cosmic narratives and poems, and religious ideals relevant to a specific sacred rite or divinity. By extension, secular drama distills from sacred drama those themes, characters, symbolisms, and performance modes that evolve from a specific ethnocultural worldview.

In a manner that parallels their religious counterparts, secular artists are usually the non-initiated mediators between culturally defined cosmic worldview and their secular audiences. As such, these artists challenge a spectrum of myths, meanings, and perceptions that are otherwise accepted on faith. The artists then can both reaffirm and/or challenge the belief system. Indeed within the context of Yorùbá religious and social order, this artistic dialectic reflects the religious dialectic imaged by Ọ̀rúnmìlà and Èṣù on the ọpọ́n Ifá (Ifá divination board). Consequently, action, setting, and audience determine the distinctions among and the context for sacred ritual, ritual drama, and secular drama. As evinced by the Ọ̀ṣun Festival, sacred ritual is the quintessence of ritual action. It occurs in seclusion and is witnessed only by designated religious initiates and specific cultural representatives. Sacred or ritual drama, on the other hand, *alludes to* the mythopoetic ritual through dramatic reenactment in an open arena. Its protagonists or major *dramatis personae* are initiates who are responsible for the symbolic presentation or the completion of a sacred ritual cycle for the benefit of the communal audience. Ritual drama appeals to the communal ethos through a series of culture-bound symbols and myths relevant to the particular theme of the festival itself. Secular drama presents the cultural values, aspirations, and historical consciousness that binds the community as a corporeal entity, and which preserves, affirms, and alludes to its sacred cosmic rituals. Its function is also to entertain an audience whose own objective is to enjoy the benefits of this event as a festival occasion. In short, secular drama intends to stimulate its audience by dramatizing aspects of the human condition or its arts.

In his essay, "Roots of African Drama and Theatre", pioneer Ghanaian scholar and artist J. C. deGraft writes,

"drama is a condensation from everyday life...which must utilize the pulsating raw material of actual human bodies, attributes, and behaviour as the sine qua non of its very medium and expression."[1]

He notes that humanity continually seeks solace and sanity from a world that seems threatening and insane, thus suggesting that dramatic art becomes the medium through which humanity addresses its aspirations and its fears. Spiritual, natural, and animal forces certainly generate powerful guideposts in humanity's attempt to secure itself, but these forces also unleash a plethora of ills and woes against which humanity must continually guard itself. *Òrìṣà, àjẹ́, and àjògùn* are woven into the sinews of human existence creating the dramatic tension found in rituals, dramas, and festivals. Human will is as awesome as the will of the Creator. Humanity is locked in eternal struggle with cosmic laws and the vagaries of nature. Whosoever or whatsoever mediates that struggle is itself a dynamic force that moves human beings from crossroads to smooth roads to crossroads, reaffirming the purview of *Èṣù* and *Ọrúnmìlà*. Humanity's first appeal is to itself, a search for resolution within its own context, an appeal to priestesses, prophets, and politicians. Approaching resolution, humanity acknowledges its own vulnerability and attempts to bridge the "gulf of transition" between itself *(ènìyàn)* and divinity *(òrìṣà)*. The *Ọ̀ṣun* Festival offers one context for exploring the complexity of the sacred and the secular that, in cosmological and dramatic terms, are interwoven thematically, symbolically, and often structurally. In this chapter, I explore how the cosmic, universal, and specifically mundane are reenacted during festival drama, as well as how they are viewed and enacted separately. This chapter explores the convergence of sacred and secular performance modes as they express a dramatic art form. DeGraft's recognition of these separate modes is useful here. With sacred ritual, he notes that the principal actress or actor is in a state of possession where she or he works out her or his own salvation, while the audience of initiates is drawn through empathy with him into communication with the daemon spirit, till they ultimately reach that state of ecstatic release which constitutes the objective of the ritual.[2]

With respect to the secular mode, DeGraft emphasizes the act of impersonation as its key factor. He says that,

the form of the act of impersonation is determined by a conscious selection and shaping of creative elements,

then drama begins to take on the lineaments of
consciously ordered art, then we are set on the long road
towards secular drama and theatre of pure entertainment.[3]

As this form of theater continues to evolve, it focuses more on
its own intrinsic artistic and aesthetic development.

It occurs then that between the sacred ritual of possession
and the secular act of impersonation lies ritual drama that forms
the symbiosis of both. This resulting symbiosis alludes to the
"ritual," that is, the avowed behavior of divinity and humanity.
During the *Ọ̀sun* Festival, the *Arugbá* emerges from the sacred
ritual of possession and remains possessed as she carries the offering to the river. She is surrounded by those who are "conscious" of her sacred ritual state, and who acquiesce to it. Her
emergence from sacred ritual into the general audience marks the
onset of ritual drama as opposed to sacred ritual. She carries the
offering before non-initiated witnesses in order to complete the
sacred ritual cycle began in seclusion. Simultaneously, her actions signal a dramatic reenactment of the first covenant made
between *Ọ̀sun* and the Òṣogbo townspeople, symbolizing the
actual settling of the town. Thus, the people celebrate the founding of Òṣogbo, which resulted in the survival of their progeni-
tors. That celebration in turn gives rise to secular drama that
comes full circle and mirrors the aspirations and fears of Òṣogbo
townspeople. As noted previously, these images of humanity and
divinity strengthen their "ritual" behavior. Moreover, where the
notion of pure entertainment becomes an element in secular
drama, DeGraft tells us that, with respect to ritual drama,

> the participants seek such desired effects as social soli-
> darity, or through which they attempt to reaffirm, keep
> alive, or commemorate such facts, beliefs, relationships,
> and attitudes as the community considers vital to its
> sanity and continued healthy existence.[4]

Consequently, both sacred and secular drama have concomitant objectives that aim at providing the human community with alternate forms of release from its fears, and a vehicle for its aspiration of control over its destiny. Delineation between the two forms reflects the necessity of addressing the "dual nature" of the world in which humanity exists.[5] The *Ọ̀ṣun* Festival and its oral literature provide the context, content, meaning, and symbolism that mirror the complexities of sacred and secular dramatic art.

Ritual Drama

Let me say here that I cannot describe the internal dynamics of the *Ọ̀ṣun* sacred ritual. First, as noted earlier, one must be initiated to be privy to those actions; second, if one is privy by rites of initiation, then one is equally constrained by that responsibility. Thus, what follows is a discussion of the ritual drama of the *Ọ̀ṣun* Festival with respect to its staging, its participants, and its symbolic meaning. These elements of the ritual are accessible through interviews with the major *dramatis personae* of *Ọ̀ṣun* worship, extrapolation from my participation in the secular festival drama, and written sources.

As noted in Chapter Four, the *Ọ̀ṣun* Festival occurs over several days in different settings. The center of Òṣogbo township, the palace courtyard of the *Atáọ́ja*, and the *Ọ̀ṣun* Grove itself provide three of those venues. In each case, the public or secular action of the principal worshippers and culture-bearers, such as the *Atáọ́ja*, follows an exclusive ritual action. From interviews and observation, these secluded acts constitute the sacred ritual aspects of the festival. According to informants, *Ìyá Ọ̀ṣun*, *Àwòrò*, and *Atáọ́ja* consistently participate in these sacred rituals of the annual festival. I am emphasizing the "festival" aspect of the ritual because I do not know how the three major officiates participate in other rituals that occur outside of that context. However, as an observer and participant in the secular and ritual drama, I felt and witnessed the effects of the exclusive sacred ritual actions upon those in the audience.

According to several informants, the Ọ̀ṣun festival begins
by consulting with the Ọ̀ṣun divination instruments
(mẹ́rìndínlógún) in conjunction with the Ifá divination oracle.
Divination takes place in the palace among the religious and cultural hierarchy of Ọ̀ṣun worship and Òṣogbo township. During
this ritual, the date of the Ọ̀ṣun Festival and the sacrificial requirements are confirmed.[6] Ọ̀ṣun's earthly representatives offer
prayers and thanksgiving to the òrìṣà. The purpose of this ritual
is to gather the requisite sacred information for the festival. As
with all religious practice, this exclusive ritual action sanctions
the inclusive communal action. Relaying the contents of this sacred communique is a secular extension of it, in part because of
the ceremonious form it takes during the public forum at the center of town. The essence of the sacred Ọ̀ṣun ritual discourse becomes the basis for dramatic reenactment with the township as
its audience.

On the evening of the olójùmẹ́rìndínlógún, Ìyá Ọ̀ṣun,
Àwòrò, and other priestesses and priests of Ọ̀ṣun engage in sacred ritual. They gather at the Ìyá Ọ̀ṣun's house which is next to
the Atáója's palace and, according to informants, pray to the divinity to join the festivities in her honor. In addition, they chant
her praises, and invoke her goodwill.[7] These ritual activities occur at set intervals (1) before the first lighting of the sixteen
candles and (2) between the processional from the Ìyá Ọ̀ṣun's
house and the Atáója's palace to the courtyard where they danced
around the olójùmẹ́rìndínlógún.

On the festival day itself, rituals are performed at the palace, at the Ìyá Ọ̀ṣun's house, and in the grove. Since the festival
day represents the climax of both the sacred and the secular aspects of the entire festival, most of the ritual performance focuses
on the ẹbọ, or sacrifice, and the arugbá, or sacrifice-carrier.
Ọmọṣadé Awọlálu notes that ẹ̀kọ (corn meal), àkàrà (bean-
cakes), iyán (pounded yam), ẹ̀fọ́ yanrìn (Ọ̀ṣun's favorite spinach-
like vegetable), goats and fowls are among those items which
comprise the sacrificial offering to Ọ̀ṣun during the festival.[8]

Ẹlébùrúîbọ̀n also points out that various non-initiate members of the community bring offerings to the shrine and the grove hoping to secure the assistance of Òṣun in addressing diverse problems. Infertility, interpersonal conflicts among co-wives or neighbors, or marital issues find redress in the mythology of Òṣun. As a "woman of power and fertility," women especially find recourse to the special healing qualities of this awesome divinity. In many respects, *ẹbọ* or sacrifice, is similar to a covenant that serves a reciprocal purpose. First, the offering opens the dialogue between *òrìṣà* and *ènìyàn*. Second, it confirms the respect for and belief in the efficacy of the divinity. Consequently, to guard its efficacy, the *arugbá* begins her preparations in ritual seclusion at the house of the *Ìyá Òṣun*. When she emerges, she carries with her not only the contents of the sacrifice, but also the most visible aspects of the sacred ritual. At this juncture, the audience becomes involved in the ritual drama as she carries the *irú* through the town from the palace to the *Òṣun* Grove. The *arugbá* now becomes the "challenger" of the "chthonic realm" on behalf of her community. Ṣoyínká's analysis of the staging and *raison d'etre* for Yorùbá ritual drama is illuminating. He contends,

> A chthonic realm, a storehouse for creative and destructive essences, it required a challenger, a human representative to breach it periodically on behalf of the well-being of the community. The stage, the ritual arena of confrontation, came to represent the symbolic chthonic space and presence of the challenger within..... It is the earliest physical expression of mans fearful awareness of the cosmic context of his existence. Its magic microcosm is created by the communal presence, and in this charged space the chthonic inhabitants are challenged.[8]

With the *Òṣun* Grove as the "ritual arena of confrontation," the highly "charged" audience follows the *Arugbá* along her ritual path. There, on the banks of the Ọ̀ṣun River, the *Arugbá*, *Ìyá Ọ̀ṣun*, *Àwòrò*, *Atáója*, priestesses, priests, community, and the spirit of the goddess *Ọ̀ṣun* confront the "cosmic totality" of their mutual, intertwined existence. There, the success or failure of the *Arugbá* mirrors that of the community and the divinity to communicate their anxieties and aspirations across the "abyss of transition."[10] Here distinction between sacred ritual and secular drama becomes most apparent. This is the climax of the festival where we are enveloped in ritual drama, that is, "drama as a cleansing, binding, communal, recreative force."[11] Now the "abyss of transition" is penetrated.

Secular Drama

A broad interpretation of secular drama is possible if we consider specific major events of the *Ọ̀ṣun* Festival as dramatic acts. The opening day represents act one; the *olójùmẹ̀rìndínlógún* becomes act two; and the festival day itself represents act three, where the climax and denouement are played out.[12] The relationship between the sacred and the secular is confirmed by the divinities who, as Ṣoyìnká and others have demonstrated, like to be entertained. The various genres of oral poetry, including *oríkì* (praise poetry), *ìjàlà* (poetic entertainment of Ògún), *orin Ọ̀ṣun* (songs of *Ọ̀ṣun*), and *Ṣàngó-pípè* (praise poetry of *Ṣàngó*), demonstrate this. Yorùbá secular drama includes certain forms of drumming that function as dialogue as well as music. This is particularly evident where communication between performers and audience occurs in the language of the drum. Finally, the form and content of secular drama becomes apparent in the staging of oral literary themes and the performers, impersonation of characters, characteristics, and movements of the deities or their earthly representatives. The intention here is strictly to entertain the audience. Indeed, the secular drama of the festival "replays" the symbols, themes, and characteristics that advance the essence of cosmic discourse found in the oral literature. Using performance modes such as music, *oríkì*, verbal dialogue, dancing, and movement, the entertainers who participate in the festival "script" their actions from *Ọ̀ṣun*'s mythology and Yorùbá cosmic beliefs. In so doing, they dramatize the philosophical meaning of the festival and delineate the sacred from the secular. Themes, symbols, actions, and language vary from one setting to another. Each act advances the plot of the festival drama toward its climax. The theme of the opening ceremony is best expressed by the women who meet the *Atáójá* at the center of the town. To demonstrate their unity, women who worship *Ọ̀ṣun* dress in the symbolic yellow patterned *aṣọ ẹgbẹ*, cloth of association, indicating group solidarity or family solidarity. These women sing to him, "*Awá kí 'lè ọba*," meaning "we greet the *Ọba*'s house (family)". The *Atáójá*'s message from the divinity *Ọ̀ṣun* obtained through the interpretation of the oracle sets the tone of the festivity and generates its subsequent action.[13] Thus, in this first act he is the protagonist, the main character, and the action revolves around him. The theme, greeting or welcoming the *Ọba*, is embellished by the gifts of food and beverage that are symbols of goodwill and welcome.

During this secular enactment, the *Atáójá*'s position within the historical and cultural context of Yorùbá culture is reaffirmed. As the descendant of Láróòyè, the first *Atáójá*, recognition and confirmation of his role in Ọ̀ṣogbo by its people symbolizes the bond between him and the township. Many *oríkì* chanters come to sing his praises and the praises of his lineage. They remind him as well as the community of Ọ̀ṣogbo history. In retracing his lineage, both he and his community reflect upon the challenges and adversity faced by their predecessors.

The opening scene in this first act is dramatic and highly charged. Royal trumpeters announce the *Atáójá*'s approach, courtesans shade him with an elaborately designed umbrella, and the court musicians sing his *oríkì* vocally and instrumentally. Women, men, and children create the contours of this pageant along the side streets. Shouts and cheers fill the air as the town-

ship gathers together around its Ọba or ruler. His beautifully em-
broidered *àgbàdà*, a full men's outer garment, as well as the
beads and crown he wears carry both historical and mythical
meanings. And although he symbolizes their continuity as a
people, the *Ọ̀pá Ọba,* the scepter of the *Ọba,* confirms his place
of authority in Yorùbá culture and history. Indeed, the narrative
of this ornate lesson in culture and history can be read in the attire and symbols that he displays in this act. Wọle Ṣoyïnká dis-
cusses the accessibility of this form of narrative to its audience
with respect to Dúró Ladipọ's play, *Ọba KoSo.* In *Myth, Literature, and the African World,* Ṣoyïnká says that,

> The initiate knows that even the paraphernalia of the
> protagonists is endowed with significant meanings, social
> and myth-referential. The outsider senses this with equal
> certainty and, while he necessarily loses something of the
> specificity, he is enabled to create with ease a parallel
> scale of references since he views it all in the framework
> of motion and stylized conflict, all obeying a finely
> regulated rhythm of relationships.[14]

Each observer recognizes that he or she is a "participant
within an integrated matrix of cultural force" to which these symbols worn by the *Atáója* refer. In this setting, the "cultural force"
pushes the historical leadership forward culminating in the actual establishment of the township. At the matrix of its myth and
history, Ọ̀ṣogbo celebrates its survival of natural and human di-
sasters. The mythology becomes the *tour de force* for the celebration of human triumph over adversity.

As secular reenactment, the townspeople proceed, as did
their ancestors, to follow the *Atáója* to the center of town. Like
the earlier migrants, Ọ̀ṣogbo inhabitants celebrate the divine wisdom of their leader and their own survival. According to custom,
appreciation is shown through gifts of food, drink, entertainment,
and camaraderie. Consequently, they thank the *Ọba* for his guid-

ance of the township and recognize his spiritual representation.[15]
Guilds, age groups, and musicians offer the entertainment
throughout the streets of Ọ̀ṣogbo. The community watches and
participates as spectators who are then drawn by anticipation into
the events. The restaurants and bars along the processional pathway fill with customers who wish to enjoy the entertainment that
accompanies it. Once he is seated, the *Atáọ́ja* becomes the focus
of the ensuing activities. He is center stage, and the secular drama
is viewed from his vantage point. The collective and individual
characters who interact with him enhance his role by expanding
its dimension. In this setting, the *Atáọ́ja* is the mythical representative of *Ọ̀ṣun*, cultural-historical leader, descendant of a founding lineage, a husband whose wives accompany him, an *Ọba*, and
through his *oríkì* as a man bearing the marks of his own heritage
and accomplishments. In his multifaceted roles, he mirrors
Ọ̀ṣun's complexity, and further suggests the extensive human
potentiality. Having defined the protagonist and presented the
theme, the first act of the festival ends with the *Atáọ́ja*'s ceremonious return to the palace.

This is the first act of the *Ọ̀ṣun* festival. As dramatic ra-
conteur, it narrates that historical event by "acting out" the pri-
mal journey to this new settlement. To demonstrate their appreciation and acceptance of the *Atáọ́ja*'s guidance for the preced-
ing year, the township shares food and drink to ensure the ruler's
survival as well as their own. Hence, they greet him according
to Yorùbá customs and beliefs. Ritual reenactment is minimized
here, extracted, as I noted previously, from its initial divination
which lends credibility to this setting.

The *olójùmẹ̀rìndínlógún* is viewed as the second act of
this festival drama. The time is 7 p.m. until dawn, the place is
the palace courtyard, and the setting is the lighting of the sixteen
lamps. As in the first act, the most sacred ritual acts occur in seclusion. The plot of this act is the calling of *Ọ̀ṣun* and her co-di-
vinities to join with humanity in her celebration. Indeed, one cannot have a party without the presence of the celebrant! The theme

of this act is the cosmic union of humanity and divinity. Ṣoyĭnká[16] of Nigeria concurs with Mazizi Kunene of South Africa, who emphasizes that,

> The gods, who are agents of the Supreme Creator, have a symbiotic relationship with man. While man needs them to reenforce his efforts in the exploration of his world, the gods also need him for their harmonious existence. Since creation is their only responsibility, they must be made to feel that they have fulfilled their primary tasks. The endorsement for their actions by man becomes part of their spiritual elevation. Hence, the need for praise and endorsement from man. It is man alone as the master of the earth who can effectively circumscribe and define the scope of the actions of the supernatural forces.[17]

Subsequently, during the *olójùmẹ̀rĭndiñlógún*, humanity takes the initiative to acknowledge this interdependence by inviting the divinities to "play."

Unlike the subtle inscriptions of the opening, the narrative of the second act is overtly stated. The cosmic balance between humanity and divinity is the theme of this act. Unlike the visible restraint in act one and act three, the people sing and dance with or behind whomever suits their fancy. They intermingle, laugh, and talk. They sing with vigor and enthusiasm, they smile and pull others along. The *Atáója* appears only three times during the long night. Although the whole event occurs in the palace courtyard, neither he nor the *Ìyá Ọ̀ṣun* nor the other religious dignitaries are the focal point here. There are no signs of an *arugbá*, and obviously no dominant presence of religious and historical authority. Only the people in the warmth of the evening inviting their *òrìṣà* to join them. Only the visible signs of the cosmic relationship between divinity and humanity are re-enacted here, humanity enjoying its own existence. Despite the presence of the *Ifá, Ṣàngó,* and *Ògún* drummers, the dramatic reenactment remains secular in that their actions reflect the will of the people to invoke the *òrìṣà* as co-participants in the festival. There is no attempt on the part of the community to reenact any ritual. In fact, the community only attempts to acknowledge that the deities like to enjoy themselves just as human beings do.[18]

As noted in Chapter Four, the lighting of the sixteen lamps (*olójùmẹ̀rindinlógún*) is highly charged and dramatized. Like the stage directions to a contemporary Yorùbá play, participants enter the courtyard from the main gate facing the palace proper. To the left of the palace is the *Iyá Ọ̀sun*'s house, and to the right of the palace flaming brightly against the midnight sky is the *olójùmẹ̀rindínlógún*. The sixteen lamps mark the center stage, and all action swirls around it until morning when the lamps are extinguished. The performers move through the courtyard toward the *olójùmẹ̀rindínlógún*, then exit as indicated on page 113. Throughout the night, a community of performers and participants define entrances and exits. These sequenced entrances and exits of the *Atáója* and *Ìyá Ọ̀sun* also demonstrate how well this event is orchestrated.[19]

Entertainment and festivity underscore the mood and actions of the township and other participants. Entering from the right of the *olójùmẹ̀rindínlógún*, drummers, dancers, and singers alike stop in front of its night fires to offer their performances to the collective reunion between divinity and humanity. In this performance mode, the human community calls the *òrìṣà* along with *Ọ̀sun* to dance, celebrate, and traverse the "abyss of transition" into a unified cosmic domain. Voices join in songs punctuated by various drum ensembles. Folks acknowledge friends and talk and dance throughout the night. Although the ambience of spiritual elevation and celebration remain well into the festival day, by dawn the crowd dwindles.

The *Ọ̀sun* Grove provides the setting for the third act, where the climax and denouement take place. The final act begins at 10 o'clock in the morning, and is set in what seems to be

a cul-de-sac bordered by the Ọ̀ṣun River. The main entrance to
the grove slopes into the center stage where the *Atáója*, his entourage, and special guests sit. As the photographs clearly show,
performance is choreographed to occur in front of him in his role
as representative of the divinity *Ọ̀ṣun*. In this role, many cultural
and religious leaders pay homage to the traditional ruler of
Ọ̀ṣogbo, the *Atẹ́wọ́gbẹja*.[20] On this day, the meaning of his complete title bears the most significance because it recalls *Ọ̀ṣun* as
the river goddess is fed by the hands of the *Atáója* who, as the
descendant of Láróòyè, honors and thanks the deity for her on-
going blessings as *Yèyé*, The Good Mother. The *Arugbá* carries
the sacrifice to the grove and the goddess *Ọ̀ṣun* accepts it from
the hands of people who worship her. As in the palace setting,
ritual prayers and other related sacred ceremonies are performed
exclusive of the general audience.[21]

There are two levels of performance which occur on the
day of the festival. One is directed toward the goddess *Ọ̀ṣun* and
the *Atáója*, and the other towards the general audience. Since
these performances occur in an open area, such distinctions may
seem inappropriate. However, as discussed, the general theme remains the bonding of humanity and divinity. Both realms are entertained each according to cultural prescription. The praise singers salute the *Atáója* and *Ọ̀ṣun* for their benevolence in favor of
the township and recall their respective deeds and histories. Most
of this action occurs in front of the throne of the *Atáója* and
Ọ̀ṣun's staff of authority, the focus of these artists.

Interestingly, the *Atáója* presides over the festival as
much a modern traditional ruler as a spiritual representative. By
modern tradition, I mean tradition that has evolved over time
within its own Yorùbá ethos. It is modern traditional because it
addresses contemporary issues from a traditional perspective.
During his lengthy presence in the grove, he changed his attire,
especially the crown that he wears. At one point, he changed his
crown just before addressing the audience. In addition to welcoming visitors and townspeople alike, he reminded them of

their historical pride in Òṣogbo, and their traditional and contemporary responsibilities. He literally changed hats, fulfilling his own dual responsibilities as cultural and political custodian of Òṣogbo township.[25]

The second level of performance occurs for the benefit of the general audience. Musicians, dancers, and acrobats attend to the need for entertainment and stimulation prior to the entrance of the *Arugbá*. Because the musicians have been mentioned so frequently in this book, I wish to focus more on the latter two groups of secular entertainers who are accompanied by the drummers. For instance, the women *Egúngún* dancers combine art and endurance with their performance, while the male stilt dancers combine endurance and acrobatics in theirs. Both are accompanied by drummers who are clearly performing as musicians rather than as verbal artists or praise-singers.

As noted in Chapter Four, the women *Egúngún* dancers intend to excite their audience. They enter the stage area to the rapid rhythm of the *bátá* drums. Once at center stage, they stop suddenly to compete with and complement one another with rapid movements of the torso. These dance movements are as graceful as they are exciting, and the roar of the crowd displays its appreciation. *Egúngún* dancers and their drummers move throughout the grove. The former move in strident, rhythmic steps, then lunge forward before each section of the crowd, and firing each section with their rapid gyrating movements. The spectators raise their voices in approval as one of the women collects the money which confirms that approval.[23]

It is an awesome experience to watch the stilt dancers enter the grove and dance their way down the sloping pathway toward center stage. Three adult dancers and a boy send a surge of excitement through the crowd as they too dance to the music of the *bátá* drums. The acrobatic feats that they perform are amazing. This ensemble dances and spins around on one stilt while a young man parades under the raised stilted leg of the other giants. And the dancing is as graceful and rhythmic as if they were dancing without stilts. Like the women *Egúngún* dancers, they perform throughout the crowd and, like many performers, they later became part of the audience (see p. 131).[24]

The narrative of this third act evolves through a mosaic of symbols, metaphors, and interlocking vignettes that create a whole mythical-historical drama. Where the *olójùmẹ́rìndínlógún* suggests the mirror images between humanity and divinity, the festival day suggests reciprocity and interdependency between them. The festival theme narrates the bond between them, especially with respect to *Ọ̀ṣun* as patroness of Òṣogbo. The preeminence of women throughout the *Ọ̀ṣun* Festival symbolizes her empowerment of them as found in the oral literature. As giver of children, she unites humanity and divinity through the womb, the symbolic matrix of immortality.

Ọmọde Ọ̀ṣun, children of *Ọ̀ṣun*, and their mothers, embellish the dramatic narrative of *Ọ̀ṣun's* graciousness and power. Their singular *aṣọ ẹgbẹ́*, with its multicolored yellow patterns is analogous to the spiritual unity they share amongst themselves and with *Ọ̀ṣun*. Dancing, drumming, and singing recount the mythical deeds of the goddess and the genealogy of the *Atáójá*. These performances ceremoniously draw upon the repository of Yorùbá beliefs, and present aspects of *Ọ̀ṣun* drama through a spectrum of golden colors, body movements, and mythopoetic symbolism of praise-poetry in song and drum. The audience "reads" these subtle forms of cultural dialogue and thus engages in the unfolding drama of the festival.[25]

The *Ọ̀ṣun* dancers provide an example of the overt dialogue of the festival through song and dance drama. These women are dressed in white to signify that they are initiates in the worship of the goddess *Ọ̀ṣun*, and therefore, abide by those restrictions. The topics covered in the songs that I recorded in the 1982 Festival ranged from the praise for the goddess to the antagonism between the Islamic community and the *Ọ̀ṣun* worshippers of Òṣogbo. These women dancers are accompanied by a women's drum ensemble that includes one male drummer. Like the goddess *Ọ̀ṣun*, the dance movements are graceful and alluring, powerful and calm. Like the ideophone found in her praise poetry that suggests the flow of the goddess and her river, "*Òwọ́-rùrù-f'ara-l'ako! Òwọ́-rùrù-f'ara-l'àpáta,*" the women sway from side to side with gentle power of their intrinsic, divine female nature, then they sway from side to side with a brisk forward motion.[26] Compare the translation of these images cited in chapter one to the dance movements described here:

> The one who, in flowing furiously along, hits her body
> against grass,
> The one who, in flowing majestically along, hits her body
> against rocks.[27]

The power of the songs and dance drama of the *Ọ̀ṣun* performers is unmistakable. Obviously, their presence heightens the anticipation of the audience as the climax draws near and the *Arugbá* approaches.

Symbiosis as the Essence of Dramatic Art

In this setting, ritual, drama, and celebration converge and diverge, thus, intersecting at the crossroads and crossing the "*chthonic realm.*" Here, the elements of ritual drama and secular drama act and react within themselves forming the quintessence of dramatic art. Even so, their unique parts are drawn in sharp relief by the actions of the actresses and actors involved. As demonstrated, sacred ritual precedes ritual drama that can, in turn, occur within the sphere of or apart from secular drama. Indeed, sacred ritual gives credibility to both ritual and secular drama by imparting to each the cultural treasure trove of myths, symbols, and themes that each variously reflects. As Kunene points out, the philosophical intent of sacred ritual directs the requisite social discourse that keeps each society aligned with its own destiny.[28] As noted above, balance is the cosmological ob

jective of Ọ̀ṣun's sacred and secular drama, while the earthly expression of that cosmic balance is the collective immortality of
human beings.

On the festival day the theme of cosmic unity reaches its
climax. The *Arugbá* carries the sacrificial offering from the palace to the grove where its contents are presented to the river goddess. The *Arugbá* 's actions constitute a plot that reaffirms the
Yorùbá belief that sacrifice, whether ritual or personal, (1) can
ameliorate problems or, at the very least, illuminate their under-
lying causes, and (2) is necessary for a successful life. As the
main character in this act, the *Arugbá* becomes the messenger of
humanity who attempts to penetrate the "abyss of transition" to
communicate with divinity, Ọ̀ṣun. Having penetrated the abyss,
the messenger of humanity confronts Èṣù, the messenger of the
òrìṣà, who, in the cosmic order, inspects the sacrifice before
passing it on to Ọ̀ṣun. Once the *Arugbá* completes her ritual assignment, communal awe and complex communal aspirations are
released in the belief that another year of salvation is granted.
The Ọ̀ṣun River is now blessed by the òrìṣà and people gather to
collect the spiritual and healing powers contained in her sweet
cool waters.[29]

Beyond the obvious *ritual persona* of the *Arugbá*, the entertainment of humanity and divinity continues until she reaches
the river with *Ìyá Ọ̀ṣun*, *Àwòrò*, and *Atáója*. Indeed, the ritual
drama signified by the *Arugbá* is enveloped in the pageantry and
festival drama of the day. Before the *Arugbá* 's entrance into the
grove, the audience acknowledges that they are enjoying a show
presented by professional and semiprofessional artists. For their
part, professional artists, such as *Babaláwo* Yẹ́mi Ẹlẹ́bùrúîbọ̀n,
know that their audience will critique their performances according to artistic merit and the traditional aesthetic principles that
define their diverse art forms.[30] How then do we assess the dramatic art of such festivals? Let us first speak in terms of cultural
preference. Mazizi Kunene confirms what oral literary practitioners and scholars know, that Africans relish a literature that is

"public, oral, and dramatized."[31] That is, they prefer a communal narrative that explores and exploits the nuances of their given
ethnolinguistic heritage and that presents a story line and images
in concert with the myths, histories, and mores maintained by
their particular cosmic philosophy. The festival event provides
one occasion for such dramatization. Thus, the action, setting,
and major *dramatis personae* are keys to determining the dramatic art of the *Òṣun* Festival. As clearly shown, sacred ritual,
ritual drama, and secular drama are staged actions that occur in
specific settings, and are orchestrated and enacted by specific
major *dramatis personae*. The context of each dramatic level
determines who witnesses or performs certain acts, and whether
those acts are private (sacred ritual) or public (ritual drama and
or secular drama).

Furthermore, the dramatic narrative of the *Òṣun* Festival
happens in the clothing, colors, paraphernalia, and verbal and
drum language of the culture.[32] Although the term "symbolism"
may seem more appropriate, it cannot fully convey the explicit
communication between sender and receiver, nor can it convey
the responses that such forms of language engender. So the traditional trumpeters who announce the entrance of the *Atáója* only
advise the audience of his approach. But the drummers who play
his *oríkì* and his genealogy convey to the audience his character,
prominence, and responsibilities. The particular crown that he
wears and the presence or absence of the beaded crown signals
for the audience the movement or scene in the festival drama.
Similarly, the presence or absence of the *Arugbá* and the *Ìyá
Òṣun*, their attire and attendants as well as the role of other singers, drummers, and musicians enhance the narrative through the
accompanying songs and interactions. The event and the actions
of the *dramatis personae* mark their place in the festival script.[33]
Festival and sacred songs reflect contemporary and historical
concerns of the society. We acknowledge, for example, the
dance-drama and songs that are the vehicles for the performance
of the *oríkì* and *orin Òṣun*. Festival songs like the following ones
further illustrate the contemporary narrative themes:

Níbo ló ní n gbé Yèyé mi sí ó
Níbo ló ní n gbe Yèyé mi sí ó
Eníláwàní-òṣì tó ní n wá ṣè mọ̀le!
Níbo ló ní n gbé Yèyé mi sí ó!

Translation:

Where did he say I should leave/put my Yèyé o?
Where did he say I should leave/put my Yèyé o?
The man with a horrible turban who asked me to
        embrace Islam
Where did he say I should leave/put my Yèyé o?

This *Ọ̀sun* Festival song reflects the tensions between the Muslim and traditional religious communities.[34] Sung in a call-and-response style, the perspectives of the *Ọ̀sun* worshippers is clearly quite secular. Compare that message and its metaphor to the following one, which was also presented during that festival in the same musical style.

Ṣèlèrú àgbo,
Àgbàrà àgbo,
LỌ̀sun fi ń wọmọ rẹ̀
Ki dókítà ó tóó dé.
Abímọ-mọ́ọ̀-dà nálè,
Ọ̀sun l'à ń pẹ̀ léégún.

Translation:

Brook water a potion
Rain water a potion
Is what *Ọ̀sun* uses to nurture her children
Before the doctor ever arrived.
A mother who nurses her newborn child without heating

the house,
Ọ̀ṣun is the one we call ancestor.[35]

Images of Ọ̀ṣun as a fertility and river goddess dominate this Festival song. Unlike the first song, the tone of this song is completely sacred. Allusions to Ọ̀ṣun's power to utilize her own watery essences to heal, nurture, and warm are allusions to a cosmic power from which her worshippers draw sustenance. Examples such as these illustrate the range of topics and themes of both historical and contemporary affairs that become the content of the Ọ̀ṣun Festival drama. Given its complexity, and its cast of thousands, the meanings and metaphors of the Ọ̀ṣun Festival act out the essence of Yorùbá cosmology and worldviews through a complex narrative mosaic of music, song, dance, dance-drama, and performance. It is not surprising that these various aural and visual mediums form a symbiosis that heightens the effect of the festival as a dramatic art form.

Notes

1. J.C. DeGraft, "Roots of African Drama and Theatre," *African Literature Today* 8 (1976): 1—25.
2. *Ibid.*
3. *Ibid*, 6.
4. *Ibid.*
5. Mazizi Kunene, "The Relevance of African Cosmological Systems to African Literature Today," *African Literature Today* 11 (1980): 190 — 205.
6. Babaláwo Ifáyẹmi Ẹlẹbùrúîbọn, Personal Interviews, 1982.
7. Badejo, Field Notes, 1981—1983.
8. Ọmọṣádẹ́ Àwọlálu, *Yorùbá Beliefs and Sacrificial Rites* (London Longmans Group, Ltd. 1979): 47 and 163—4.
9. Wole Ṣoyïnká, *Myth, Literature, and the African World*, p 2—3.

10. *Ibid*, 4.
11. *Ibid*.
12. *Ibid*, pp. 26 and 140 – 160. See also, Bádéjọ, Field Notes, *op. cit.*
13. Bádéjọ, Field Notes.
14. *Ibid*, 56.
15 *Ọ̀ṣogbo. Oyo State Town Series* (Ibàdàn: Ministry Of Local Government and Information): January 1977, 12 – 14.
16. Ṣoyïnká, *op. cit*, 143 – 147.
17. Kunene, *op. cit*, 199.
18. Ṣoyïnka, 1 – 36.
19. Bádéjọ, Field Notes.
20. *Ọ̀yọ́ State Town Series, op. cit.*
21. Bádéjọ, Field Notes.
22. *Ibid*.
23. *Ibid*.
24. *Ibid*.
25. *Ibid*.
26. Bádéjọ, D.L, *A Goddess of Our Own: Collected Poems of the Yorùbá Goddess Ọ̀ṣun,* transcribed and translated by Yiwọ́la Áwọlayè, Ilorin University (work-in-progress).
27. *Ibid*.
28. Kunene, *op. cit*, 190.
29. Bádéjọ, Field Notes, 1982.
30. Wande Abímbọla, *Ìfá* (Ibàdàn, Nigeria: Oxford University Press, 1976).
31. Kunene, *op. cit.*
32. For a fuller discussion of these various narrative forms, see Andrea Benton Rushing, *A Language of Their Own: A Photographic Exhibit on Yorùbá Attire* (Amherst College, 1987). Tunji Vidal, *The Poetic and Musical Forms of Yorùbá Songs* (Unpublished seminar series, Department of African Languages and Literatures,

University of Ife, Nigeria,1981); also J.H. Kwabena Nketia, The Linguistic Aspect of Style in African Languages, In *Current Trends in Linguistics*, 7: 733 – 756, 1971.

33. Bádéjọ, Field Notes, 1982.
34. Bádéjọ, *A Goddess of Our Own.*
35. *Ibid.*

Chapter Six

THE SOCIAL VISION OF THE *ÒṢUN* FESTIVAL DRAMA

All world religions provide – or at least attempt to provide – tenets and parameters that, ostensibly, guide social interaction; so, too, with traditional African religions. The complexity, counterpunctual actions and interactions of the Yorùbá pantheon, as Wọle Ṣóyínká has noted, speaks to divinity's verisimilitude with humanity. *Òṣun* worship, as enacted through the dramatic art of her annual festival discloses but one perspective, not only of Yorùbá religion, but also of its wider social impact.

As demonstrated in chapter one and chapter five, *Òṣun*'s oral literature and the three "acts" of the festival itself contain aspects of a cosmological, sociocultural, historical, and political ethos that translate and constitute the realities of Yorùbá life. In this instance, the path which *Ògún* cut through the abyss works both ways. Here the *òrìṣà* are guardians for humanity's most sacrosanct principles. As keepers of the word, *awo* implying the secret words of creation and transformation, the divinities codify humanity's best potential as well as our most profound failure. In this regard, the *òrìṣà* are keepers of humanity's cumulative knowledge of itself. Consequently, humanity's sacrifices to the *òrìṣà* become the mechanism for unlocking that knowledge. It is possible, therefore, to view preservation of the human ideal, which is contained in the divine corpus of oral literary traditions. The divinities are (as Ṣoyìnká describes the Igbo deity, Ulu, in Achebe's novel, *Arrow of God*) exponents of

> communal will, an element of the gods own precarious existence. The god can initiate nothing, it seems his role is that of an executor of decisions already taken, or affirmer of secular ethos.[1]

What, then, are the principles that the Yorùbá hold sacred, and how do they view the secular world from their cosmic vantage point? An answer can be gathered from piecing together the characteristics and metaphors of the pantheon. Since *Ọ̀ṣun* is a major *òrìṣà* in that pantheon, her oral literature and festival drama offer a glimpse of that worldview. For our purposes, this chapter will explore the historical themes as its basis or direction, the political themes as its validation of leadership or control, the sociocultural themes as the yardstick by which it measures interpersonal behavior, and the cosmological themes as its framework.

Historical Themes

Like other Yorùbá towns, Ọ̀ṣogbo evolved through a series of events and, as indicated below, seems to have been developing from about the fifteenth century. In *The History of the Yorubas*, Reverend Samuel Johnson notes that Ọ̀ṣogbo was built during the "second period" which he terms as the "period of growth, and prosperity and oppression."[2] Although no dates are given, Johnson cites its founding as a countermove by the *Ọwá* of Ìjẹ̀ṣà when Kori, the fifth *Aláàfin* of Ọ̀yọ́ established a military post at Ẹdẹ to protect trade relations with the Ìjẹ̀bùs.[3] The title of *Tìmì* was conferred upon the new ruler in Ẹdẹ, and *Atáója* likewise was given to the new Ọ̀ṣogbo ruler. It is noteworthy that the famous battle between Tìmì of Ẹdẹ and Gbọ̀nkáà of Ọ̀yọ́ so powerfully dramatized in Dúró Ládipọ's *Obá KòSo*, occurred during this era. Johnson does not indicate whether the area was already settled, but allusions in the oral literature suggest that it was sparsely inhabited. Although references are vague, lines such as, *they (first settlers) met Òṣun here (Òṣogbo)*, are repeated in both the *Ìfá* divination corpus[4] and *oríkì Òṣun*,[5] suggesting that Òṣogbo, like other sixteenth century settlements, may have been a frontier town in the midst of shifting empires.

From all indications, Òṣogbo served solely as a military outpost at that time, and not as a settlement. If as Robin Law notes Èdẹ was founded before the sixteenth century[6], then, it is likely that this first settling of Òṣogbo also occurred before the sixteenth century. However, it seems that several subsequent events changed the nature of this frontier outpost and the town of Òṣogbo began to develop. Johnson contends that the settling of Òṣogbo was primarily a countermove of the Ọwù who intended to guard their mutual trade interests with the Ijèbus at Àpòmù market. If this is indeed true, then Òṣogbo's location at the junction between Ọyọ́, Èdẹ, and Ijèbu explains Òṣogbo's rapid commercial growth and autonomy as well as the constant referral to *Òṣun*'s wealth. Given its rich natural resources, Òṣogbo township was an ideal setting for the development of arts, crafts, and local trade. Johnson proposes, along with the numerous references to both present and past towns in *Òṣun*'s oral literature, that migration to Òṣogbo from other areas occurred in waves over a long period of time as discussed in chapter five. These migrations and their *raison d'etre* impacted on Òṣogbo's sociocultural structure.

Both oral and written records confirm that, as a military outpost, Òṣogbo gained prominence as the Ọyọ́ empire declined and competing regencies vied for control of northern and southern trade routes.[7] Consequently, Òṣogbo became a hub within the changing boundaries of the Ọyọ́, Owu, Èkìtì, and Ìbàdàn empires. As mentioned, its location and military provisions seemed a safe haven for refugees fleeing the ravishes of declining empires, warfare, and slave-raiding. In the oral literature, there are constant references to towns that evolved from these empires throughout this era. References to Ìjùmù, Ìpọlé, Ilésà, Èfọn, Iwó, Irègùn, and others allude to the migration of people from these areas to Òsogbo. As the *oríkì* and *orin Òṣun* suggest, many of these immigrants fled a series of clashes among contending Yorùbá forces. These movements may have began as early as the fifteenth century when, as Akinjobin notes, the Nupe attacked Ọyọ and drove them from their old capital.[8] Certainly, these types of migrations must have been well under way during the seventeenth century.[9] Indeed, the oral reference to the Tìmì of Ẹdẹ, an Ọyọ leader, meeting Láàròyè, an Ọwú leader from Ìjèsàland, intimates a political and cultural convergence of early Yorùbá regencies at Òsogbo.

Lastly, with the north-south flow of the Òsun River into the Lagos Lagoon, drought victims, fishermen, and traders certainly found the area attractive. Another source, Ọyọ State Local Government documents cite the late eighteenth century as the era in which Òsogbo was founded. This particular founding or migration is also supported well in the oral tradition and written sources. The government document cites drought in Ìpolé, a neighboring town, as the impetus on this occasion. Akinjogbin's article, *"The Expansion of Ọyọ and the Rise of Dahomey, 1600-1800,"* offers a similar connection between "prolonged drought" conditions in the area and migrations from previously settled kingdoms such as "Ọwú, Kétu, Ilésà, Ìlá, and Òkò (later Ìjèbù) as well as some of the Èkìtì kingdoms."[10]

At the turn of the nineteenth century, another wave of migrants settled in Òsogbo. These people were attempting to escape the Fulani slave-raiding from the north and the warfare in Ọyọ to the west. By the middle of the nineteenth century, Ìbàdàn, another trading center, had developed into a formidable rival of the declining Ọyọ empire as well as the expansionist interests of the northern Fulani.[11] With the Ọwú defeated, Òsogbo became an

Ìbàdàn town. In fact, the Ìbàdàn's rescued Òṣogbo when they delivered the final defeat to the Fulani around 1838.[12] The oral literary references to *Ọ̀ṣun* saving the town concur with Ojo's documentation that Òṣogbo "was sited on the defensible bank of the Oshun River, nearest the deepest pool which does not dry up in the dry season."[13]

Since control of southern trade routes through Àpòmù in Ìjẹ̀bu was a major factor in the earliest settling of Òṣogbo, it is likely that traders from the former center settled in Òṣogbo during the nineteenth century. It would also appear that the confluence of the *Ọ̀ṣun* River with the Erinle River to the east and her tributary, the Ọbá River to the west, impacted greatly upon the fishing industry that still thrives in Òṣogbo today. Again the oral literature abounds with references to *Ọ̀ṣun*'s children, which include the many fish of her river. But the most significant reference to fisheries remains *Ọ̀ṣun*'s image as the fish-goddess whom the ruler of Òṣogbo feeds (worships) reflected in the title *Atẹ́wọ́gbéja,* discussed in chapters four and five. Indeed as Ojo and other scholars demonstrate, Yorùbá oral literature and the culture it preserves contain those environmental and occupational references that have influenced its historical development.

Political Themes

If the historical themes illustrate migration patterns, especially toward the Ọ̀ṣun River at Òṣogbo, then the political themes illustrate the tensions and struggles for power and/or leadership that impacted upon the new township. For our purposes here, we will consider those tensions and struggles as they are reflected in the leadership positions and titles that command authority in the oral literature and confirmed by written sources. The following discussion reaffirms the parallel structuring of the political and religious systems, which as Fadipe notes, "The priesthood of every *òrìṣà* is organized on the model of the political system."[14] He also says that the "organization of worshippers is very important" and that "whoever has been elected the head ... is generally the priest and/or priestess of that *òrìṣà* for the whole town and, where the town is the capital, the state."[15] In other words, the religious structure parallels and institutionalizes the political one.

As demonstrated elsewhere, the title *Atáója* originally was conferred on Láàròyè, who was the seventh *Owá* of Ìpolé, a town southeast of Òṣogbo in Ìjèṣàland. Reverend Johnson points out that his principal duty is "to worship the fish in the river *Ọ̀ṣun*,"[16] while Ojo states that he is the "arch-priest of the goddess" whose "act of benevolence" caused "Òṣogbo to be sited close to the deepest pool along the course of the river."[17] As an Ìjèṣà tributary, the political organization of Òṣogbo probably resembles the Ifé political structure more closely prior to the nineteenth century than it has since becoming a district of Ìbàdàn after the Fulani Wars.[18]

Oral literary references, which confirm that *Ọ̀ṣun* is one of the original *òrìṣà* who descended at Ilé-Ifè to organize the world, also suggest Òṣogbo's spiritual ties and her religio-political allegiance to Ifè. More importantly, the titles *Ìyá Ọ̀ṣun* and *Ìyálóde* refer to religious and political as well as economic titles and positions of female leadership that, despite Fadipe's disclaimer to the contrary, were central to the economic and political structure, and allude to *Ọ̀ṣun* as a title for female rulership. A closer look at their roles and functions reveals these women's "real power."[19]

Unlike the *Tìmì* of Ẹdẹ, the *Atáója* remained a tributary ruler of Ọwú until it lost the war to the Ìbàdàns. Where the Tìmì challenged the authority of the *Aláàfin* of Ọ̀yọ́, the *Atáója* continued as a religio-political functionary of some central authority outside of Òṣogbo. In spite of this, he also remained the solid source of authority within Òṣogbo township. Such continuity provides a sense of security for the many waves of refugees who flooded the township over the past three and half centuries.

As a local, traditional religio-political Yorùbá leader, the *Atáója*'s functions and duties mirror that of other Yorùbá obás.

A clear example of this lies in the relationship between the *Atáója* and the *Ìyá Ọ̀ṣun*. In his *History of the Yorubas*, Johnson details the relationship between the *Aláàfin* of Ọ̀yọ́ and his "official mother," or "*Ìyá Ọba*." This title means that "she is supposed to act the part of mother to him," and that "it is her privilege to be the third person in the room where the King and the Basorun worship the *Ọ̀run* (heavenly mysteries) in the month of September every year."[20] Similarly, the *Ìyá Ọ̀ṣun* is the "official mother" of the *Atáója* as well as the caretaker for the goddess *Ọ̀ṣun*.[21] She officiates at the *ose, or four-day weekly worship of the goddess*, and at the calling of the *òrìṣà Ọ̀ṣun* to her annual festival.[22]

The *Ìyá Ọ̀ṣun Òṣogbo* is the chief priestess of the titled *Ìyá Ọ̀ṣun* found in other townships. These women also are known by the generic title for local chief priestesses, *Ìyálọ́ṣá, the mothers of the òrìsà*. With respect to *Ọ̀ṣun*, however, they are also referred to as *Ìyá l'Ọ̀ṣun, mothers of Ọ̀ṣun,* who are responsible to the *Ìyá Ọ̀ṣun Òṣogbo* in their practice of *Ọ̀ṣun* worship. In addition, the *Ìyá Ọ̀ṣun Òṣogbo* presides as the chief priestess over a hierarchy which, in some respects, resembles that of ọba's. As the head of the hierarchy of *Ọ̀ṣun* functionaries, she directs the *Àwòrò Ọ̀ṣun, Balogun Ọ̀ṣun, Ìyáláṣẹ*, the *Arugbá* as well as the other *Ọ̀ṣun* worshippers.

The *Àwòrò Ọ̀ṣun*, the senior priest, is ranked next to the *Ìyá Ọ̀ṣun*, and assists *Ìyá Ọ̀ṣun* in carrying the sacrifice to the *Ọ̀ṣun* River. Although men and women alike worship the goddess *Ọ̀ṣun*, this is the only title in the religious hierarchy that is held by a man. *Balogun,* or commander-in-chief, is another important political title that is widely distributed throughout Yorùbáland. Signifying a war leader, the title *Balogun* exists in both districts and towns.[23] Third in rank to the *Ìyá Ọ̀ṣun*, the *Balogun Ọ̀ṣun* is the bodyguard who also leads the male devotees. She makes the preparations for the annual festival and is the caretaker of the shrine.[24] Similar to this latter charge, the *Ìyálaṣẹ Ọ̀ṣun* is responsible for the food for *Ọ̀ṣun* and her devotees. While devotees and worshippers hold other occupations, such as market women and men, dyers, and farmers, the *Àwòrò, Balogun,* and *Ìyálaṣẹ Ọ̀ṣun* work strictly in the service of the *òrìṣà.*[25]

The *Ìyá Ọ̀ṣun* is also in charge of the *Arugbá,* or the one who carries the calabash for sacrifice. She performs her rituals in the same place where the *Atáója* performs his. *Arugbá* is chosen from among his close relatives and formerly had to live with the *Ìyá Ọ̀ṣun.* Today, the *Arugbá* attends school, but she must still live in the *Ọ̀ṣun* shrine for one month yearly. From the time she is chosen until her marriage, she must not carry anything on her head, except the *igbá,* or calabash, which contains the annual offering to *Ọ̀ṣun.* Once she is married, her husband is bound to fulfill her obligations to the worship of *Ọ̀ṣun* when she cannot. *Ọ̀ṣun's* oracle, *mẹ́rìndínlógún* or sixteen-cowries divination, is used to select both the *Ìyá Ọ̀ṣun* and the *Arugbá.* Both are accorded special social privileges such as choosing their provisions from the market without compensation to the sellers. This privilege confirms the role of the *Ìyá Ọ̀ṣun* as the *Ìyálóde,* mother of the outdoors, which includes the markets, and the relationship among the political, economic, and religious functions in the society.

Like the title *Balogun,* the title *Ìyálóde* is a generic one. Johnson defines the *Ìyálóde* as the:

> queen of the ladies (of the palace). (It) is bestowed upon the most distinguished lady in the town. She has also her lieutenants Otun, Osi, Ekerin etc, as any other principal chiefs of the town. Some of these Iyalodes command a force of powerful warriors, and have a voice in the council of chiefs. Through the *Ìyálóde,* the women of the town can make their voices heard in municipal and other affairs.[26]

Fadipe's explanation of the role of the *Ìyálóde* furthers our discussion. He notes:

> in many Yorùbá towns, especially among the Ọ̀yọ́-

Yorùbá, women are organized principally for political purposes in what is called *Ẹgbẹ́ Ìyálóde*, literally, the association of the *Ìyálóde*, the latter being the official title of its president. It is essentially a town organization and its members are chiefly craftswomen and traders. Any representation made by this body to the political authorities are listened to with respect whether they are concerned with their trading interests or with some broader political issue.[27]

Both the *Atáója* and the *Ìyá Ọ̀ṣun* hold dual responsibilities that are consistent within Yorùbá culture. Both are at the head of parallel structures which respectively institutionalize Yorùbá political and religious philosophies. Yet unlike the *Ìyá Ọ̀ṣun Ọ̀ṣogbo*, who is the center of *Ọ̀ṣun* worshippers, the *Atáója* historically owes allegiance to external centers of power.

One possible reason for this discrepancy can be found in the migration patterns mentioned earlier and in one line in the *odù Ifá* stating that the settlers "found *Ọ̀ṣun* there" when they arrived at the banks of the river. As one of the *ÌrúnMọlẹ̀*, *Ọ̀ṣun*, according to Yorùbá cosmology and history, migrated from Ilé-Ifẹ̀ as the other *òrìṣà* did. It is also possible that *Ìjamọ̀*, a present-day town of Ilé-Ilújí near Ondo[28] from which *Ọ̀ṣun* came according to the oral literature, was also the previous name of the area we know today as Òṣogbo. In either case, it seems (1) that *Ọ̀ṣun* was the progenitor ruler of that area, and (2) the location was settled before the fifteenth century.

The same *odù Ifá* says that Olutìmìhín and Láàròyè made a pact with *Ọ̀ṣun* enabling them to settle in the area. Having granted permission, she asked the newcomers to move away from her grove, so that her children could come out and play. Although the expression, *her children,* also refers to the plant and animal life of the area, it strongly indicates that there was a prior settlement in the area, possibly ruled by a queen with whom the founders made a treaty. Certainly, the profuse oral literary ref-

⦿ erences to *Ọ̀ṣun* as an *Ọba*, a ruler, and warrior make this case. Furthermore, an aboriginal population under her rulership would have been referred to as her children whose vested interest in the local dyeing industry would have warranted protection. Thus the need to protect the indigo trees and the trade in parrot feathers supported by the flora and fauna of the *Ọ̀ṣun* Grove. Indeed, Òṣogbo's strategic location along the connecting trade routes between northern and southern markets as well as its position as a military outpost for changing capitals points to her political importance. Both factors would have enhanced the power of the *Ìyá Ọ̀ṣun* in her capacity as the *Ìyálóde*, and reenforces *Ọ̀ṣun* as a female title.

Religious issues are another source of political tension alluded to in the *orin Ọ̀ṣun* (*Ọ̀ṣun* Festival songs). The Fulani intrusion into Yorùbá territory was intended to spread Islam as much as it was to capture people for slave-trading. Although the Ibadans checked the Fulani advances around 1838, and the Christian missionaries presented a formidable presence during the colonial era, neither event prevented the Muslim faith from its steady move southward. Today, Islam still penetrates the southern regions in search of converts. The traditional religious practices, such as the worship of *Ọ̀ṣun*, stymies such conversions. In 1982, the tension again arose between the traditionalists and the Muslims over the *Ọ̀ṣun* Festival in Òṣogbo. This tension is captured in the festival songs, like the one cited in chapter five,

Níbo l'o ní n gbé Yèyé mi sí o?
Eníláwàní-òṣì t'o ní n wá ṣè 'mọle!

Where did he say I should leave my Yèyé o?
The man with a horrible turban who asked me to embrace Islam.[29]

"To leave my Yèyé" means to abandon the worship of *Ọ̀ṣun*. For these women to abandon the practice of *Ọ̀ṣun* means more than just converting to another religion. It also means losing political and economic power in the ruling structures and local market economies in which they hold historical and traditional positions.

Those positions are solidified by the group identity afforded the women of Ọ̀ṣun. In another festival song, they sing:

> Ọmọ ẹlẹ́gbẹ́ ni wá ò ee
> Ọmọ ẹlẹ́gbẹ́ ni wá ò àà
> Bọ́isi̇̀ tí ò fẹ́ẹ́ wá k'ó jòkó
> Ọmọ ẹlẹ́gbẹ́ ni wá.

> We are members of the group
> We are members of the group
> Boys who do not like us should sit (stay behind)
> We are members of the group.[30]

This group solidarity symbolizes the worship of Ọ̀ṣun and enhances women's positions in all aspects of Yorùbá life. As noted above, the *Ẹgbẹ́ Ìyálóde* is the guild of craftswomen and traders whose talents and business acumen are enshrined in the oral literature of Ọ̀ṣun. The goddess represents more than fertility: she is also the mother of three markets, a dyer, and a child of Ijumu where kolanuts[31] are plentiful. She is a craftswoman and a trader who has bequeathed to women who *have power like hers* political and economic power that is legitimized within the religious practice. And finally, she is a ruler and leader of women, an eternal reminder of female rulership and power.

Ultimately, Ọ̀ṣun worshippers, like many other traditionalists, seek peaceful coexistence with other religions. For them, Ọ̀ṣun worship is a source of personal strength, political power, and economic independence. As such, it is a functional way of life that seeks no greater ambition than the protection of its own membership. That is illustrated in this song:

Bàbá enírungbọ̀n, jẹ́ á ṣẹẹbọọ wa
Bàbá enírungbọ̀n, jẹ́ á ṣẹẹbọọ ti wa
Àwa è mọ̀mọ̀ pé ẹ mọ́mọ̀ kirun l'ọ́júmó
Bàbá enírungbọ̀n, jẹ́ á ṣẹẹbọ ti wa.

The bearded man, let us do our own festival,
The bearded man, let us do our own festival
We did not say you should not pray daily
The bearded man, let us do our own festival.[32]

Sociocultural Themes

Aside from the historical and political themes, the action of
the festival acknowledges a parallel sociocultural hierarchy that
is maintained and mirrored by a religio-political structure. Leadership, social and familial control, the mutual responsibilities of
the community and individuals, and relationship between female
and male positions in the society are implied within this sociocultural framework. The populace expects the *Atáója* and the *Ìyá
Ọ̀ṣun* to minister to its political and spiritual needs. These
Òṣogbo officials are the trustees of the people's will to survive,
and the people, in turn, invest them with continuous support.
Hence, the *Ìyá Ọ̀ṣun* and the *Atáója* symbolize the religio-political order, which, ostensibly, acts on behalf of the communal will.
As such, they are agents whose positions represent sociocultural
stability and continuity that underlie a communal sense of well-
being. And within the framework of this communal security the
individual supposedly masters its social and cultural nuances as
well as her or his role in its furtherance.

For these reasons, sociocultural themes in the *Ọ̀ṣun* Festival drama are, broadly speaking, reflections of the general issues and concepts found in the larger Yorùbá society. Age groups
and guilds direct the individual along prescribed pathways, while
the gerontocracy and patriarchy attempt widespread social control. As demonstrated above, each micro-political, economic, and

religious unit exerts a partial measure of the composite political influence. However, tensions between individual and group controls, between male and female, and between the various Yorùbá ethnic divisions remain at the base of social conflict and interaction. These tensions are also found in the oral literature and often seek redress during the festival.

Yorùbá sociocultural vision is bound only by the immortality of its people. Tensions, conflicts, and contradictions are resolved within the context of cosmic time. Resolution is continuous not instantaneous; it requires diligence and sacrifice. Despite seemingly boundless parameters, the sociocultural vision is fragile. Its basic premise rests at the crossroads of earthly and spiritual being and is symbolized by the moment of birth. This may explain why *Òṣun* is often referred to as the mother of *Èṣù*, the guardian of the crossroads. The security of the living, the acknowledgment of the ancestors and divinities, the individual participation at the religious vortex create a holistic view of the world itself and a context for resolution. Sociocultural balance is attainable solely through unification among the ancestors, the living and the unborn. When the *Arugbá* carries the *ẹbọ* or offering, she carries the embodiment of that principle. Sacrifice reciprocates divinity's healing of social wounds and ills; therefore it is central to ritual efficacy. Obviously, sacrifice and resolution are particularly significant for the *Òṣun* Festival where the celebrated *òrìṣà* symbolizes fertility, power, and continuity.

Òṣun, as one of the original *òrìṣà*, is principal among the other *òrìṣà* who are also able to give children. With a history of high infant mortality rates, Yorùbá women seek fertility as a weapon against it. The forest belt and numerous waterways breed mosquitos and other disease-bearing insects. In times of drought, water easily becomes a festering caldron of cholera and other fatal illnesses. Towns and villages are decimated by an outbreak of any of these diseases. As such, reproduction is of paramount importance lest the group perish.

As mainly agriculturalists and traders, labor is particularly crucial. Since male and female alike work the land, numerous children mean more productivity. However, because the female eventually marries and carries her labor to her husband's family, male children become more desirable.[33] Moreover, since the Yorùbá are patriarchal, land and other forms of inheritance remain with the paternal line. This form of social organization renders women subject to male domination, a theme which is discussed below. Another factor in the desire for increased fertility was the slave-raiding and internecine warfare that it produced. As found in Ọ̀ṣogbo history, migration, resettlement, and defense were major factors in the township's founding. Kidnapping played a major role in the process of acquiring slaves. This factor depleted the potential indigenous labor pool and created great suffering. In addition to the maternal stress which is obscured in the oral and written literature, the death or abduction of one's children means insecurity for women whose social welfare is inextricably tied to the ability of their children to care for them during their senior years.[34] Also, the women's position in their marital home often depends on the number of living and tangible children, especially males, which she has. Since reproduction is considered part of a woman's contribution to communal productivity, infertility is considered non-productive. Infertility particularly affects women whose social mobility during their adult years is influenced by the presence of their children.[32] The prevalence of the *Ẹgbẹ Ìyálọṣá*, followed by the *ọmọde Ọ̀ṣun*, during the three major acts of the festival illustrates the extremely critical role fertility plays in the lives of Yorùbá women.

Because Yorùbá social and political institutions are deeply hierarchal, social mobility and status are crucial to both men and women, and bound by the pillars of the gerontocracy and the patriarchy. As noted above, the structure of the political institutions is replicated throughout specific regions and impacts on the religious and sociocultural organization. For both, age permits leverage within the social structure, especially the family unit. For women, the position in the marital home, her place in the religious priesthood, her rank in the marketplace, and her role in the political structure have far-reaching consequences for her social mobility and success. For example, the *Arugbá* remains a devotee of the goddess even after she has married. But her husband must agree to allow her to perform her regular rituals, and he is obliged to perform them himself when she is incapacitated.[36] Similarly, for other devotees and priestesses of *Ọ̀sun*, marriage enhances rather than limits their ritual duties or roles in the religious hierarchy because they too become mothers.

Another sociocultural theme of the festival is the accumulation of wealth. One *odù Ifá* notes *Ọ̀sun*'s wealth, and tells how she offers her wealth as a sacrifice in order to have children. The *Ìyáloja* as the president of the women's guild of craftswomen and traders wields considerable power within the social as well as the political structure. As the authority who speaks for and directs market people and artisans, she bridges the religious, political, and economic spheres of the society. As a spokeswoman for other townswomen, she provides a powerful feminine voice. Her position then elevates all women in the society whom she represents.

Although rarely acknowledged, woman power in the political arena not only exists but also impacts upon the social system. While the presence of the gerontocracy and the patriarchy dominates women as well as voiceless men, *Ọ̀sun* festival drama and oral literature suggest otherwise. Clearly, *Ìyá Osun*'s position parallels that of the *Atáója* as demonstrated in the various processionals and her role as his *official mother*. In her capacity as *Ìyálóde*, the *Ìyá Ọ̀sun* ensures that the pact with the goddess is fulfilled annually on behalf of women in general, and Ọ̀sogbo township in particular. She gives hope to childless women and protects the interests of marketwomen and craftswomen. The position of the *Ìyá* Ọ̀sun presents to Ọ̀sogbo women an image of their integral role in the vision and maintenance of their society.

Cosmological Themes

If women have these positions and play these roles in the society then, as many *odù Ifá* illustrate, women are central to the
cosmic order. The mysterious forces of disease and death, motherhood and childlessness, wealth and poverty, empowerment and
oppression are recurrent themes in the *Ọ̀sun* Festival drama and
oral literature which seek resolution through sacrifice. As with
all religions, the cosmos is the inexplicable realm of ultimate
power. There, just beyond the reach of ordinary human beings
lie the mysteries of life and death, of human vulnerability and
empowerment. In that context, we are reminded that the *òrìṣà*,
àjẹ́, and *ajogun* are considered extraordinary beings who have
access to these mysterious powers. The *òrìṣà* are *Olódùmarè*'s
ministers whose purposes are beneficial to humankind. The *àjẹ́*,
powerful beings, represent the spectrum and power of life's possibilities. The *ajogun*, on the other hand, represent life's collective obstacles such as disease, death, poverty, infertility, and so
forth. In Yorùbá cosmology, the awesome knowledge of the *àjẹ́*
allows them to influence human and natural events. That power,
discussed in chapter two, mirrors the awesome feminine repro-
ductive powers. The power of *Ọ̀sun*, and by extension all women,
lies in her image as a goddess of fertility who gives children to
childless women. Thus, in the cosmic realm; *Ọ̀sun*'s role as an
òrìṣà, a giver of children, and her *power as an àjẹ́* becomes a
metaphor for her *real power*, that is, the power to advance or
abate the continuous existence of human beings and human
progress. As a divine benefactor, *Ọ̀sun*'s role as leader of the àjẹ́
may appear contradictory. However, upon closer examination,
her role reflects not only cosmic but also social reality; that is,
the gamut of powerful forces complement one another.

The cosmic realm embraces the range of power symbolized by *àjẹ́*. It recognizes their mutual co-existence as realities
and yardsticks by which to measure any eventuality. It accepts
the dialectic that resides between and within nature and human-

ity as the natural order of things. And it utilizes sacrifice as the requisite instrument for the maintenance of balance and harmony. Within the Yorùbá cosmos, sacrifice means relinquishing one thing to gain another, to forfeit some measure of self in order to progress, to shed a layer of old skin to shine anew. Finally, as demonstrated in the *Ifá* divination corpus, the cosmic realm acknowledges that no living entity, including the divinities themselves, are above the equanimity of sacrifice and the vagaries of life's fortunes.

What has this to do with *Ọ̀ṣun* and her festival? Like the other divinities, *Ọ̀ṣun* is in charge of an aspect of the cosmic realm. Where **Ẹ̀ṣù**, for example, is in charge of the *àṣẹ, the secret knowledge of the creation of the world, Ọ̀ṣun* is in charge of the *àjẹ́, or powerful beings.* Like other *òrìṣà, Ẹ̀ṣù* and *Ọ̀ṣun* function for the benefit of humanity.[37] Consequently, the divinities in their interaction with human beings may tempt and falter, err and cajole, celebrate and discipline, but they must ultimately serve the aspirations, resolve the imbalances, and answer the inquiries of humanity. So *Ọ̀ṣun*, as leader of the *àjẹ́*, must protect their covenants of the *àjẹ́*, but for her to initiate any destructive action is tantamount to her own annihilation. Hence, limits are set and boundaries are drawn even within the cosmos. Both *òrìṣà* and humanity acknowledge their respective imperfections as aspects of universal truths. For its part, humanity finds amid the vast plethora of possible causes for such imperfections an *òrìṣà* who serves as a vehicle of redress.

To the Yorùbá woman, childlessness is regarded as a major imperfection. As mentioned elsewhere, children are a source of wealth and security in the marital home as well as in the larger society. They are expected to provide for the needs of their elderly parents, especially the mother. However, malevolent forces, the *ajogun*, threaten the survival and development of new life. Sacrificial offerings, prayers, and worship of a specific *òrìṣà* are among the mechanisms used to avert destruction. Smallpox, cholera, and dysentery are among the oftentimes fatal diseases that cause such a high infant mortality rate in the region. These illnesses added to the frequency of miscarriages, *abíkú,* alluded to in the oral literature, make survival beyond infancy and early childhood a most arduous task for parents, especially mothers. Surely it must seem to Yorùbá women, as to all women, that the mystery of childbearing and childrearing demands a special vigilance lest the precious life be swept away and reclaimed by the Source from whence it comes. But surely the most awesome threat to the survival of human life is human living itself. Jealousy, hatred, maliciousness, greed, and contemptuousness within the human family are certainly not the exclusive property of the Yorùbá people. These diseases of the heart, intangible as they may be, continue to plague the whole of humanity. Such invisible forces demand restraint. Appeal to *Ọ̀sun* as the leader of the *àjẹ́* suggests an attempt to forestall these universal threats from such inexplicable sources.

Nor does such an appeal suggest that humanity has relinquished its own power and self-control to that of a spiritual being. On the contrary, the oral literary narratives demonstrate that migration involving political structures, changing economic fortunes, and social upheavals are the results of human intervention in its own affairs. For the Yorùbá, the spiritual and the mundane are completely *interdependent.* In such a synergistic environment, as Professors Idowu and Abímbọla note, everyday life is, itself, a religious act.

Finally, like life itself, male and female are reciprocal principles of the cosmic and social order. *Ọ̀sun*'s place in Yorùbá creation, the position of the *Ìyá Ọ̀sun* and the *Ìyálóde* as well as the invaluable role of reproduction and production in the social, political, and economic structure demonstrate that women are powerful icons central to communal harmony and well-being.

Notes

1. Wole Ṣóyínká, *Myth, Literature, and the African World* (Cambridge: Cambridge University Press): 1976, 95.
2. Reverend Samuel Johnson, *A History of the Yorubas From the Earliest Times to the British Protectorate*, 155–158, 669.
3. *Ibid.* 156.
4. Babaláwọ Ifáyẹmi Ẹlẹ́bùrúîbọ̀n, Personal Interviews, 1981–1983.
5. D. L. Badejo, *A Goddess of Our Own.*
6. R.C.C. Law, *The Oyo Empire c1600–c1838.* (Oxford: Clarendon Press, 1977); A.L. Mabogunje, *Owu in Yoruba History*, (Ibadan: Ibadan University Press, 1971): 3; and Johnson, *A History of the Yorubas, op. cit.*
7. *Ibid.*
8. Akinjobin, "The Expansion of Oyo and the Rise of Dahomey," in *History of West Africa*, Ajayi and Crowder (eds.), vol. 1, 311.
9. See note 6 above.
10. Akinjogbin, *op. cit.* 304–343.
11. Law, *op. cit.*
12. *Ibid.*
13. Afolabi Ojo, *Yoruba Culture: A Geographical Analysis* (Ife: University of Ife Press and London: University of London Press, Ltd, 1966).
14. N.A. Fadipe, *The Sociology of the Yoruba* (Ibadan: Ibadan University Press, 1970): 254.
15. *Ibid.* 285.
16. Johnson, *op. cit.* 156.
17. Ojo, *op. cit.* 164.
18. Fadipe, *op. cit.* 199.
19. Filomena Chioma Steady, ed., *The Black Woman Cross-Culturally* (Rochester, New York: Schenkman Books, Inc, 1981): 34–36.

20. Johnson, *op. cit.* 63.
21. Babaláwọ Ifáyẹmi Ẹlẹ́bùrúîbọ̀n, Personal Interviews, 1983.
22. Mr. Babayinka and Ms. Susan Wenger, Personal Interviews, 1983.
23. Johnson, *op. cit.* 132.
24. Johnson, *ibid.* Also, D.L. Badejo, Field Notes, *op. cit.*
25. Badejo, *ibid.*
26. Johnson, *op. cit.* 77.
27. Fadipe, *op. cit.* 253.
28. Wande Abímbọla, Personal Interview, 1990.
29. Bádéjọ, *A Goddess of Our Own, op. cit.* Also, Bádéjọ, Field Notes, *op. cit.*
30. *Ibid.*
31. *Ibid.*
32. *Ibid.*

Chapter Seven

GENDER, POWER, AND AFRICAN FEMINIST THEORY

Women's power in Yorùbá cultural history is as ancient as it is contemporary. The annual festival and oral literature of Ọ̀ṣun demonstrate this. Unlike Judeo-Christian and Islamic doctrines, women goddesses and rulers figure prominently in Yorùbá cosmological thought. Consequently, in traditional African thought, women's power, like men's power, evolves from *the* Divine Source of all power. Like their male counterparts, Yorùbá women are born with *àṣẹ* (power), hence, women's power is autonomous, complementary, spiritual, and intrinsic. As Rowland Abiodun states,

> the word, *àṣẹ*, is variously translated and understood as power, authority, command, specter ... the vital force in all living and non-living things or a coming-to-pass of an utterance, a logos proforicos. To devotees of the *òrìṣà* (deities), however, the concept of àṣẹ is more practical and immediate. *Àṣẹ* inhabits and energizes the awe-inspiring space of the *òrìṣà*, their altars (ojú-ìbó), and all their objects, utensils, and offerings, including the air around them.[1]

The *òrìṣà Ọ̀ṣun* emanates her *àṣẹ* as a human being and a deity. She is a vital source as her name, attributes, and activi-

ties indicate. Also the word *Ọ̀ṣun* itself means a source that seeps
out and establishes something, a beginning like a township or
settlement. *Ọ̀ṣun* alludes not only to a deity, but also to a quintessential, creative matrix, a source of power. She is then conceptually and cosmologically *pèrègùn*, eternal source of and title for
female rulership. *Ọ̀ṣun* as a title explains the multiplicity of
Ọ̀ṣun(s) throughout Yorùbá-speaking, especially `Ìjèṣà, territory,
as well as the references to *Ọ̀ṣun* and other *women like her* as
leaders. *Ọ̀ṣun* as title further explains the reverence and awe in
which women's power is held by men, and confirms the ideal of
parity between women and men in the sociopolitical and religious structures.

Ifi Amadiume demonstrates in an Igbo example[2] that
power, especially personal power, is *human,* not gender-specific.
Genderless linguistic constructs in the Yorùbá language illustrates the essentially human status in such roles as *òrìṣà* (divinity), *ènìyàn* (human being), *ọba* (ruler), and *àgbàlagbà* (elder)
as well as the pronouns *ẹ̀* (he or she for respect) and *ò* (she or he
familiar). These terms argue that gender and sex roles are frequently asymmetrical, and often obscure. Similarly, *ìyá* or
mother becomes *ìyálóde* literally meaning "mother of the outside," and socially is translated as "president" or "leader of
women's organizations," implying that mother is a leader, like
Ọ̀ṣun. Further, *ìyàwó* literally "wife," is applied to a married
woman not only by her husband but also by his male and female
relatives as *ìyàwó* or "our wife." The term "*ìyàwó*" also applies
to male *and* female initiates who *marry* an *òrìṣà*. So, a male initiate as well as a female initiate to *Ọ̀ṣun* is *ìyàwó Ọ̀ṣun,* "the wife
of *Ọ̀ṣun.*" These linguistic examples coupled with *Ọ̀ṣun*'s role in
Yorùbá cosmology and social structure underscore an African
feminist theory that challenges the hegemony of the Western
social order. It does so, because unlike Euro-American feminism,
women are demonstrably central to African cultural realities and
practices.

Undoubtedly, there are contradictions within this theory

with respect to gender and sex roles, but many, although not all, of these contradictions in contemporary thought arise from the imposition of Islamic and Western sexism and cultural values. In view of the oral literary examples cited here, in traditional Yorùbá thought sexism is checked by cosmic ideals, gender and linguistic constructs, parallel sociopolitical and religious structures, and complementary female-male roles. Power (*àṣẹ*) then, is not male but human, and women, as the bearers of humanity, are consummate icons of power. The annual *Ọ̀ṣun* Festival and oral literature attest that even within the patriarchal Yorùbá system, women are central to the proper function and survival of humanity. The mythical images of *Ọ̀ṣun* and the corresponding positions that women hold in the political, economic, social, and religious spheres reiterate this. Indeed, this central, active, participatory role in traditional societies makes African women, as Filomena Steady notes, the *original feminists*.[3] *Ọ̀ṣun Ṣẹ̀ẹ̀gẹ̀sí Olóòyà-iyùn* is a model of this humanistic feminism which extends Steady's seminal African feminist construct by drawing from and including a spiritual, cosmic, and sociolinguistic premise. As illustrated in this book, the cosmological basis lays the philosophical foundation for the social, political, economic, and religious structures and interactions within Yorùbá culture.

Subsequently, the structure of *Ọ̀ṣun's* festival drama along with her symbolism and themes offer one example of a cultural-historical foundation for African feminist theory. In this regard, the function and meaning of the *Ọ̀ṣun* Festival suggest not only a religious, but also a political framework that is, at once, wholistic and exclusive. It is wholistic because, as Steady points out, African Feminism is humanistic.[4] Simultaneously, it is exclusively female because as Sudarkasa illustrates, African women's institutions are reciprocal and interdependent. From a theoretical perspective, the sacred and secular drama of the *Ọ̀ṣun* Festival along with her praise-poetry envelope the dichotomy suggested by this unity of wholeness and exclusivity.

By speaking directly to and for women who constitute the

source of human continuity, the *Ọ̀ṣun* Festival, like most African festivals, becomes an elegant forum for the disclosure of this unity of opposites. As giver of children and leader of the *àjẹ́*, *Ọ̀ṣun's* mythical images testify that women are mysterious because they recreate themselves as well as men, indeed women birth the ruler and the ruled alike. This exclusive female bond creates the rationale for the *obínrin ẹgbẹ*, or "women's associations." Simultaneously, the festival reinforces its wholistic nature, since the *Atáója* co-rules Òṣogbo with *Ọ̀ṣun* in the person of the *Ìyá Ọ̀ṣun* while *Ìyá Ọ̀ṣun* conversely performs annual sacred rituals in his presence. This is further substantiated by the fact that once married, the *Arugbá* 's (sacrifice carrier) husband is equally bound to the sanctions of *Ọ̀ṣun* worship and must perform his wife's rituals when she is unable to do so.[5] Balance, reciprocity, and the sanctity of gender roles are the messages of the festival's drama.

From a literary perspective, African feminist theory extols images of women who embody power in their femininity, love of self as part of their community of selves, the conscientiousness of creativity, and the labor of human freedom. A Yorùbá proverb says, *ìwà l'ẹwà*, "character is beauty."[6] In a sociocultural context, the poised female character is enveloped in a cosmic ideal which outpictures an image of beauty for Yorùbá women in art and cultural practice. It envisions women as a true matrix and our literary images as a reflection of life's contradictions and complements. Women are revealed and (re)visioned as parallel and complementary partners with men. Yes, male sexism is present, and it is at once acknowledged and challenged. A line from the *orin ọdún Ọ̀ṣun* (*Ọ̀ṣun* festival songs) clearly ridicules and dismisses it: *Bóìsì tí ò fẹ wá jòkó* ("Boys or men who don't like us, can sit down, that is, stay behind") because *ọmọ ẹlẹgbẹ ni wá ó* ee, ("we are members of a group, that is, sisterhood").[7] Sexism, then, is a human and social contradiction that is resolved only in a human and social context. Truly, sexism threatens the vibrancy of the human community to which *Ọ̀ṣun* and her sisters give birth. Yet, as the Yorùbá creation myth recounted in chapter two shows, African women have the power to challenge any threat to the cosmic and social order. The male divinities attempt to negate *Ọ̀ṣun* threatens to destroy humanity and nullify divinity. Thematically, this narrative illustrates that sexism generates chaos, and implies that men do come to terms with women's roles even within a patriarchal system like the Yorùbá. This example reaffirms the comparison with *Nnobi* (*Igbo*) women's centrality in the patriarchal Igbo society. Although Yorùbá and Igbo religious, political, and social structures vary, females and female deities hold pivotal positions in their respective social and cosmic structures. Additionally, in both ethnolinguistic cultures, women's business acumen and marketing skills enhance their social and political positions.[8]

The oral literature also shows the consequences of personal weakness. *Ọ̀ṣun*'s refusal to sacrifice her gown prevents her from being the first divinity to receive the knowledge of the *Ìfá* oracle. Unlike her co-wife and sister goddess *Òyá*, *Ọ̀ṣun* is vain. As a result, *Òrúnmìlà* successfully acquires the knowledge of the *Ìfá* oracle from *Olódùmarè*. Such thematic weaknesses in nature solidify the reciprocal emulation between humanity and divinity. In spite of this, or because of it, *Ọ̀ṣun*'s primary concern lies with the continuity and protection of her human progeny. So, among all the *òrìṣà*, it is *Ọ̀ṣun* who ends the war of the Town of Women (cited in chapter three) and reunites male and female.[9]

Obviously, *Ọ̀ṣun* represents the complexity of the female principle and a spectrum of African feminist themes in the orature. Here, women's voices and community consciousness are consolidated within the social order. In this mythological context, women like men have their own abilities, influence, and power. Women are neither men's competitors nor their inferiors. Like their male counterparts, weaknesses and failures are assessed according to both personal and communal guidelines rather than sex-specific expectations. The major exception here is childbirth, one of women's productive roles. To be woman is to reproduce as well as produce. The orature implies that male oppression and sexism cause an intolerable imbalance, and that gender roles are meant to be complementary rather than antagonistic.

The festival drama offers only one perspective of Yorùbá social vision. During the preparatory stages and reenactment, the *Ìyá Ọ̀ṣun* and *Atáója* coadminister both the spiritual and political needs of the festival and the township. Together, they symbolize the balance and complementary functions within the sociocultural and political order. As a unit, they represent the balance between the male and female mores as well as the complementary responsibilities of both. The affirmation of their historical and sociopolitical titles reflect the parallel structure, roles, and voices in the social vision. Their reciprocal roles in the realm of spiritual and political leadership are exchanged and interchanged, indicating a wholeness that acknowledges sex-specificity merely as a component of the social order.

Offering a sacrifice and singing the praises to the goddess *Ọ̀ṣun* as mother and nurturer captures the essence of a powerful being who must be placated if disaster is to be averted. The image of *Ọ̀ṣun* as leader of the *àjẹ́*, or powerful beings, symbolizes the mystery of women. This special female ambience bonds women together and gives them a special knowledge of human needs, wants, and potentiality. As custodians of earth, fire, water, and wood, women are, metaphysically speaking, agents of change, gifted with the ability to transform these natural elements into human sustenance.

African feminist criticism discloses the historical and contemporary roles of women in leadership and support systems. *Ọ̀ṣun* as a model establishes that African women are historically part of the political, social, cultural, and economic sectors. It shows that *Ọ̀ṣun*, as a mythical image of womanhood, is queen mother *and* ruler, the *subject* of political and economic actions, the challenge *and* the support of the social order. *Ọ̀ṣun*'s mythology maintains that matriarchy operates well with and within the patriarchy forming a sisterhood that is defined in organizational terms as *ẹgbẹ*, or association.

When women's organizations are institutionalized into membership societies, the title *Ìyálóde*, or "mother of the outside," is conferred upon their presidents. As indicated above, *ìyá* becomes the core morpheme in similar constructions, thus equating "mother" with "leader." *Ìyálọja* (mother of the market), is the title for the president or leader of the market and market women. In her *oríkì*, *Ọ̀sun* is praised as *ìyálóde* and as one who has business acumen, signifying her roles as a business woman, tie-dyer, and an astute market leader. Women's organizations are also hierarchical, as demonstrated by the titles and roles of the religious *Ìyá Ọ̀sun Ọ̀sogbo* and the familial - social term *ìyálè*. The former refers to the head/leader of all *Ọ̀sun* worshippers in Ọ̀sogbo and also refers to the *Ìyá Ọ̀sun* (senior *Ọ̀sun* priestess) from other towns who are subordinate to her. *Ìyálè* literally means "mother of the house," and socially refers to the senior or head or leader wife in the polygynous household. These illustrations exemplify sisterhoods or societies that consolidate women's endeavors and their power.

This concept of sisterhood defines the art of mothering itself in Yorùbá culture where co-wives are also co-mothers in polygynous households, in extended families, and communal locales. As cited above, the term *ìyàwo* exemplifies the all-encompassing view of the central familial roles of mother and wife. The coordination of familial communal activities at marriage, birth, naming ceremonies, festivals, and funerals embodies the principles of social cohesion and the primacy of female organizational expertise. Like *Ìyálóde Ọ̀sun*, these women leaders organize large numbers of females and males around specific tasks and special interests.

The *language and style* of both festival drama and oral literature underscore traditional literary characteristics. Hyperbole, repetition, protracted metaphors, and complex tropes are especially characteristic of the orature. As part of the content of festival drama, *Ọ̀ṣun*'s *oríkì* (praise poetry) and *orin ọdún* (festival songs) ignite their audiences with the artistry of Yorùbá oral genres. Hyperbole, in her praise poetry, presents *Ọ̀ṣun* as "a strong water" or the goddess "who tucks her vagina inside to go fight another *òrìṣà*." Similarly, other forms of address and references to *Ọ̀ṣun* as *ọkọ mi* (my husband), and *oba mi* (my lord) intimate her role as an *òrìṣà* who "marries" her initiates as well as reminding us of her intrinsic power. Such appellations are repeated throughout the poetry and songs of the festival. Its various acts and forms saturate the audience with the meaning imparted by such imagery, so that the tone and ambience of the festival underscores *Ọ̀ṣun*'s image as a women of power, femininity, and fecundity.[10]

In another example, protracted metaphors such as *òwó-rùrù-f'ara-lako* and *òwó-rùrù-f'ara-làpáta* use ideophones to signify *Ọ̀ṣun*'s beauty and power. Clearly, her beauty enhances her power, as the two images interlock creating one awesome icon. The everflowing river, as a symbol, followed by the ideophones, "The one who, in flowing forcefully along, hits her body against grass, the one who, in flowing furiously along, hits her body against rocks" reinforces *Ọ̀ṣun* as a beautiful, sensual, serene, and powerful woman leader. It suggests her consistency and fortitude, a major theme of the festival drama. The contrasts between the soft grass and the hard rocks accentuates the image of "The Good Mother" who nurtures and defends, who is mysterious and ever-present irrespective of conditions. Clearly then, her courage and ability to move forward with majesty elaborates on this woman's power, that is, "one who wears a big chieftaincy title."[11]

As noted in chapter six, such symbolism and meaning suggests that female rulership may have preceded male leadership in Òṣogbo. It illustrates that the pact Olútìmìhín and Láróòyè made with *Ọ̀ṣun* as ruler of Òṣogbo parallels the balance of power and rulership between women and men in mythology and in life. The fact that history, genealogy, and migration patterns are contained between the lines of her complex tropes further substantiate this possibility. Extinct towns, market places and items, rulers and titles disclose *Ọ̀ṣun's* status as an ancient divinity who still is worshipped in many contemporary towns. *Ọ̀ṣun Òṣogbo, Ọ̀ṣun Ẹ̀wùjí,* and *Ọ̀ṣun Ìjùmù* recall some ancient and modern Yorùbá towns discussed in chapter six. This factor indicates the broad base of *Ọ̀ṣun* worship outside of Òṣogbo (where her major shrine is located). It also reveals migration patterns from other townships to Òṣogbo. It attests to the image of *Ọ̀ṣun* as *The Good Mother* who extends herself to protect her children, and partially explains the appeal of the festival to people from outside Òṣogbo.

Like these examples from the *Ọ̀ṣun* festival and oral literature, African feminist criticism extols the image of strong and beautiful women. Such women, irrespective of obstacles, continue to flow along, like the "strong waters" that symbolize *Ọ̀ṣun.* Images of the goddess as a beautiful warrior and mother ruler centralize African womanhood. Both culturally and historically, they proclaim that the woman of African descent is fully engaged in her own life and the life and struggles of her community. The flow of her river and *Ọ̀ṣun* worship in other townships also connotes her engagement with the life and lives of those communities, irrespective of location. Moreover, deference to the *Ìyá Ọ̀ṣun Òṣogbo* exemplifies the necessity for autonomous female leadership and organization, suggested by the use of the word *Ọ̀ṣun* as an ancient title of female rulership.

In essence, *òrìṣà Ọ̀ṣun* images an elegant woman of wealth, power, femininity, and fecundity, that is, the communal mother of an African world. Nor is she without her own talents and individuality. Like other women, she is a worker, trader, crafts-woman, singer, poet, and dancer. As the guilds and professional groups indicate, she is expected to explore and *exploit her own* innate talents. Consequently, as a theoretical framework for African feminist criticism, the *Ọ̀ṣun* oral literature and festival drama codify these complex images of African womanhood as a source of empowerment for women globally. As such, cultural-historical realities and concepts are essential to the growth of our communities.[12]

Following her example, African feminist theory is wholistic in its advocacy for women's issues and is legitimized within its own right *and* within the context of a society of men and women. At the *Ìyá Ọ̀ṣun*'s home, women's voices harmonized in unison, praise *Ọ̀ṣun* in a call-and-response mode accompanied only by a *kalongo* (bell) and chanted *a cappella*. On the festival day, *Ọ̀ṣun* worshippers and priestesses sing festival songs reminiscent of an AABA blues score. There, women's voices, accompanied mainly by female drummers, are raised in social protest, political commentary, reverence, and solidarity.[13] The festival as context for cultural drama and orature confirms, as Sudarkasa points out, that social, political, and economic institutions are forums for social control and debate belonging to females as well as males.[14] The joyous and the sorrowful are both invited to transcend their personal moments and move across the *abyss of transition*. The oral literature discloses that the voices of the disaffected and the disinherited also constitute part of the human chorus. The powerful *àjẹ́*, the malevolent *ajogun*, childless women, refugees of wars, drought, and pestilence – all are embodied, along with the food-sellers and the new, singing mothers, in the festival and orature of human sounds and images. As a humanistic theory, African Feminism denies none of her children's voices.

Although Igbo and Yorùbá social and political structures differ, the image of inner strength and a theme of spiritual, economic, and political sisterhood are dominant in both cultures. These virtues, it is believed, are at the core of conquest over adversity. So, while sisterhood and social cohesion are the ideal, enmity among women and between women and men is likewise a social reality. Tension exists among co-wives, women of rival lineages, and among an *ìyàwó* and her female in-laws.

As demonstrated by such awesome power found in *Ọ̀ṣun*'s mythology, African Feminist Theory remains committed to the preservation of our collective humanity. Correspondingly, when confronted with marginalization by some of the òrìsà, Òsun arrests their chauvinism. Clearly, her power evolves from the same Omnipotent source as theirs. This power (àsẹ) along with her inner strength are key to her conquering spirit. Nurturing is a form of resistance to human annihilation. The expression of such nurturing encompasses the willingness and ability to engage in physical struggle as intimated by the female title Balogun Òsun. Òsun, the leader of powerful beings, becomes a warrior and protectress who battles that which threatens her children. Symbolically, as the custodian of nature's transformative elements, Yèyé, The Good Mother, is footsoldier and cavalrywoman, defending those whom she births and nourishes. In this role, she confirms her own deftness as a leader of and participant in the social order. Indeed, she is Mother Earth and likewise Mother of the Earth.

Finally, Òsun is mother and woman, and as woman, she is audacious, gracious, and beautiful. Her power enriches her femininity, making her beautiful in the eyes of the community that she issues forth and protects. Her beauty comprises her physical, spiritual, and effectual mode within both female and communal forums. Her movements, like the river that bears her name, flow graciously and forcefully throughout that community. Her countenance remains an expression of African womanhood. Òsun's mythology and her festival drama embody a belief in woman power and sacrifice, that is, in the belief that to give is to get, and to get is to give, while to give and to get is to empower. Kí Òsun tí ó wá l'àsẹ, ami o. Ẹ sẹ Òsun Òsogbo. Òrìsà mi ooo, Pẹlẹ ooo.

Notes

1.   Rowland Abiodun, "Understanding Yorùbá Art and Aesthetics: The Concept of Àsẹ," *African Arts* (Los Angeles), July 1994, 68 - 78.

2.   Ifi Amadiume, *Male Daughters, Female Husbands: Gender And Sex in an African Society* (London, Zed Press, 1988).

3.   Filomena Steady, "The Black Woman Cross-Culturally" An Overview," in Filomena Chioma Steady, ed., *The Black Woman Cross-Culturally* (Rochester, Vermont: Schenkman Books, Inc, 1981).

4.   *Ibid.*

5.   Babaláwo Yẹmi Ẹlẹ́bùrú̀ìbọ̀n, Personal Interviews, 1982.

6.   Niara Sudarkasa, "The Status of Women in Indigenous African Societies," in (eds) Rosalyn Terborg-Penn, Sharon Harley, and Andrea Benton Rushing, *Women in Africa and the African Diaspora* (Washington, D.C. Howard University Press, 1987). See also Rowland Abiodun, "Verbal and Visual Metaphors: Mythical Allusions in Yorùbá Ritualistic Art of Ori," *Word and Image, A Journal of Verbal/Visual Inquiry*, 3:3 (1987): 252-270.

7.   D.L. Bádéjọ, Field Notes, 1981-83. See also Badejo, *A Goddess Of Our Own.*

8.   *Ibid.* See also, D.L. Bádéjọ, "Femininity as a Literary and Social Function of Power in the Oral Literature of the Yorùbá Goddess *Ọ̀ṣun,*" in Jacob Olupona and Toyin Falola, eds, *Religion and Society in Nigeria* (Ibadan University Press Limited, 1991) 77-92; see also Amadiume, *op. cit.*

9.   William Bascom, *Sixteen Cowrie Divination* (Bloomington: Indiana University Press, 1969).

10.   D.L. Bádéjọ, *Femininity, op. cit.*

11.   D.L. Bádéjọ, *A Goddess, op. cit.*

12.   D.L. Bádéjọ, *ibid.*

13.   D.L. Bádéjọ, "The Goddess *Ọ̀ṣun* As A Paradigm For African Feminist Criticism" *Sage: A Scholarly Journal on Black Women* (Summer 1989): 27-32.

14.   D.L. Bádéjọ, *Femininity, op. cit.* Sudarkasa, *op. cit.*

PRONUNCIATION KEY

The following pronunciation key is a guide to understanding the
Yorùbá tonal marks included in this text. Yorùbá is a tonal
language whose meaning is best understood in context. This
pronunciation key is designed to assist non-Yorùbá speakers to
approximate its beautiful sound. As noted in chapter one, tones
are marked by

low tone `	=	do
mid tone (no mark)	=	re
high tone ´	=	mi

so that,

Ọ̀ṣun	=	do-re	=	Oh - shun
Ṣẹ̀ẹ̀gẹ̀sí	=	do-do-mi	=	Sheh-geh-see.

The dot under the vowels and consonants also affects the
pronunciation and meaning of various words. These too are
subject to tonal markings. Note that Yorùbá words typically
break at the vowels.

an	=	awn	(silent w)
ẹ	=	eh	(silent h)
ọ	=	awe	(silent w)
ọn	=	own	(silent w)
ẹn	=	ehn	(silent h)
ṣ	=	sh	

[examples]

àṣẹ	=	do-re	=	ah-sheh

òrìṣà	=	do-do-do	=	oh-ree-shah
Ẹ̀fọ̀nté	=	do-do-mi	=	Eh-fown-teh
ènìyàn	=	do-do-do	=	eh-nee-yahn

The other vowels are pronounced as follows,

a	=	ah
e	=	eh
i	=	ee
o	=	oh
u	=	ew (as in few)
y	=	yeh (silent h)

[examples]

àgbo	=	do-re	=	ah-bow (silent w)
ewì	=	re-do	=	eh-wee
ìyá	=	do-mi	=	ee-yah (silent h)
odù	=	re-do	=	oh-dew (silent w)
Yèyé	=	do-mi	=	Yeh-yeh (silent h)

The Yorùbá language also includes frictives, that is, forceful sounds. These are,

gb	=	as in rugby
p	=	as in explicate

[examples]

arugbá	=	re-re-mi	=	ah-rew-gbah (silent h)
Ṣàngó-pípè	=	do-mi-mi-do	=	Shan-goh-pee-peh

Lastly, there are four vowels which singularly carry meaning.

Notice that these vowels are genderless when written or spoken out of context.

a	=	we
o	=	you
ẹ	=	you (plural)
oun	=	her, him

Pronunciation and tonal markings vary among the different Yorùba dialects. Elision, context, and form (spoken, sung, or intoned) all affect the movement of tones and the meaning of the language.

GLOSSARY

This glossary only includes selected Yorùbá words, representing the most frequently used and significant terms in the book.

ÀÀWẸ̀. Medicinal preparation.

ABÍKÚ. A child born repeatedly to the same mother. Women who have several miscarriages are said to be tormented by *àbíku* children.

ABIYAMỌ. This term refers to a nursing mother.

ABỌ́. Medicinal infusion.

ADÉ. Crown. When found in a person's name, it refers to royalty.

ÀGBO. Medicinal waters.

AGẸMO. An *òrìṣà* worshipped mainly in Ìjẹ̀bù-Odẹ̀.

ÀÌKÚ. Without death, or longevity.

ÁÌWẸ́. The special pot that *Ìyálòṣà* (*Ọ̀ṣun* priestesses) use for medicinal preparations.

ÀJẸ́. Powerful beings.

AJOGUN. Malevolent forces found in all aspects of life.

ÀKÙKỌ. A male bird, a cock.

ÀKÀRÀ. Fried bean cakes made from black-eyed beans.

ÀMÀLÀ. A dumpling-like starch made from yam flour.

ARUGBÁ. The title of the virgin sacrifice-carrier who takes the offering to the Ọ̀ṣun River during the annual festival.

ÀṢẸ. The quintessential power that *Olòdùmarè* used to create the universe and all life. The *òrìṣà,* Èṣù, is the custodian of the *àṣẹ,* and guardian of the crossroads. *See* Èṣù.

AṢO ẸGBẸ́. Clothe of association. Families and organizations frequently wear attire made in the same colors and patterns.

ÀYÀN. The Yorùbá name for the African silkwood tree. It is also the name of the drums belonging to the *babaláwo* and *Ifá.*

BAÁLÈ. Father of the house.

BABA. Father.

BABALÁWO. Father of secrets as in secret knowledge (sacred *Ifá* texts) and confidente of personal secrets (spiritual advisor).

BABALOṢÀ. Father of divinity. It is a title for male priests.

BALÓGUN. A title for war chiefs.

DÚRÓSÍMÍ. A name given to a male *abíkù* infant. It means "stay or wait with me."

ẸBỌ. Sacrifice. *See* IRÚ.

ÈFÓ̩. The name for any green vegetable, usually referring to a spinach-like leaf.

Ẹ̀GBẸ́. A society or organization.

Ẹ̀MU. Palm-wine. The liquid substance found in certain palm trees.

ÈNÌYÀN. Also written *ÈNÌÀ.* it means "human beings, people".

Ẹ̀SẸ̀. A generic name for diviniation poems.

Ẹ̀ṣù. Custodian of the *àṣẹ,* and guardian of the crossroads.

Ewì. A generic name for poetry.

Gìlògìlò. One of several hundred ideophones in the Yorùbá language, it means "a very radiant beauty."

Ìbà. Homage.

Ide. Brass. One of *Ọ̀ṣun's* symbols and part of her paraphenalia.

Ìjálá. The name of the hunters' poetry associated with *Ògún.*

Ikú. Death.

Ilẹ̀. Land, homeland.

Irú. Communal sacrifice or offering carried in a sacred calabash.

Irún Mọlẹ̀. The original deities (*òrìṣà*) sent to earth (*ilẹ̀*) by the Supreme Creator Essence (*Olódùmarè*) to prepare the world for human habitation.

Irúlá. Okra seeds.

Ìwì. A particular type of *Egúngún* poetry.

Iwin. A spirit or custodian (of a deity).

Ìwòrì Méjì. A catagory of *Ifá* poetry.

Ìyá. Mother.

Ìyà mi. Another title for the female *àjẹ́, our mothers.*

Ìyá Ọ̀sun. Mother *Ọ̀sun.* Title of the head of *Ọ̀sun* worship.

Ìyálasẹ. An *Ọ̀sun* priestess who prepares the food for the shrine and for offering.

Ìyálọ́sà. A generic name for any priestess meaning "mother of the *òrìsà*". See BABALỌSA

Ìyálódẹ. The title for the president of the market. It also means "mother of the outside."

Iyán. Another dumpling-like starch made from pounded yams.

Ìyẹ̀rẹ̀. A special type of *Ifá* poetry.

Jólóyé. A special dance performed to celebrate a peaceful and productive reign. It requires a specific attire to be worn.

Méjì. Two.

Ọba. Title given to a ruler.

Odó Idẹ. "Golden mortar" belongs to *Ọ̀sun*'s paraphenalia. She is said to be the owner of the golden mortar which symbolizes both her wealth and her womanliness.

Odù. The name of an *Ifá* chapter. Also a wife of Òrúnmílá.

ỌFọ̀. A spell or a curse.

ỌGBọN. Wisdom.

ỌKọ. Husband.

OLOBO-TÚJẸ̀. A plant found in the Ọ̀sun Grove that resembles an aloe vera. It also refers to female genitals.

OLÓJÚMẹ́RÌNDÍNLÓGÚN. Sixteen lamps. These are lit on the fourth night of the opening ceremonies to invite *Ọ̀sun* and her companion *òrìṣà* to join the human community in celebrating the *Ọ̀sun* festival.

ỌLọ́Rọ̀. Owner of the word, a confidante. It also is the title of the first Ọ̀sun crown.

ỌLọ́Sẹ́. Whipping boys. Young men who participate in the festival as symbolic tamers of negative forces.

ỌMọ. Child.

ọ̀ọ̀NI-IFẹ̀. The title of the paramount ruler of Ifẹ̀.

ọ̀PÁ-ọBA. The staff of the ruler.

ọ̀Pẹ̀Lẹ̀. Divining chain. It is used to cast *Ifá* divination.

ỌPọ́N IFÁ. The *Ifá* divination tray used by the *babaláwo* during consultation with a client.

ORÍ. Head. One chooses an *orí* or head which means that one chooses a destiny.

ORÍKÌ.   Praise-poetry or praise-name.

ORIN.   Song.

ÒRÌṢÀ.   Deity or deities.

ÒRUN.   Heaven.

ÒYÈKÚ.   A chapter in the *IFÁ* corpus.

ṢÀNGÓ-PÍPÈ.   A special poetry genre belonging to *Ṣàngó*.

ṢÈKÈRÈ.   A musical instrument.

YÈYÉ.   The good mother, *ÒṢUN*.

BIBLIOGRAPHY

Primary Sources

Abímbọlá, Wándé. Conversations with author. Amherst, Massachusetts, April-June 1990.

Àṣàbi, Mrs. Ṣàngótúndùn. Interview with author. Òṣogbo, Ọ̀ṣun State, Nigeria, February 1981.

Babayínkà, Mr. and Susan Wenger. Interview with author, Òṣogbo, Ọ̀ṣun State, Nigeria, 1983.

Bádéjọ, Diedre L. Oríkì Ọ̀ṣun (Praise Poetry of Ọ̀ṣun). Audiotape. Recorded 1 February 1981. Òṣogbo, Ọ̀ṣun State, Nigeria. Personal Collection.

—. Orin Ọ̀ṣun ati Orin Odùn Ọ̀ṣun (Ọ̀ṣun Songs and Ọ̀ṣun Festival Songs). Audiotape. Recorded 8 August 1982. Òṣogbo, Ọ̀ṣun State, Nigeria. Personal Collection.

—. Excerpts from Ifá Religious Corpus as Rendered by Babaláwo Ifáyẹ́mí Ẹlẹ́búrùíbọn. Audiotape. Recorded 29 January 1981 and 28 August through 3 September 1982. Òṣogbo, Ọ̀ṣun State, Nigeria. Personal Collection.

Ẹlẹ́búrùíbọn, Ifáyẹ́mí. Interviews with author, 1981—1984.

`Iyá Ọ̀ṣun Òṣogbo and Àwòrò Ọ̀ṣun Òṣogbo. Interview with author. 8 April 1983.

Jakuta, Chief Adébáyó. Personal Correspondence with author. 5 February 1988.

Secondary Sources

Abímbọ́lá, Wándé. *Ifá: An Exposition of Ifá Literary Corpus.* Ibadan: Oxford University Press Nigeria, 1976.

—. *Ifá Divination Poetry.* New York: Nok Publishers, Ltd., 1977.

—. *Ifá: An Exposition of Ifá Literary Corpus.* Ibadan: Oxford University Press, 1976.

—. *Sixteen Great Poems of Ifá.* UNESCO. 1975.

—. *Yorùbá Oral Literature.* Ilé-Ifẹ̀: University of Ifẹ̀, Nigeria, 1975.

Abíódún, Rowland. *African Art Studies: The State of the Discipline.* Washington, D.C.: Smithsonian Institution, National Museum of African Art. 1987.

—. Understanding Yorùbá Art and Aesthetics: The Concept of Àṣẹ. In *African Arts,* Los Angeles, July 1994, 68—78.

—. "Verbal and Visual Metaphors: Mythical Allusions in Yorùbá Ritualistic Art of Orí." In *Word and Images: A Journal of Verbal/Visual Inquiry,* 3,3 (1987): 134 — 149.

—. Women in Yorùbá Religious Images. In *African Languages and Cultures.* 2,1 (1989): 1-18.

Adédéjí, Joel. "Oral Tradition and the Contemporary Theatre." In *Research in African Literatures*, 2, 2 (1971): 134—149.

—. "The Place of Drama in Yorùbá Religious Observation." In *Odù: Journal of African Studies*, University of Ifè, 3 (1966) : 88—94.

Afolayan, Adebisi. *Yorùbá Language and Literature*. Ifè: University of Ifè Press, 1982.

Agiri, Babatúndé. "Yorùbá Oral Tradition with Special Reference to the Early History of the Òyó Kingdom." In *Yorùbá Oral Tradition*, ed. Wándé Abímbólá. Ifè: Department of African Languages and Literatures, University of Ifè, 1975.

Ajayi, J.F.A. and Robert Smith. *Yorùbá Warfare in the Nineteenth Century*. Cambridge: Cambridge University Press, 1964.

Akínjóbìn. "The Expansion of Oyo and the Rise of Dahomey." In *History of West Africa*. ed. J.F.A. Ajayi and Micheal Crowder. vol. 1, 311. New York Columbia University Press, 1973.

Amadiume, Ifi. *Male Daughters, Female Husbands: Gender and Sex in an African Society*. London: Zed Press, 1988.

Áwolálú, Qmósáde. *Yorùbá Beliefs and Sacrificial Rites*. London: Longman Group, Ltd, 1979.

Babalóla, S. A. Interview with Gerald Cashion: "Studies in Yorùbá Folklore." in *Folklore Forum*. Bloomington: Indiana University Folklore Institute; Bibliographic Special Series, 11, 1973, 63-70.

—. *The Content and Form of Yorùbá Ìjálá.* London: Oxford University Press, 1976.

Bádéjọ, Diedre L. *A Goddess of Our Own.* work-in-progress.

—. Femininity as a Literary and Social Function of Power. In *Religion and Society in Nigeria.* Ibadan: University Press, 1991, 77—92.

—. "The Goddess Ọ̀ṣun as a Paradigm for African Feminist Criticism." In *Sage: A Scholarly Journal on Black Women.* Atlanta, Georgia: The Sage Women's Educational Press Inc. Vol. 6, no.1 (Summer 1989), 27—32.

Bádéjọ, Peter. *Aṣa Ibílẹ̀ Yorùbá.* University of California at Los Angeles, 1980.

Baker, Houston. *Blues, Ideology, and Afro-American Literature.* Chicago University Press, 1984.

Bamgboṣe, Ayo. "The Form of Yorùbá Proverbs."

Bascom, William. *Ifa Divination: Communication Between Gods and Men in West Africa.* Bloomington: Indiana University Press, 1969.

—. *Sixteen Cowries: Yorùbá Divination from Africa to the New World.* Bloomington: Indiana University Press, 1980.

Biobaku, S. O. *Sources of Yorùbá History.* Oxford: Clarendon Press, 1973.

DeGraft, J.C. "Roots of African Drama and Theatre." In *African Literature Today 8 1976.*

Eliade Mircea. *The Sacred and the Profane: The Nature of Religion.* Translated from the French by William R. Trash. New York: Harcourt, Brace, and World, 1959.

Fadipe, N. A. *The Sociology of the Yorùbá.* Ibadan: Ibadan University Press, 1970.

Henige, David. *Oral Historiography.* London: Longman Group Ltd., 1982.

Johnson, Samuel. *The History of the Yorubas: From the Earliest Times to the Beginning of the British Protectorate.* Westport, Connecticut: Negro Universities Press, 1970.

Kunene, Mazizi. "The Relevance of African Cosmological Systems to African Literature Today," In *African Literature Today,* 11: 190—205, 1980.

Law, R.C.C. *The Oyo Empire 1600—1838.* Oxford: Clarendon Press, 1977.

Mabogunje, A. L. *Owu in Yorùbá History.* Ibadan: Ibadan University Press, 1977.

Nketia, Kwabena J.H. "The Linguistic Aspect of Style in African Languages." In *Current Trends in Linguistics,* 7: 733—757, 1971.

Ogunbiyi, Yemi. *Drama and Theatre in Nigeria: A Critical Sourcebook.* Lagos: Nigeria Magazine, 1981.

Ojo, Afolabi. *Yoruba Culture: A Geographical Analysis.* Ifẹ̀: University of Ifẹ̀ Press and London: University of London Press, Ltd., 1966.

Okonjo, Kemene. "Women in Contemporary Africa." In *African Society, Culture, and Politics*. ed. Christopher Mojekwu, Washington, D.C.: University Press of America, 1978.

Olatunji, Olatunde. "Iyèrè Ifá: Yorùbá Oracle Chants." In *African Notes*, 7,2, nd.

—. "The Yorùbá Oral Poet and His Society." In *Research in African Literatures*, 10, 2: 179—207, 1979.

Oludare, Olajubu. "Iwi Egúngún Chants: An Introduction." In *Research in African Literatures*, 5, 1 (1974): 31—51.

Olupona, J. Kehinde. *Kingship, Religion, and Rituals in a Nigerian Community: A Phenomenological Study of Ondo Yorùbá Festivals*. Stockholm, Sweden: Almqvist and Wiksell International, 1991.

Olupona, J. Kehinde and Toyin Falola. *Religion and Society in Nigeria*. Ibadan: University Press Limited, 1991.

"Ọ̀ṣogbo," In *Oyo State Town Series*. Ibadan: Ministry of Local Government and Information. January 1977.

Rushing, Andrea Benton. "A Language of Their Own: Photographic Exhibition of Yorùbá Attire." Amherst College, 1987.

Sodipe, J.H. and Brian Hallen. *Witchcraft, Magic, and Religion*. London: Ethnographica Ltd., 1986.

Ṣoyinka, Wole. *Myth, Literature, and the African World*. Cambridge: Cambridge University Press, 1977.

Steady, Filomena. "African Feminism: " In *Women in Africa and the African Diaspora*, ed. Rosalyn Terborg-Penn, Andrea Benton Rushing, and Sharon Harley. Washington, D.C.: Howard University Press, 1987.

—. " The Black Woman Cross-Culturally: An Overview." In *The Black Woman Cross-Culturally*. Rochester, Vermont: Schenkman Books, Inc., 1981.

Sudarkasa, Niara. "The Status of Women in Indigenous African Societies." In *Women in Africa and the African Diaspora,* ed. Rosalyn Terborg-Penn, Andrea Benton Rushing, and Sharon Harley. Washington, D.C.: Howard University Press, 1987.

Thompson, Robert Farris. *Flash of the Spirit: African and Afro-American Art and Philosophy.* New York: Vintage Books, 1984.

Walker, Alice. *In Search of Our Mothers' Gardens.* Orlando, Florida: Harcourt, Brace, Jovanovich, 1983.

Index

A

ádé (crown) 71
Ádétayùn Ọ̀ṣun priestess 11
àbíkú (child who is born to die)
  miscarriage 68, 172
abíyamo (nursing mother) 35
Abímbọ́lá 70
African Feminism
  and humanism 175-177, 184
African feminist theory 176-184
  cultural-historical foundation 177
  literary perspective 178
àgbàlagbà (elder) 68, 176
Àgbo, medicinal waters 84
àïku (longevity) 68
àjẹ́, (powerful beings), 2, 11, 34-36, 40, 43, 73-80, 91-96, 184
  Ọ̀ṣun as leader of 1
ajogun (warriors against humanity) 77, 133, 184
Akan of Ghana 9
Aláàfin of Ọ̀yọ́ 156
àmàlà
  favorite food of Ṣàngó 37
androgynous Olódùmarè 51
Àpòmù market 159
ara (body) 80
arugbó (sacrifice carrier)
  and *Ọ̀ṣun* festival 104, 116-120
arugbá 104-111, 114-121, 134-147, 169
  characteristics 116
  ritual assignment 148
    and *irú* 135
    as challenger of the chthonic realm 137

àṣẹ (life-force) 42-43, 69, 77-84, 91, 173-179
àṣẹ (quintessential creative power of the universe)
  and *Olódùmarè* 50-51
   and *Ọ̀ṣun* 9
Àṣekunlà 13
aṣọ ẹgbẹ́ 139, 146
Àtáója (traditional ruler of Òṣogbo) 34
  political and spiritual leader 10
  as guardian of *Ọ̀ṣun* 108
  as mediator 105
  as representative of *Ọ̀ṣun* 105
  as symbol of *Ọ̀ṣun* 109
  meaning 105
Atáója (ruler of Òṣogbo) 104-111
  and center stage 118
  and Most Royal Beaded Crown 120
  as cultural-historical leader 141
  and Ọ̀pá Ọba 120
  presiding over *Ọ̀ṣun* Festival 144
Atáója addresses
  Ọ̀ṣun festival 121
Atẹ́wọ́gbẹ́ja 114, 144-159
áwo 155-160
Àwòrò
  role of 104-114
Àwòrò (chief priest of *Ọ̀ṣun*) 104, 116
Àwòrò Ọ̀ṣun 161-162

B

Bálogùn Ọ̀ṣun
  as war leader 120
  as body guard 161
bátá drums 145
babaláwọ (*Ifá* priests) 51, 54
  also fathers of secrets 65
babaláwo 82, 86, 90-97
  Ifá priest-diviner
    traditional priest-scholars 84
Bascom 86

beautiful, wealthy woman 80
Bọye 94

C

childbirth 179
childlessness 171
chthonic realm 74, 147
circularity of existence 55
concept of sisterhood 181
cosmic adjustment 69, 70
cosmic balance 142
Cosmic Harmony 80
cosmological thought 69, 93
cosmological vision 74
cosmology 67-84
crossroads
    purview of Èṣù and Ọrúnmílá 133
cultural caretakers
    cultural knowledge
        cultural literacy 54
cultural practice 83, 95
cultural-historical foundation 177

D

DeGraft 133
destructive-creative synergy 69
disharmony or rupture 68
Dramatic Art 147
dramatic art form 151
dramatic reenactment 142
dramatis personae 132, 149

E

égun 36
    ancestors
        Egúngún 44
ẹbọ, or sacrifice 50-69, 95, 136
Ẹdẹ 10, 157-160

èfọ́ yanrìn 136
Ẹ̀fọ̀n 158
Ẹ̀gànrẹ̀fẹ́fe 94
Ẹgbẹ́ Ìyálóde 163-168
ẹgbẹ́ 7, 29
ẹmu or palm wine 81
Ẹ̀ṣù 130, 148
ẹsẹ 72, 86
ẹsẹ Ifá 2, 74
Edídágèrègére 94
Èkìtì kingdoms 158
Èṣù, guardian of the crossroads 74

F

female character
  and cosmic ideal 178
female deity 74
female *Egúngún* dancers 119
female leadership 160
female principle 70, 72, 78, 80
female rulership 160
fertility 83
festival calendar 53-54
Festival discourse 63
festival drama 70, 98, 156, 180
  language and style in 181
  sacred drama 103-105, 135-138
  secular drama 138-140
    and oral literature (orature) 114, 149
    orin odùn (festival songs) 149-151
    odù Ifá 1
Fulani 164-165
Fulani horsemen 115

G

giver and sustainer of life 80
group solidarity 165

H

healer
  Ọ̀ṣun as 12-13, 32, 41-45
  Ọ̀ṣun worshippers as 8
Healing the rupture 69
Historical Themes 156-159
Human will 133
humanistic feminism 177

I

Írẹ̀tẹ̀ Àlào 84
ìbà 3, 11, 38-42
icons of metamorphosis and synthesis 83
Ifá 1, 11, 45, 157
Ifá Festival 71
Ifá 69-96, 102
  and mediation 105
Ifá as the repository 71
Ifá as the voice of the divinities 71
Ifá corpus 52, 53
Ifẹ́ political structure 160
Ìjamo 163
Ìjẹ̀bu 159
Ìjẹ̀ṣa 8, 31, 36, 156
  tributary 160
Ìjùmú 7, 30, 156
ikú 77
Ilẹ̀-Ifẹ́ 48, 57, 74
Ilésa 158
ilú àyàn 71, 118
images of
  African womanhood 183
Immorality 68
Ìpole 158
Ìrègùn 158
ÌrúnMọlẹ̀ 2, 74-89
Irùn Imọlẹ̀ 2

ìwà 50
Ìwo 158
ïya 176
Ìyá Ọ̀ṣun 164
Ìyá Ọ̀ṣun Òṣogbo 3
Ìyálójà 8
Ìyálóde 8
Ìyá lÓṣun, mothers of Ọ̀ṣun 161
Ìyá nlfa 91
Ìyá Ọba 161
Ìyá Ọ̀ṣun 8, 120, 121, 160
   definition 105
   primary caretaker 116
Ìyá Ọ̀ṣun (chief priestess of Ọ̀ṣun) 104-108
Ìyá Ọ̀ṣun Òṣogbo 161-164, 182
Ìyálásẹ 116
Ìyálàsẹ (caretaker of the àṣẹ) 104-111
Ìyálasẹ Ọ̀ṣun 161-164
ïyále 181
Ìyálóde 160, 181
Ìyálóde, mother of the outdoors 162-164
Ìyáloja
   role of 169
Ìyálosá, the mothers of the òrìṣà 161
ïyàwó 176
ïyàwó Ọ̀ṣun 176
Ìyẹ̀rẹ̀ Ifá 54, 66

J

júbà 13, 107

K

kì 49
kinetic spiritual energy 80
Kunene, Mazizi 67, 99, 148

L

Laróòyè 10
leader of the *àjẹ́* 80
leader of women, *Ọ̀ṣun* 86
life-forces 68

M

male principle 70, 74
male-female principle 69, 72-75
marriage to Ṣàngó 76
master *Ifá* priests 91
mẹ̀rindínlógún 28, 76, 108
Mẹ̀rindínlógún of *Ọ̀ṣun* 71
myth and history 138
mythical-historical drama 146
mythopoetic ritual 132
mythopoetic symbolism 70, 77

N

network of deities 48

O

Ọba 163
Ọbà, the goddess of the Obà River 82
Ọbá KòSo 81
Ọbàtálá, the sculptor of the human form 81
ogbọ́n 79, 96
Ọ̀kànràn Sòdẹ̀ 78, 91
ọla 13, 42
ọlọ́sẹ (whipping boys) 104, 122
ọmọ 28, 31, 35, 42
Ọmọde Ọ̀ṣun 108, 119, 146, 168
Ọ̀pá Ọba 107, 109, 140
ọpẹ̀lẹ (divining chain) 71
ọpọ́n Ifá (*Ifá* divination board) 132
Ọ̀rìṣa-ńla 74
Ọ̀rúnmìlà, the god of divination 1, 73-76

Ọ̀run (heavenly mysteries) 161
Ọ̀ṣun 185
    images of 151
Ọ̀ṣun   See also Ọ̀ṣun festival
    and female rulership 106
    and settling of Ọ̀ṣogbo 97
    as ancient ruler 106
    as giver of children 1
        warrrior woman 107
    as the mother of Èṣù 167
    earthly representatives of 136
    feeding the goddess of the river 121
    icons 108
    meaning of 106
    mythical images of 177
    statues and symbols of 119
Ọ̀ṣun,
    rulership of Ọ̀ṣogbo 97
Ọ̀ṣun Ápáránìrà 52
Ọ̀ṣun as title 176
Ọ̀ṣun dancers 146
Ọ̀ṣun Èwùji 183
Ọ̀ṣun Festival 99, 106-116, 135, 175-179
    and Muslims 164
    as dramatic art 131
    dramatization of 131
Ọ̀ṣun Festival 71, 82, 103-114
    and musicians 109
    and Ọ̀ṣun worshippers 103
    and other òrìṣà worshippers 104
    and ritual discourse 136
    and secular drama 132
    and secular reenactment 140
    as ritual drama 131
    as sacred ritual 131
    climax of 104
    drama and oral literature 170
    pageantry of 107-116

ritual (sacrosanct) drama 121
    festival (secular) drama 121
sacred ritual 147
structure of 177
vicars of 105
Òṣun festival 105
    as drama 103-113
    defined 103
Òṣun Festival Drama 155
Òṣun Festival Proper 118
Òṣun Festival song 150
Òṣun Festival
    role of babaláwo in 105
Òṣun Grove 3, 10, 12, 30, 35, 39, 114, 115, 135, 143
Òṣun Ìjùmu 183
Òṣun, leader of *àjẹ́*
    and covenants with *àjẹ́* 97
Òṣun Òṣogbo 182
Òṣun Òṣogbo 1-10, 31, 34, 35, 37
Òṣun priestesses 108, 120
Òṣun River 121, 143, 158, 159-162
    images of 97
Òṣun River 115
Òṣun Ṣẹ̀ẹ̀gẹ̀sí Olóòyà-iyùn 1, 177
Òṣun sanctuary 121
Òṣun shrine 2
Òṣun, the goddess of fertility 74
Òṣun, the Good Mother 45
Òṣun titles 106
    and female rulership 106
Òṣun worshippers 165
    Ìyá Òsun and Àwòrò
    administrators of 116
Òṣun's image 159
Òṣun's mythology 185
Òṣun's oral literature 115
Òṣun's role in the cosmic order 79
Òṣun's wealth 157
òṣẹ́ 86

Ọ̀ṣẹTúrá, an odù Ifa 73-78, 95
Ọ̀yọ́ State Local Government 158
Ọbá 21
obínrin ẹgbẹ, or women's associations 178
Odánílòjùwẹ̀rẹ̀wẹ́re 94
odu 90
odù Ifá of Òrúnmìla 71
odù Ifá 2, 34, 77-79, 82, 90-97, 106, 163-169
Odùdúwà 52
Ògún 27, 80, 89, 95, 155
    statue of 118
Ògún, the god of war and iron 74
Ohenemahene (Queen Mother) 9
Ọ̀jiyàòmẹ̀fún 83, 84
okyeame 9
olóbò-tújẹ̀ 39
Olójùmẹ̀rindínlógún 71
Olódùmarè 2, 74
Olójùmẹ́rindínlógún 89, 109, 118, 136, 138, 141
    mẹ́rindínlógún
        Sixteen lamps 1
        preparation for 109
Olórò 29
Olútìmíhin 10
oral literary references 159-160
oral literary themes
    male oppression and sexism 179
    staging of 138
oral literature 155-157, 177-179
oral poetry
    genres of 138-141
orature 49, 61
oríkì 3, 4, 6, 8, 11, 35, 43, 45, 77, 97
oríkì Ọ̀ṣun 73
oríkï 149, 157–158
    orin odún 1
original feminists 177
orin Ọ̀ṣun 149, 158
òrìṣà 74, 155, 162-164

òrìṣà mythologies 81
òrìṣà Òṣun 103, 175-184
Òrìṣà-ńlá or Ọbàtálá, 81
Òrúnmìla 7, 13
Òṣogbo
    founding of 105
    Olútímíyìn and Èlàáróyi 97
    mythical and political history of 104
Òṣogbo history 168
Òṣogbo market
    and Ògún shrine 107
Òyá, goddess of the wind and the Niger River 82

P

patriarchal Yorùbá system 177
Pèrègún 6-8 17, 27
philosophy 48, 54
political history 53
political themes 159
    and Oríkì
    and Oríkì Òṣun 5
Preparations for
    Òṣun Festival 105-109
proverb 81, 178

R

reciprocity and balance
    male and female 180
religious vortex 167
Resolution 132, 167
restitution 72, 96
Ritual Drama 132-140
    empowerment 121
    reenactment 141

S

Ṣàngó   30-38, 75
  as the god of thunder and lightning 74
  ruler of Òyó 77
Ṣọlágbadé Ẹ̀wùjí 19
Ṣọ̀pọ̀no 89
Ṣoyinka 117
sacred waters 121
Sacrifice 68, 69, 72, 73, 76, 84, 85, 90, 92, 94, 95, 96, 97
  ẹbọ 49. *See also* ẹbọ́ (sacrifice) *Ẹ̀ṣù*
Sexism 176-184
Sixteen Great Poems of *Ifá* 77
social discourse 55
social vision 54, 155
Sociocultural Themes 155, 166-169
spiritual power 48
staged 103-107
Steady 73
Sudarkasa 177

T

Tìmì of Ẹde 158-160
title of Tìmì 156
Town of Women 86, 179
traditional African religions 155

W

warrior-woman 80
Wealth in *Ìrẹ̀tẹ́ Àlào* 85
wisdom of the ancestors 71
woman power 78, 169
womb 9, 40
women
  as icons of power 177
  as partners with men 178
women *Egúngún* dancers 145

women rulers 8
Women's intrinsic power 86
Women's power 85, 175-183

Y

Yẹmẹsẹ 53
Yèyé, the Good Mother 80-89, 165, 185
Yorùbá proverb 10
Yorùbá
   cosmology 47, 75
   cultural and political history 115
   philosophy 47
   social order. *See* festival drama
      Ọ̀ṣun festival Òṣogbo
   social vision 180
Yorùbá cosmic beliefs 139
Yorùbá cosmological thought 175
   Ọ̀ṣun's role in 114
Yorùbá cosmology and worldviews
   49, 51, 53, 67, 68, 69, 70, 72, 81, 93, 98, 151
Yorùbá cultural history 175-183
Yorùbá culture and history 140
Yorùbá language 70, 176
Yorùbá musical form 117
Yorùbá oral literature 159
Yorùbá political and religious philosophies 163
Yorùbá regencies 158
Yorùbá religion 155
Yorùbá ritual drama 137
Yorùbá social order 48, 49
Yorùbá sociocultural vision 166–180